THE CURIOUS
BARTENDER

THE CURIOUS

BARTENDER

THE

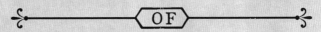

ARTISTRY AND ALCHEMY

OF

CREATING THE PERFECT COCKTAIL

TRISTAN STEPHENSON

PHOTOGRAPHY BY ADDIE CHINN

RYLAND PETERS & SMALL

LONDON • NEW YORK

Designer Geoff Borin
Editor Rebecca Woods
Head of Production Patricia Harrington
Art Director Leslie Harrington
Editorial Director Julia Charles

Prop Stylist Sarianne Plaisant
Indexer Hilary Bird

First published in 2013 by
Ryland Peters & Small
20–21 Jockey's Fields
London WC1R 4BW
and
519 Broadway, 5th Floor
New York, NY 10012

www.rylandpeters.com

10 9 8 7

All photography by Addie Chinn, apart from:
Peter Cassidy: backgrounds on pages 1, 3–19, 57, 155–157,
160–166, 168–171, 174, 177–178, 181, 184–187
Laura Edwards: backgrounds on pages 59–62, 65–69,
72–74, 76–78, 80–81, 85–87, 89
Kate Whitaker: backgrounds on pages 111–114, 116–121,
124–125, 127–131

Illustration credits:

page 3 © istockphoto/aleksandarvelasevic; page 10 ©
istockphoto/whitemay; page 15 © www.victorianpicture
library.com; page 16 © www.victorianpicturelibrary.com;
pages 18–19 illustrations © Selina Snow; page 21 ©
www.victorianpicturelibrary.com; page 87 © istockphoto/
Duncan 1890; page 100 © istockphoto/nicoolay; page
121 © istockphoto/nicoolay; page 150 © istockphoto/
Grafissimo; pages 172–173 © istockphoto/ilbusca; page
177 © istockphoto/nicoolay; page 185 © istockphoto/
nicoolay; page 195 © istockphoto/nicoolay

ISBN: 978-1-84975-437-8

A CIP record for this book is available from the
British Library.

US Library of Congress CIP data has been applied for.

Printed in China

CONTENTS

INTRODUCTION

◆

Hello and welcome. I'm really glad you could make it.

Contrary to the common public perception of the service industry, the art of bartending is not a simple one. This book focuses on much of the science involved in mixing drinks, but I think it's important to stress from the start that bartending itself is an art. Science can be learned and recipes can be memorized, but that's only half the struggle. The other half of the job is playing the raconteur, providing the service and, of course, making it look easy. That kind of stuff is difficult to learn and very hard to teach. Much of it comes with confidence (as it did with me), but there needs to be a certain spark there, the desire to entertain, the ability to engage in mindless mundane chat and the will to do it again and again. Some special people like Dave, the 50-something pub barman I worked with in Cornwall when I was 18, have perfected their craft over decades of standing, pouring, chatting and hosting, to the point where the whole act is entirely seamless.

That said, the facts and know-how do come in handy. I have spent the last ten years gathering as much knowledge as possible about the craft of the cocktail, and this book is a culmination of those efforts. What follows in this introduction is the pared-down story of how my career has developed, along with the people who have influenced me and the discoveries that have shaped me.

THE START

I didn't ever plan on being a bartender. I recall my career meetings at school being more centred around graphic design, performance and movie making. But I suppose that the profession I ended up joining isn't actually a million miles from my original aspirations. Just like a graphic designer, I get to be creative, to shape something from a concept through to reality. Like a stage actor, I have a platform from which I can preach and perform. And like a director, I am the puppet master – a kind of night-time engineer.

After dropping out of university, I wound up back in my home county of Cornwall working in the local pubs and restaurants. Despite feeling like a bit of a failure, all was not lost. What I didn't know then and I do know now is that over the following five years I would be lucky to have a succession of managers and bosses who would allow me almost complete creative freedom and the chance to develop. After spending over a year as a commis chef in a local pub, I moved on to a newly opened restaurant in Polzeath, Cornwall, called the Blue Tomato. I was 19. The aim was to improve my cooking and move up the ranks. Sadly, the kitchen turned out to be fully staffed, so I ended up working on the bar. There were only two bartenders in the operation and I was the lower-ranking one, so when the bar manager walked out after only two days of trading, I was immediately promoted. After less than a week of getting stuck into my new occupation, I was managing my first bar; my career as a cocktail bartender was off to a flying start!

The one major drawback to my promotion, however, was that I had no-one to show me the ropes. I was literally reading cocktails from specification sheets and making them for guests, on my own, for the first time. I was writing order sheets and shut-down procedures without templates, or, in fact, any certainty that order sheets and shut-down procedures were even a real thing! I didn't know it at the time, but the 16 drinks that the restaurant owner had picked at random for the list could not have been a better selection of classic cocktails to cut my teeth on. Everything from the Martini, Manhattan, Julep, Old Fashioned and Whisky Sour were on there – all drinks that I still love to make and that are included in this book. One morning, I got to work early since I planned on making the entire list of drinks as a means of learning them off by heart. Two hours later, the bar looked like a bomb had hit it, but there were 16 perfectly presented drinks to show for it. My boss walked in and I remember her saying, 'Well, I think we've found our cocktail bartender'. Without that encouragement, I'm not sure I would have stuck at it.

And I must have been doing something right – the bar got busy and the drinks were received very well. All of my time became consumed with perfecting the cocktail list, researching new drinks and reading lots of cocktail books and bartending manuals. I started featuring a cocktail of the day, which, to begin with, were pulled out of Simon Difford's original *Sauce Guide to Cocktails* (2001), but after around 18 months, and 500 cocktails later, I began creating my own cocktails and selling them instead. The buzz of conceiving, mixing and presenting a drink, then seeing someone enjoy it, and maybe even order it again was an addictive feeling for me. I worked with the chefs in the kitchen to use unusual (at least for the time) ingredients, such as kaffir lime leaves, coriander and caraway in my drinks. I also began using boutique vodkas, specialist liqueurs and Japanese whiskeys (which were all but unheard of in the UK back then).

THE MIDDLE BIT

After two years and two busy summer seasons at the Blue Tomato, I was ready to move on. Fortunately, the fates had conspired and Jamie Oliver was set to open the third branch of his Fifteen restaurant chain in Watergate Bay, Newquay, a 30-minute drive away for me. I applied for the bar manager job, which was probably the top bartending job in Cornwall at the time, but might as well have been the top bartending job in the world at the time as far as I was concerned! After the interview, I phoned to make sure I had made the right impression and the job was offered to me there and then. I was incredibly excited to be working at such a high-profile venue along with, I assumed, other like-minded people. The project had cost around £1.5 million, and I'd have my own shiny new bar, complete with eager bar team and even more eager guests!

It turned out that the bar had been badly designed and that I didn't actually have a team at all (just me again), but these were issues that I overcame over the opening months. After all, it's challenges such as those that set you up for opening your own venues, which at that time was the most inconceivable of dreams. I pulled in a couple of friends who had worked for me at the Blue Tomato and we set about getting the drinks programme off the ground. The best thing about Fifteen was the access to incredible, locally sourced seasonal ingredients. After only five months, I had redesigned my initial cocktail list to include a selection of mostly original, seasonally inspired ingredients. I had use of a local forager who would furnish me with wild burdock, scurvy-grass, sea buckthorn and nettles, to name a few. The restaurant also sourced ingredients from nearby biodynamic producers, who supplied me with a whole range of edible flowers, including mallows and borage. I got obsessed with ingredients, provenance and organic produce, even to the point where I had my team manufacturing our very own 'healthy' soft drinks range, including cola, dandelion and burdock, ginger beer and lemonade. I also worked on food and drink pairing projects, developing dishes with the Fifteen chefs to match classic and contemporary cocktails. Furthermore, I developed a deep and abiding love for the world of coffee. Working closely with Origin Coffee in Cornwall, I trained and perfected my craft, which a few years later resulted in me harvesting, processing and roasting my own coffee from the Eden Project in Cornwall. In 2007 and 2008, I competed in the UK Barista Championships, being placed seventh and third respectively.

There was much more to learn on the cocktail side of things, but the late nights were getting the better of me (and my wife Laura). After two and a half years at Fifteen, I was offered a brand ambassador job at the world's largest premium spirits producer Diageo. Many people told me I would be crazy to leave Fifteen. After all, I had managed to get Jamie Oliver to make one of my drinks on TV, and appeared on a few TV shows myself – fame and fortune were potentially just around the corner. But the new job would allow me to meet new people, learn and develop.

The job was quite an undertaking, since it meant that I would be training bartenders from some of the top bars in the UK. I remember anxiously asking Thomas Aske, a fellow brand ambassador (who would later become my business parter), how he handled the bartenders who were really clued up or knew more than he did. Thomas reassured me that I had nothing to worry about. I made sure of that fact by immersing myself in books on spirit production, flavour chemistry, cocktail history and history in general. I set about contacting distillers and archivists in order to equip myself with as much knowledge as possible, and I became more and more capable of answering even the most difficult questions posed by bartenders.

In my spare time, I began brewing beer and cider at home, and I transformed my garage into a distillery, complete with a 30-litre/10-gallon stainless steel still that I blew my first year's bonus on. I put into practice my limited plumbing knowledge, gleaned from a previous summer job, and plumbed in cooling and heating circuits for my brewery/distillery setup. Meanwhile, I became a member of a beer-tasting panel at the then quite small Sharp's Brewery in Rock, learning as much as I could from the Head Brewer, Stuart Howe, about yeast and fermentation science. During the same period, I was lucky enough to visit dozens of distilleries across the world, including facilities in France, Mexico, Holland and Scotland, further improving my understanding of how spirits are made. I also began to tentatively investigate the hot topic of 'molecular mixology', a phrase that I later grew to hate!

From the start, I realized that combining forward-thinking gastronomic techniques with timeless, classic cocktails was going to be fun. It had the wonderful attraction of fusing science with history – bringing both the modern and the classical together, and allowing the drink to tell a richer story. What could be better? During that early inception period, many of the techniques, such as the often-abused foam and the over-applied spherification, were receiving criticism from the classical bartending fraternity, and I could see their argument. But for me, it always seemed obvious that many of the modern practices could work in harmony with classic cocktails without upsetting the DNA too much. All it required was the correct, sympathetic application.

One of the main things I took from my time as a brand ambassador was an understanding of bars in general. I trained at Michelin-starred restaurant bars, huge nightclubs, grand hotel bars, boutique hotel bars, dive bars, classic cocktail bars, pubs and pretty much any other type of bar you can think of. I got to see how they managed operations, what worked, what didn't.

THE BEGINNING (AGAIN)

After two and a half years (see a pattern here?) at Diageo, I was ready to move on again. But this time it was different. My ever-understanding wife Laura and I would need to move out of Cornwall and up to London. It was time to open my own bar, and along with Thomas Aske (my former Diageo colleague), that's exactly what we did.

Having been spectators for the years leading up to Purl's opening, Thomas and I had seen some amazing drinks produced by some of the world's best bartenders. A lot of those drinks had been presented during cocktail competitions, but few of the most fantastic cocktails made their way onto actual lists in bars. It seemed to us a shame that normal consumers never got a chance to try modern ritualistic drinks, or cocktails served in vintage glassware or original drinks with a real story behind them. We set about to make this right, and in opening Purl attempted to create a haven for cocktail lovers.

Purl was designed to be somewhere that oozed historical cocktail appeal, with nods to *The Savoy Cocktail Book*, Professor Jerry Thomas and many other influences from across the years. Our first cocktail list was half classics done right, and half forward-thinking, ultra-modern drinks with all the techniques available at our disposal (a bit like this book, actually).

We took steps to ensure that we could produce these technically advanced drinks night after night. The bar turned into a kitchen with *mise en place* commencing in the late morning, hours before we were due to open. We had portable fish tank pumps fitted to all three stations (see page 49), cream whippers (see page 32) and soda siphons in speed rails, liquid nitrogen (see page 44) on tap and 10 kg/22 lb. of dry ice being delivered a day. We got through a 20 kg/45 lb. block of crystal-clear ice each day, hand cracking it with ice picks, and we upgraded our Hoshizaki ice machine three times to keep up with our ice requirements. Purl was a huge success and quickly became renowned as one of the top bars in the UK as result of the theatricality, innovation and creativity of the cocktails we served.

Following Purl, we opened The Worship Street Whistling Shop in London's Shoreditch, modelled on a Victorian gin palace and equipped with its very own lab for ingredient preparation and drinks development. Here, I worked closely with Ryan Chetiyawardana, developing new and exciting ways of unravelling and reconstituting cocktails at a molecular level. We built stills out of pressure cookers and glass funnels, used rotary evaporators (see page 52) to cold distill delicate ingredients and utilized all manner of acids, salts (see pages 27–29) and powdered ingredients in the quest for making the best drinks we possibly could.

This was a great time for me – it was like learning about cocktails for the first time again. I avidly began researching the science of flavour, from the compounds in food and drink that provide taste and aroma, right through to the human nervous system, multi-sensory flavour perception and the neuroscience of flavour. My research led me to the work of expert chemists, biologists, psychologists and flavour scientists such as Tony Blake, Charles Spence, Hervé This, Gordon Shepherd and Harold McGee.

My curiosity piqued, I inevitably started to conduct my own controlled experiments, too, furthering my understanding of the factors that affect cocktail enjoyment.

PRESENT DAY

This book aims to bring together the core values of what I believe makes a great cocktail. As with most subjects, we have to look back before we can look forward. The history and culture surrounding spirits and cocktails is as rich and diverse as any other topic you could care to mention. Much of my inspiration comes from days gone by, whether it be from the drinks themselves, the surroundings in which they were drunk, common folklore, anecdotes of the era or even something as simple as a glass that may be unique to the time. Combining the history with an eye on the science is the tricky part. Bartenders have long debated between the traditional way of doing things and the right way of doing things. How is it possible to retain the identity of a drink that may be over 100 years old while messing with its components in the pursuit of perfection? There are many drinks in this book that I have aimed to improve through the careful use of specially selected ingredients and techniques. The goal was to keep the function the same, but to create a better user experience, employing all of the modern tools and materials available to me. Naturally, my idea of a perfected drink may be someone else's nightmare; as with food, we all have our own unique flavour preferences born out of positive experiences in the past. Recreating those experiences is the key to meeting or exceeding expectations.

Some of the recipes in this book are long, but hopefully that won't put you off reading and enjoying them. The aim is to take you, step by step, through the thought processes and (hopefully) leave very little to chance. I have certainly found over my career that understanding the little details gives you a greater view of the big picture. This book, unlike any other cocktail book, will delve into those details. It might be that you attempt to accurately recreate some of the recipes in the book – I'd love it if you did. Or it might be that you pick and choose the pieces that interest you or are relevant to one of your own drinks. Either way, I hope you find the information contained within these pages useful and inspiring.

Cheers!

HOW TO USE THIS BOOK

◆

The book is broadly separated into three sections – techniques, recipes and a glossary of terms, suppliers and equipment. This is not a simple encyclopedia of recipes; it is in some parts a manual and in others a documentation of drinking history and the methods of a modern bartender.

The Techniques section covers all of the classic bartending practices, from how to stir a cocktail or select an ingredient, right through to clarifying fruit juices and using liquid nitrogen. Many of the subjects will be referred to within the Cocktails chapters, so you can use the Techniques pages as a reference.

The recipes are ordered according to spirit category – meaning that, for example, all of the vodka-based cocktails are grouped together. I have, however, also produced a flavour map of the drinks in this book (see pages 18–19). The map plots every classic cocktail to an axis of flavour, meaning that you can select which drink you would like to make based on a specific style of cocktail or occasion.

All of the cocktails in the book are grouped in pairs. Some of the drinks have been created specifically for the book, others began development almost a decade ago and some are among the first drinks that I ever made behind a bar (and are a great starting point for any amateur cocktail enthusiast). There are a total of 33 classic drinks, with details on history, creators and recipes. Every one of these cocktails can easily be made at home with only a small selection of bar equipment (and sometimes even that isn't required!). Each classic cocktail is paired with another drink, one that I have created myself based loosely on its classic counterpart. Some of these original cocktails have been deemed by me

to be seriously advanced stuff, impossible to replicate without the necessary kit. I have included them as they make fascinating reading for the amateur, and have provided enough details so that they may even be attempted by other bartender readers. These drinks are labelled 'Mixology Impossible'.

Unless otherwise stated, each recipe makes one serving. You can, of course, double, triple or decuple (multiply by ten) the ingredients to make more – just make sure that all of the ingredients are treated equally! There are a handful of recipes that produce in excess of 20 servings, and this is due to the fact that they may need batching up and barrel or bottle ageing, or that they are traditionally served in a larger container, like a punch bowl.

Many of the recipes in this book also have sub-recipes – a recipe within a recipe. More often than not, the sub-recipe will produce a large enough quantity for multiple individual servings of the finished cocktail, and I provide notes on storing these homemade ingredients. The recipes are listed in the order in which they need to be constructed. It's always worth checking through all of the ingredients needed for every stage before you start. For example, the CL 1900 (see page 174) has three different elements that are made in the order that you need them – the 7X Flavour goes into the Cola Formula and the Cola Formula is used to make the finished drink.

As you are reading this book, it is a given that you will own the basic equipment – shaker, jigger, etc. Any specialist equipment that you may not have at home is flagged up in bold within the method, so you can see at a glance what you might need to complete the recipe.

FUNDAMENTALS

◆

Even though this book contains some complicated recipes and advanced techniques, it is also designed to be used by the amateur home bartender or cocktail enthusiast. With this in mind, I have written this section, which covers the fundamental elements of the bar craft. So whether you're picking up a shaker for the first time or you're years into a bartending career, it's possible that there's something to learn in this section of the book. Enjoy!

BASIC EQUIPMENT

These days there are virtually no limits to the range and variety of bar equipment available to bartender and enthusiast. Contrary to what you might think, you really don't need a lot of equipment to make great drinks. At least half of the drinks in this book can be produced with a cocktail shaker, mixing beaker, barspoon, jigger, strainer and ice only. If you want to give yourself a bit of a head start, I'd add a good set of digital scales (particularly if you want to experiment with some of my original variations), fruit peeler, decent knife and a large syringe. I have travelled the world with little more than the above items and still managed to knock together some crowd-pleasing cocktails when the circumstances required me to.

It's easy to assume that the quality and price tag of your equipment will reflect the quality of your drinks. But we're not building a house here; some of the techniques that the modern bartender uses can have complex elements, but most of the equipment we use to achieve them need not be such a high specification. Lemons and limes don't have to be squeezed with a fancy geared citrus press (also known as a Mexican elbow), and instead of silver ice tongs any combination of finger and thumb will suffice.

When bartending on shift at one of my bars, I will, of course, present drinks using the arsenal of tools available to me, as this is an important part of the theatre of the bar. But when making a tasty nightcap, illuminated only by the glow of the fridge door, you had best believe that I've called upon some unconventional equipment to achieve standard tasks. Below is a list of common bartending equipment and their uses.

BARSPOON

If you are going to spend some money on a nice piece of bar kit, let it be this. Barspoons come in a variety of lengths and breadths, and some have flat discs on the end, others have a kind of pitchfork, and some have nothing at all.

The disc is designed to aid in floating liquids on top of one another. Many bartenders use it for muddling instead, but this is something I would not advise, having seen the effects of metal shattering the side of a highball glass.

The pitchfork end is somewhat of an anomaly. Logic would tell us that it's for picking up olives or cherries etc., but in reality, it's certainly not a replacement for a pair of tongs. Some Japanese bartenders (which is from where this type of spoon originates) have informed me that it is literally for visual effect, flashing light as the top of the spoon spins around.

JIGGER

Jiggers come in all sorts of shapes and sizes, but they all do the same thing – measure liquid. The size you go for is really a reflection of how big you like your drinks, since any cocktail can be made with any jigger (egg cup, thimble), as long as the ratios of the ingredients are kept the same.

The fashionable way to go at the time of writing is a double-ended cone-shaped jigger. One side will typically hold 50 ml/2 oz. and the other 25 ml/1 oz. There are, of course, smaller and larger versions to suit all drinks (some with smaller increments included inside) for adherence to local spirit measurement law enforcement.

Some bartenders prefer to use chef's measuring spoons, a set of six or so common measures on a keyring. While these are excellent for accuracy, they are a little fiddly to use and to clean.

The best compromise is a couple of steel jiggers that have graded measurements on the inside. This should allow you to measure a whole range of quantities easily and accurately.

SHAKERS

Just like jiggers, shakers come in a lot of styles. If you can track down one of the books that documents shakers from different eras, you will undoubtedly be impressed and perhaps even a little perplexed with the variety of contraptions mankind has conceived for the simple practice of shaking ice and liquid together.

Nearly all modern shakers are made from stainless steel. Steel is a reasonably good material for a cocktail shaker, since it is inexpensive and doesn't tarnish easily. Steel also has a lower thermal conductivity than copper, aluminium and silver, so it won't cool down or heat up quickly. For a cocktail shaker, this is a good thing: it means that the chilling power of the ice is being used to chill the cocktail, not your shaker and the air around it. Using a shaker made from silver, copper or aluminium would do the opposite: much of the chilling power of the ice would be quickly absorbed into the shaker walls, ultimately resulting in slightly more dilution in the cocktail.

There are some metals that have recently been used to construct highly non-conductive shakers. Titanium is one of them, since it has around 1% of the conductivity of copper. At such a low level of conductivity, it almost behaves like an insulator. Titanium is also highly chemically resistant and highly resistant to corrosion. Obviously, there are associated expenses with buying a shaker made from expensive materials such as titanium, so you can expect to pay in the region of £150/$230 for one of those beauties! A plastic shaker would achieve even lower levels of thermal conductivity

and cost a lot less. Perhaps the ultimate shaker, which to my knowledge doesn't currently exist, would be made from styrene foam. Styrene foam is used commercially as an insulator, since it has virtually no thermal conductivity. You won't look very cool with a plastic or styrene shaker, mind you!

The volume of the shaker may have some bearing on the degree of aeration and/or emulsification (where using surfactants or egg whites – see pages 48–51) that goes on, with larger shakers, having more air space, being the more effective at this. Obviously, larger shakers can also fit more drink in them, too, which is always a good thing in my book!

(See Ice, Shaking & Stirring, pages 22–26, for more advice on the relative pros and cons of different cocktail shakers and the science behind shaking and stirring drinks.)

MIXING BEAKER

Back when I first picked up a barspoon, mixing beakers were few and far between. Stirred drinks were generally made in the glass part of a Boston shaker, which is silly, because a Boston glass has no lip to pour from, so it meant that you had to pour quite quickly to avoid the drink flowing down the side of the glass!

These days there are a variety of mixing beakers available, ranging considerably in price. The two most important things when choosing a mixing beaker are how well it pours and how well it suits your stirring action, with the former being crucial, since stirring action can be adjusted but a poor beaker will never ever pour well.

Mixing beakers are generally constructed of glass or crystal. Recently, Japanese Yarai mixing beakers have become popular due to high-quality construction and good functionality. They do come at a high price, but hey, you only need to buy one.

Gallone (gallon) mixing glasses are also popular. Hand blown, they are made on the famous glass-producing island of Murano, near Venice, Italy. They are especially useful as the lip curls over the top of the glass in a way that prevents ice from exiting the glass. This not only means that you can pour the liquid out without the use of a strainer, but you can also stir the drink by simply swirling the beaker – so no barspoon required either!

GLASSWARE

Even though you will see me write extensively about the importance of good-quality, relevant and varied service ware, if the truth be told, 90% of cocktails can be served in one of three glasses – the coupe, highball and old fashioned. Settle on a sensible-sized coupe that can handle both a tiny Martini or a shaken higher-volume drink like a Sidecar – 150 ml/5 oz. is usually about right. It won't look like a half-full bucket when serving a Martini, and it won't be full to the brim when mixing a Cosmopolitan. Your highball and old fashioned will usually be around the same volume, only one will be taller and more narrow (highball) and the other more squat and wider (old fashioned). Think about what drinks you like to make the most and consider which size will suit them. I'm a fan of sticking to a glass that fits the need, rather than shopping around and varying the collection.

All that said, I have been known to quite contentedly consume cocktails from tea cups, egg cups or mixed directly back into the bottle. If the drink tastes good, it tastes good; most often the service ware is there only to improve the experience and enhance the environment. If that environment is a camping trip, then why not drink a Manhattan from an enamel camping mug – what vessel could possibly be better suited?

For chilled cocktails, the glasses should always be chilled before use. Serving a cold cocktail in a room-temperature glass is like serving a curry on a cold plate – the food cools down a lot quicker, and likewise, a drink will warm up a lot quicker. Ideally, use glasses directly from a freezer.

You can also chill glasses on the fly by adding a few lumps of ice and some water, then quickly stirring for a minute or so. Taking the time to ensure the glass is at the correct temperature can have a profound effect on your guests' drinking experience.

INGREDIENTS

All ingredients are equal, but some are more equal than others. While some cocktails require highly specific brands or styles in them, most of the time the exact product that you choose won't be of critical importance. It's a common understanding that a cocktail is only as strong as its weakest link, but in reality not all links in the chain are of equal size or importance.

Take a Dry Martini for example; the gin is an important consideration as it is at the forefront of the flavour profile, so a little more care in selection is required. In a cocktail such as the Negroni, however, where the gin battles against far more powerful flavours than that of dry vermouth in the Dry Martini, there is clearly less need to be fastidious about the brand of gin. In fact, unless you're using a gin with wildly extreme botanicals, or one that tastes bad, in all likelihood your Negroni will taste nice with most brands of gin. I liken it (like a lot of things) to cooking. If you're making spaghetti alla Bolognese, for example, the exact cut of minced/ground beef is not as important as the quality of the pasta or tomatoes, or the cooking time. If you're grilling a steak, however, the cut of beef becomes a very important factor. Which is more important in a Bloody Mary – the brand of vodka or the quality of the tomato juice? (See pages 106–109.)

What I'm trying to say here is that in most cases it's ok to select a single brand from each of the main spirit categories (vodka, gin, rum, tequila, whisky, bourbon, Cognac) and stick with it for the majority of your cocktail making. This practice will save you a lot of space and expense, and ensure that your spirit cupboard or back bar doesn't contain a bunch of dusty, neglected bottles. My main piece of advice is that you make sure you pick one that is versatile, of a premium quality and pleasing to drink neat. In this book I will usually stick to one or two brands of booze for each category, but I will also point out any drinks where I believe that a specific style, age or brand of liquor is required. This is most relevant to the rum category where the cocktails are as diverse as the rum category itself.

Likewise, with the dry or fresh products listed in this book, sometimes I will emphasize a need for quality, but in understanding an ingredient's contribution to the drink, you should get a fair idea of how important the ingredient's quality and, where relevant, style is to the final outcome.

THE SCIENCE OF FLAVOUR

◆

There's a lot going on when you take a sip of that Martini. Tongue, mouth, nose, eyes and even ears work in harmony to glean every ounce of relevant information about the drink that you're sipping on. In fact, flavour is among the most complex perceptions created by our brains. Let us first see a description of how flavour is produced, taken from the 1825 book *Physiologie du Goût* ('The Physiology of Taste') by flavour psychologist Jean Anthelme Brillat-Savarin:

Man's apparatus of the sense of taste has been brought to a state of rare perfection; and, to convince ourselves thoroughly, let us watch it at work.

As soon as an edible body has been put into the mouth, it is seized upon, gases, moisture, and all, without possibility of retreat.

Lips stop whatever might try to escape; the teeth bite and break it; saliva drenches it: the tongue mashes and churns it; a breathlike sucking pushes it toward the gullet; the tongue lifts up to make it slide and slip; the sense of smell appreciates it as it passes the nasal channel, and it is pulled down into the stomach (...) without a single atom or drop or particle having been missed by the powers of appreciation of the taste sense.

It's common knowledge that as much as 80% of flavour is deciphered by the nose, not the mouth. This is mostly true, though it's difficult to quantify exactly how much the nose does in comparison to all the multi-sensory inputs that the brain utilizes. The brain's ability to combine taste, touch and smell into a unified flavour image is called synesthesia.

SMELL

Much of this 'flavour mapping' work is conducted through retronasal smell, that is 'backward' smell, through the back of the nose. As we gargle, swill, masticate and swallow, tiny aromatic molecules, only visible on an atomic level, are exhaled up through the throat and out of the nose. As they pass through the nasal passage, they come into contact with the olefactory epithelium – the nose's direct hard-wire to the brain. The olefactory epithelium sends minute signals to the olfactory bulb, which converts signals into a smell image, the main component of flavour.

Contrary to whatever bad publicity you may have heard about the human sense of smell, it is truly an incredible thing – better, in fact, than even the most advanced molecule-detecting equipment that our brains have been able to devise.

TASTE

Taste and the palate also play an important role in flavour perception. Taste begins with taste buds, a collection of sensory cells, each with fine hairs that respond to stimuli. Taste buds are located within the tiny visible folds on the surface of the tongue, known as papillae. The different receptors in taste cells detect five primary tastes – salt, sweet, sour, bitter and umami (a savoury-like taste common in tomatoes, soy sauce and Parmesan cheese). These tastes are detected all over the tongue, though some areas have higher concentrations of specific receptors. Signals are sent to the brain for processing, along with other sensory input.

The tongue and mouth also conduct the important role of detecting mouth-feel. Although more relevant to eating than drinking, mouth-feel can have a profound effect on our appreciation of cocktails. Mouth-feel is not a wholly understood science, but it is known to include such sensory

submodalities as touch, pressure, temperature and pain, each of which affect the image of flavour in different ways. Ever noticed how flat cola and fizzy cola taste different? That'll be the pain receptors in your mouth altering the flavour image when triggered by the tickling of CO_2 gas in the bubbles.

VISION

In the most basic way, our eyes tell us whether something will fit into our mouths, and whether or not it's likely to hurt us. But going deeper, the way that a drink looks plays a huge part in how we determine its flavour. I'm not just talking about pretty garnishes (although they do help), but fundamental things such as colour, size, glassware and temperature indication (frost, steam). My favourite experiment, which I have conducted on more than a few occasions, is feeding someone blue tomato juice (made by agar clarification and blue food colouring – see pages 41–42). Even though the taste and aroma have not been altered at all, most subjects fail to recognize the drink simply because the colour has no relevance to the fruit. Once a lady that I gave blue tomato juice to told me that it tasted like laundry fluid – clearly she was heavily influenced by the bright blue colour.

SOUND

Even sound has an important part to play in the discovery of flavour. The French playwright Molière described in his 1666 play, *The Doctor in Spite of Himself*, the sound of wine as 'glouglou':

How sweet from you, My bottle true;
How sweet from you, Your little glouglou.

And it is true that red wine has an entirely unique sound over other liquids. The 'gloug-gloug' sound of wine as we swallow is the muscle activity in our throats processing red wine's unique texture. The sound of ice clinking in a cocktail shaker or a stream of liquid flowing into a martini glass should not be underestimated as important elements of the overall drinking experience.

OTHER FACTORS

There is a huge variety of other factors that are thought to contribute towards the 'flavour map' of a drink. Even our sense of well-being, comfort and the environment around us affects flavour. Hot soup is better when you're cold and a chilled glass of Sauvignon Blanc tastes better when you're hot. Likewise, continental beers never taste as good as when sipped on a hot sandy beach in their country of origin. Your mother's shepherd's pie will always taste better (or worse) than any other, since it evokes a sense of nostalgia.

In summary, the human appreciation of flavour is a marvellous thing, and something that should be exercised, enjoyed and tested wherever possible. The complex neural pathways that process the data input from our senses all converge in a part of the brain called the 'primate neocortex'. Here, we experience a conscious flavour perception, something that is tangible within our minds. And perhaps the smartest trick of all is that of the brain reflecting the data back down to the tongue and fooling us into thinking the whole experience took place in our mouths!

COCKTAIL TASTE SCIENCE

Looking at the last 200 years of cocktail evolution, we have seen some clues as to why we have landed upon such an eclectic selection of drinks. Many of the advances in cocktail preparation give key indicators as to why we prefer to enjoy drinks one way more than another, and it's these drinks coupled with the complexities of the human perception of flavour that have laid the path for cocktail creators over the years.

We can now go a step further, into the component tastes of a cocktail, and see both how they affect our sense of perception and how they affect each other in the context of a cocktail. Primary taste sensations of saltiness or sweetness are well known to us, but what is not as fully understood is the complex relationships that these tastes have with each other and how they play a role in balancing drinks.

SUGAR

Sugar is energy. Pure energy. As humans we love the stuff – hell, you can add sugar to pretty much anything and we'll probably enjoy it more. There is a primal desire for sugar programmed into every one of us right from birth.

Sugar does have the effect of slightly reducing the perception of alcohol in a drink. Exactly why this is the case is not clear, though it might be partly due to sugar reducing the volatility of the alcohol (how readily it will evaporate). It could also be a result of the brain's 'reward' system, wherein the effect of the alcohol is lessened as a result of the positive sweet trigger. Our reward system recognizes the calories present in the sugar and chooses to ignore the negative chemesthesis effects (see opposite) of the alcohol. Liqueurs are the perfect case in point. Think about how a 40% ABV liqueur slips down a lot easier than 40% straight vodka.

Tests have shown that sugar suppresses the intensity of bitter, acidic and salty flavours, too. But it does more than that: it actually makes those other tastes more pleasurable than if they were stand-alone – the satisfaction of a bittersweet glass of ale, the refreshing acid sting of a kiwi fruit, the indulgence of salted caramel.

BITTERNESS

Bitterness is by far the most complicated of the taste senses. It is thought that the tongue detects over 100 different types of bitterness (salt is just salt), and the molecules that have a bitter taste come in various different shapes and sizes. Unlike sugar, we are programmed with an aversion to bitterness. It's thought that this is as a result of most bitter substances being poisonous in big enough quantities. (The flip side of this is that in smaller quantities bitter ingredients are often medicinal – the anaesthetic effect of chewing on a clove, the anti-malarial properties of quinine and the stomach-settling qualities of holly bush tea. It's for this reason that certain primate species have been observed chewing on bitter plant roots and tree bark when they are feeling unwell.)

Remember your first cup of black coffee? Or your first lager? Chances are that it didn't go down all that well and that's because mother nature wants you to hate bitterness! Bitterness on its own is not nice, and it would require a huge amount of sensory training to convince your brain otherwise.

But we're not going to give in that easily! The problem for Mother Nature lies in the fact that bitterness has a strange drying effect on the tongue that makes you want to refresh your palate. When we drink something intensely bitter, it's almost like an instant thirst inducer, meaning that another sip is required. And another. So when bitterness is accompanied by aromatics and sweetness (and salt – see opposite), it can become incredibly addictive! The best example of this is the classic gin and tonic – surely one of the greatest refreshments the world has known.

Adding bitters to mixed drinks helps us to engineer a more interesting and complex cocktail by fusing together intense bitterness with other taste and aromatic stimuli.

ACIDITY

When we eat or drink something intensely sour, we screw our faces up and wince in the wake of it. Intense sourness is experienced negatively, since its consumption generally has no nutritional benefits – why waste energy eating it?

On the plus side, however, acidity does an excellent job of balancing other taste sensations. If you have ever eaten 'miracle fruit' – an African berry that when consumed temporarily blocks certain taste receptors, resulting in everything tasting sweet – you will have noticed how bland a world it is when there is no acidity to balance sweetness. Without sourness, ripe fruit is simply sweet; even the accompanying aromatics in a fresh peach fail to deliver that heady feeling of gustatory perfection, since there is no acid to balance the sweetness or to grip the palate.

In cocktails we often use sourness, balanced with sweetness, to emulate the taste of ripe fruit. Limes and lemons are mostly used, since they have a relatively neutral flavour profile dominated almost entirely by their sourness. For more on acids, see pages 27–29.

SALT

According to Hervé This's 2006 book, *Molecular Gastronomy*:

> *Salts selectively suppress bitterness (and probably other disagreeable tastes as well) while intensifying agreeable tastes.*

In my experience, a small addition of salt (0.1–0.3%) almost always improves the taste of a cocktail, cordial, liqueur or syrup. The one major exception being if the product is already noticeably salty – through the use of a salty ingredient, perhaps. It is ironic, then, that it is such and under-utilized ingredient in cocktails. A great example of where it is used is in the Gin Rickey. This drink is basically a Gin Fizz (see page 60), or Tom Collins, but with lime juice substituted for lemon juice. Yet in some cultures, most notably India, the sugar is omitted and a small amount of salt is used in its place. What, on paper, appears be a very sour drink actually becomes softer and really very tasty. Salt is a much more common beverage ingredient in hot climates, since in the right quantities it is thought to aid in maintaining hydration.

Salt lowers perception of sourness significantly, but only slightly affects the intensity of bitter or sweet things.

UMAMI

The discovery of the fifth taste, umami, seems like a new thing, but it was actually over 100 years ago, in 1908, that Kikunae Ikeda at the Tokyo Imperial University established its existence. Not salty, sweet, sour or bitter, umami produces a strange sensation that can best be described as 'savoury'. Umami is not a taste that crops up all that often in cocktails. Sure, the tomato juice family of drinks – Bloody Mary (see pages 106–109), Red Snapper et al. – have their fair share of savoury kick, but it pretty much ends there. Given the strong savoury connotations of umami (if you've never tried it, miso soup or just pure monosodium glutamate are a safe bet as long as you can ignore the saltiness of the soup), it's not all that surprising that bartenders use very little, since one of the main functions of a cocktail is to whet the appetite, not suppress it.

ALCOHOL

Almost all spirits have some flavour, even the vodkas. This may come from residual fusel oils or higher alcohols remaining from the distillation process, or traces of the product that the spirit is made from. In the case of vodka, this might be a slight cereal note, or a buttery potato flavour.

Pure ethanol (alcohol) is almost completely flavourless. But when mixed with water at certain specific concentrations, it does have a slightly bitter-sweet taste. In addition to this, ethanol and acetone (a flavourful ketone) both have a dehydrating effect on the palate, which in turn gives a sense of astringency. Chemesthesis is a term meaning the feel or sensibility of a chemical, ethanol in this case, on the skin, taste buds, mucous membranes, throat and stomach. Alcohol plays havoc with certain nerve channels and the result is the perception of burning. It just so happens that the same nerves triggered by alcohol are the ones triggered by capsaicin (the stuff that makes chillies hot). While pain isn't a taste, per se, it does have a knock-on effect on our perception of tastes and aromas.

SWEET

OLD FASHIONED

MAI TAI

ESPRESSO MARTINI

CORPSE REVIVER

TEQUILA & SANGRITA

SAZERAC

NEGRONI

MARTINEZ

FISH HOUSE PUNCH

MANHATTAN

ROB ROY

STRONG

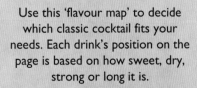

MARTINI

BRANDY CRUSTA

THE FLAVOUR MAP

Use this 'flavour map' to decide which classic cocktail fits your needs. Each drink's position on the page is based on how sweet, dry, strong or long it is.

SIDECAR

MARGARITA

DRY

DAIQUIRI

SWEET

ZOMBIE

FLIP

JULEP

EGG NOG

HOT BUTTERED RUM

CUBA LIBRE

BLOODY MARY

PURL

BRAMBLE

MOSCOW MULE

PALOMA

MOJITO

LONG

SINGAPORE SLING

RAMOS GIN FIZZ

WHISKY SOUR

AVIATION

COSMOPOLITAN

DRY

TECHNIQUES

ICE, SHAKING & STIRRING

FUNDAMENTALS

It might seem like a no-brainer to stress the importance of how you shake, stir and use ice, but it is easy to overlook the complexity of these techniques, and in doing so, overlook some crucial variables that can be manipulated to your advantage. Both the temperature and the degree of dilution of a cocktail are key contributors to the enjoyment of the cocktail, so insuring that they are managed correctly is a hugely important part of the bartender's craft.

The common belief is that colder drinks taste better. As temperature lowers, the drink becomes less viscous and the texture becomes thicker and more pleasant. Alcohol evaporation is suppressed so that the initial hit of liquor feels softer and increases gently as the drink warms on the tongue. Low temperature also provides a greater feeling of refreshment and cleansing to the palate. However, the negative side of very cold drinks is that they're not as smelly. Vapour pressure is a term that describes how readily a liquid vaporizes – it's the liquid's vapour that we smell when we stick our noses into a glass of wine. Vapour pressure lowers as temperature lowers, meaning that colder drinks have less aroma.

Good chilling goes hand in hand with the melting of ice. Many bartenders have created elaborate routines to limit dilution, but the truth is that a bit of dilution in a drink can actually be a positive thing. But when does not enough dilution become too much? Looking at different bottles of gin, you can see from the wide variety of bottle strengths that producers are careful to package the product at exactly the right ABV to best show off the flavour. The same is true for cocktails; the ABV of a finished drink will affect both the taste of the drink and the aroma, where a little extra water can persuade a greater number of aromatic molecules to escape the glass (which is why water is often added to whisky).

Much of the time dilution is a subjective science, but I have found that sometimes the amount of water in a cocktail is of critical importance and can easily ruin a drink when insufficient care is taken. The key is understanding how and why chilling and dilution occur, then adjusting our techniques, like a chef adjusts cooking time, to meet the needs of each individual cocktail.

THE PHYSICS OF ICE

Your room temperature spirits and liquors store heat energy and when mixed with ice the two components attempt to equilibrate.

The liquor is chilled by the ice in two ways that take place simultaneously. The first and most obvious of these physical reactions is the direct conduction of heat from the liquor to the ice – the liquor is cooled because the ice is colder. It takes 209 joules of energy to warm 100 g ice up by 1°C (this is known as the specific heat of ice), and that energy is 'stolen' from the liquor by the ice, which in turn cools the liquor down.

The second, less obvious (but more important), reaction that takes place is the melting of the ice and the associated energy required to do it. In contrast to the specific heat, it takes 33,400 joules of energy to melt 100 g of ice into 100 g water (this is known as the heat of fusion of ice). In the context of a cocktail, the energy required is once again stolen from the liquor.

Ice used directly from the freezer will chill a cocktail with marginally less dilution than ice that has sat around for 20 minutes. This is for two reasons, the first of which is that ice taken directly from the freezer will be colder (about -18°C/ -0.4°F) than ice that has been exposed to room temperature air for a while. This means that some of the chilling power of the freezer ice will come from its low temperature, about 3,760 joules per 100 g of ice. The rest (and vast majority) of the chilling power still comes from the melting however – a potential 33,400 joules if 100 g ice in total is melted. Ice that has had time to warm up and sit around, or ice that is taken directly from an ice maker, is about 0°C/32°F – its melting point. That ice will chill a cocktail only through energy absorbed by the heat of fusion.

The second (and more important) reason that 'warmed-up' ice dilutes a drink more is that it usually has surface water on it. Since the ice is constantly melting from the outside in, this thin film of water can add up to a significant quantity (especially on crushed ice) when a large scoop is added to a cocktail shaker. That immediate dilution also means it becomes harder for the ice to do its chilling job, since it has more overall liquid to

contend with. That in turn results in increased dilution of the drink as the ice melts. It's a nasty chain of events that as a bartender it is certainly best to avoid. My advice is to use refrozen ice, or drain away the surface water by running it through a salad spinner (or swinging it around in a cloth bag) before use – you'll be surprised how much water hides in all those nooks and crannies!

A glass of ice water will never be lower than 0°C/32°F, since it would have to freeze to drop below zero. But many strong cocktails can be chilled as low as -8°C/17.6°F. This low temperature is only possible because alcohol (ethanol) has a much lower freezing point than water. An unshaken cocktail with 25% ABV (such as a Whisky Sour) will have a freezing point of around -15°C/5°F, and the ice will continue to melt and chill the drink well below 0°C/32°F, even though the ice is actually warmer than the cocktail. As the ice melts to facilitate chilling, the alcohol content of the liquid decreases. This in turn means that the theoretical minimum temperature to which the ice can chill the drink increases as time goes on.

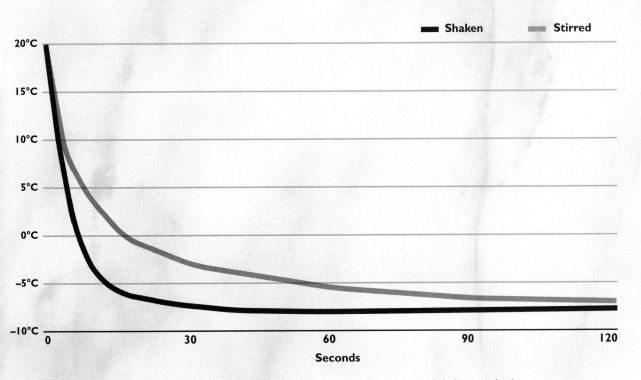

The decrease and eventual plateau in drink temperature over time by stirring and shaking methods.

The shape and size of the ice you use makes very little difference to the final temperature and dilution of the drink. Crushed, cubed and even big rocks of hand-cracked ice of the same weight will all eventually achieve about the same level of dilution and temperature. Only the time it takes to achieve it changes because the surface areas of the the different ice types vary. Stirring with crushed ice might take a Martini down to -5°C/23°F in ten seconds, but stirring the same Martini with the same weight of hand-cracked ice can take over two minutes to achieve the same level of temperature and dilution.

SHAKING

In a shaken cocktail, the drink's ingredients are combined in a cocktail shaker and shaken with ice for a short time, typically under ten seconds. Shaking a cocktail chills it quickly. This is, in part, because the agitation of the ice and liquid speeds up the process of equilibrium, but also because the ice cracks and breaks, increasing its surface area. Shaking a drink for more than 20 seconds will have very little further effect on temperature or dilution (see graph on page 23). This is because as the cocktail approaches its freezing point its temperature plateaus. At this point, the level of dilution will also plateau, since the ice is only required to stabilize the temperature of the drink, not chill it.

Shaken drinks are also 'aerated' to a degree – the action of whipping up the cocktail with ice causes air bubbles to become trapped in the liquid for a time. We are able to detect these tiny bubbles on the palate and they can profoundly affect the tactile experience of the cocktail and the way in which flavour is perceived.

The Japanese bar scene has contributed a number of great things to Western bartending over the past few years, the most useful of all being the wide selection of quality barware and tools. Another significant influence that has come out of Japan has made a lot of Western bartenders reconsider the way in which they shake. When I first heard about the 'Japanese hard shake', I assumed it was a way of shaking a drink hard (makes sense), but if anything it should refer to how hard it is to master.

The aim is to bounce the ice off every surface of the shaker by moving the shaker in a highly specific pattern. It looks a lot like a dance step, but with a cocktail shaker. The intended result is a drink that, quite simply, tastes better. The pioneer of the technique, Uyeda San of Tender Bar in Tokyo, is adamant that the drink is better in every way, but in tests I have discovered that the pattern in which you shake (as long as it's not excessively slow) makes no difference to the temperature or dilution of the cocktail. Once again, science wins over.

That leaves only the element of aeration. Sadly, measuring aeration and viscosity is much harder to do and requires in-depth qualitative testing to be able to truly determine whether the hard shake really does make a better drink.

STIRRING

A strong drink can be chilled to -3°C/27°F in under ten seconds by shaking it with cubed ice, but to achieve the same result by stirring with cubed ice will take over 30 seconds. This is because a stir is, in a sense, a very slow shake. You can be forgiven for assuming that a stirred drink has more dilution because it takes longer, but the physics are the same whether the drink is shaken or stirred – if a cocktail is stirred for long enough, it will reach almost exactly the same temperature and dilution as if it were shaken. I say almost, because the longer exposure to the warm air surrounding the beaker will create some extra dilution in the drink.

The most important thing to understand about stirring is that it takes rather a long time – over a minute in many cases if you're aiming for really low temperatures. Remember that chilling and dilution plateau in the same way as shaking; after around 120 seconds (depending on the size of the ice) the drink won't get much colder and it won't get much more diluted (see graph on page 23).

WHAT'S THE BEST ICE TO USE IN THE COCKTAIL?

Despite a strong argument for large lumps of hand-cracked ice in a finished drink, it's also important not to let head rule over heart. Some drinks are inseparably intertwined with iconic visual appeal and when constructing these libations, great care must be taken not to pervert the history that has brought them to our recipe books today.

For example, drinks like the Mojito (see pages 156–157) or Caipirinha (cachaça, whole lime wedges and sugar) generally use crushed ice, partly due to its speedy cooling capacity, but the ice also plays a big part in the presentation of the drink, too. If ever you have been served a Mojito with cubed ice, you would have noticed that the mint leaves clumped together and likely floated near the top of the drink. Crushed ice allows the bartender to encapsulate the mint leaves of the drink within layers of frozen nuggets, evenly distributed through the glass, changing the visual impact from that of a stagnant pond to a perfectly layered, icy mint tomb. Likewise, the tropical connotations that are implied by crushed ice have no place in the seductive leather-embossed, cigar-smoked ritual that surrounds a cocktail such as the Old Fashioned (see page 146). For an Old Fashioned, a single lump of hand-cracked ice perfectly reflects the discerning character present within any man with the required status to order one.

MATERIALS

Recently, I have taken a much stronger interest in the materials that I use to stir and shake drinks. Early test results have shown huge differences in drink temperature and the associated dilution based on the size and thermal conductivity of the shaker or mixing beaker.

Larger shakers have more material for the ice to chill and so result in more dilution. This is bad if you're only making one drink, but a large shaker filled with ice and four Cosmopolitans would actually produce less dilution than four small shakers making the same four drinks. This is because the volume to surface area ratio of the larger shaker is smaller; in other words, it holds more stuff using comparatively less metal.

Understanding the effects of different shakers on the final drink will help us develop more specific guidelines for classic cocktails. I envisage a time in the not-too-distant future where we select specific equipment for specific drinks based on the target temperature and dilution of that drink. If you like a splash of water in your Daiquiri to take the edge off, why not try shaking it in a small copper three-piece shaker instead? You might find it provides the extra dilution you're after!

The chart below lists the four most common shaker types, detailing the typical size and materials it is made from. These are rough guidelines since many of these shakers will come in a variety of sizes.

Shaker type	Material	+'s	–'s
Three piece (cobbler)	Steel, copper, plastic, titanium	Built-in 'strainer'.	Usually quite small.
Parisienne	Steel	Easy to clean, elegant, relatively large.	Requires strainer.
Boston	Glass and steel	Easy to clean, large, visible ingredients.	Crude, requires a strainer, breakable.
Tin-on-Tin	Steel	Easy to clean, inexpensive.	Requires strainer.

SEASONING COCKTAILS

◆

Seasoning a cocktail is not something that we normally think necessary to do. In the kitchen, salt, acids and umami flavours are commonly used to add depth and breadth to a dish. So how do we do it in cocktails?

SALT

As I mentioned in the The Science of Flavour section of the Introduction (see page 17), salt is universally recognized to improve flavour in the correct quantities. I have personally introduced salt to more and more of my creations over the last few years for the simple reason that they taste better with a pinch of salt. Salt suppresses the perception of bitterness and astringency, and, as with food, it is highly effective in accentuating the positive characteristics of a drink. The important distinction to make here, though, is that in most cases the salt shouldn't be noticeable; for me, that means keeping the usage down to around 0.25–0.7% of the total weight of the drink.

Traditionally, alkaline salts have been used in the production of seltzer water and soft drinks as an acidity buffer. Salt has the effect of softening acidity slightly, and as such has been used to soften the slightly nasty carbonic acid present in carbonated water and in the production of acid phosphate, a traditional acidulent for flavoured sodas.

I tend to use classic sea salt (sodium chloride) flakes mostly. They are easy to handle, highly soluble and good for extracting flavours when left to infuse with dry ingredients (to make flavoured salt, for example). However, there are other options in the form of ingredients that are naturally salty. Bacon is becoming a commonly used salty ingredient as either a fat wash – the process of mixing rendered fat with a liquid, then allowing it to stabilize and filtering it back out – or infused directly into spirits and liqueurs. Marmite or Vegemite can also provide a nice saltiness and an accompanying savoury note. Soy sauce and fish sauce both have a reasonably high salinity, too, but use carefully and be aware of differing salt levels between styles and brands before chucking it straight into a drink! Shrimp paste has a salty/sweet character; the first time I was served shrimp paste in a Bloody Mary I was blown away by the flavour.

Flavouring salts is easy to do and can be very effective. Try storing sea salt flakes with a range of dry ingredients in airtight containers, from whole vanilla pods to lavender flowers. You'll be surprised how much flavour the salt takes on, and it can then be used as either an ingredient or part of a garnish.

ACIDS

The bar craft has historically used lemons and limes as souring agents. They do a very good job of balancing sweetness and adding a 'fruity' flavour to the drink. Acid is important in many drinks, since it activates the salivary glands on the side of your tongue, resulting in loads of nice saliva to swish the drink around the mouth. There are plenty of alternatives to citrus fruit, though, and in many cases these other ingredients can be very cost effective, too (lemons and limes are not cheap). Below are a few examples. (Remember: the lower the pH, the more sour the ingredient.)

CITRUS
The obvious choice for many a bartender. Citrus is natural, stores reasonably well and provides theatrical and aromatic effect when freshly squeezed into a drink. Lime is generally the most sour of the family and can be as sour as 1.8 pH.

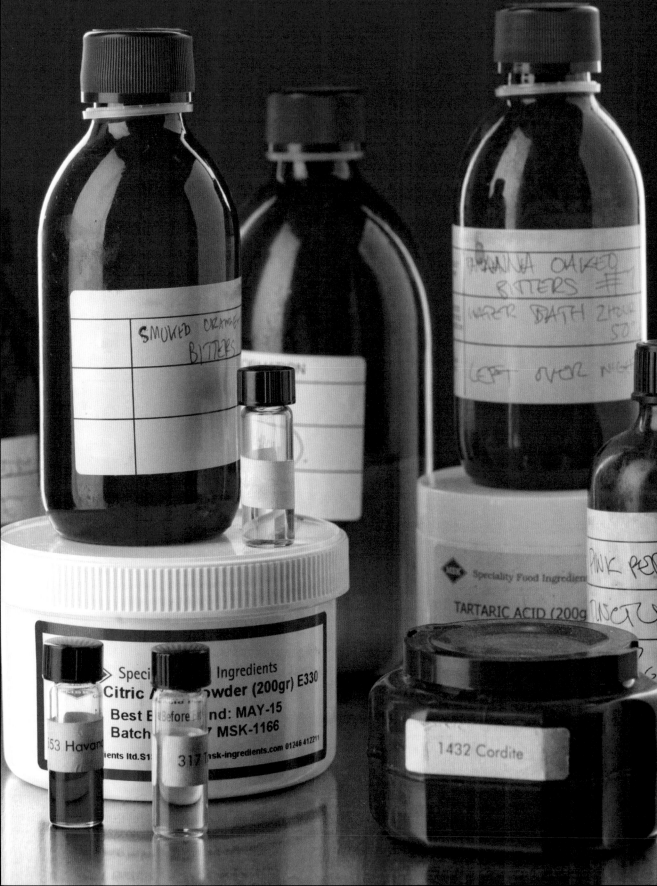

Lime is comprised of both citric and ascorbic acid, whereas lemon is almost entirely citric acid and around pH 2.3 (see Pure Acids, below, for more on acid styles). Orange and grapefruit have a similar pH to one another of around 3.7 (oranges have more sugar in them, so feel less sour).

PURE ACIDS

The cheapest, easiest and least romantic way to use acids is to simply purchase them in their pure, powdered form. This usually requires a pH testing kit, as you will need to dilute the acid to a usable level. I normally dilute to around pH 2.5 so as to emulate the intensity of lemon juice, but you can go stronger and use the solutions in a dasher bottle as you would with bitters. Here are some of the commonly available acids with some tasting notes:

- **Acetic Acid:** common in vinegar – powerful pungency
- **Ascorbic Acid:** vitamin C, present in most citrus fruit – crisp and bright
- **Citric Acid:** citrus fruit – bright, sharp and clean
- **Lactic Acid:** found in dairy products – burnt milk, sour cream, buttermilk
- **Malic Acid:** green apples, nectarines – fruity, bright, tangy
- **Tartaric Acid:** from grapes – intense and clean, quickly drops off

Measuring pH is a useful thing to do if you want to be sure of the intensity of your acids. This can be done with pH strips, which, when dipped in the solution, change colour based on the acidity of the liquid. You can also buy inexpensive digital pH readers that are not much bigger than a marker pen. These are dipped into the liquid and then show a digital reading.

OTHER FRUIT

There are various fruity alternatives to our citrus friends. Some of them may be sourceable locally to you and so tick boxes where provenance and food miles are concerned. Here's a brief rundown of the predominant acids in common fruits:

Apples – malic
Cherries – citric
Currants – citric, tartaric

Blueberries – citric
Cranberies – citric, malic
Gooseberries – citric

Grape – malic, tartaric
Lemon – citric
Nectarine – malic
Passionfruit – malic
Pear – malic
Rhubarb – malic, citric, oxalic
Tomato – citric, malic

Kiwi – citric
Lime – malic, citric
Orange – citric
Peach – malic
Pineapple – citric, malic
Strawberries – citric

Many of the fruits listed above contain other acids in trace amounts, but I have only listed the ones that you can actually detect.

VINEGAR

As used in shrubs (see Cured Margarita, page 192), vinegar might sound like a strange choice, but in the right quantities or when coupled with citrus juice it can add amazing depth. Vinegar contains acetic acid and is usually between 2.5 and 3.5 pH depending on the style. Some vinegars, such as balsamic, have significantly more flavour than others and this is something to bear in mind when using them. My personal favourite is sherry vinegar – it's only around 3.5 pH, but adds a nice sherry flavour to cocktails.

UMAMI

If you're in the mood for a touch of savoury flavour to your cocktails, there are various options. Tomatoes and Parmesan cheese provide a fair whack of umami flavour, as do dried mushrooms, kombu seaweed and soy bean paste. Some of those may sound more desirable in a cocktail than others, but in small quantities any of them can enhance certain types of drinks, especially smoked or smoky-tasting cocktails.

Of course, you can always cut straight to the taste and buy monosodium glutamate (MSG) powder, which is excellent for enhancing my Ultimate Bloody Mary (see pages 107–109).

INFUSION & EXTRACTION

— ◆ —

Manufacturing liquors, bitters, cordials and tinctures has become a staple part of the barcraft in recent years. While the classicist's approach requires very little in the way of 'homemade' ingredients, any budding bartender intent on making their own drinks must be comfortable with the idea of making their own ingredients. The production of these ingredients can all be classified under the heading 'infusions'. Think of it like making a cup of tea!

One of the advantages of pre-infusing liquids is that the product can be stored and reused with confidence in its consistency. Making a redcurrant liqueur will yield better long-term results and require less time overall than 'muddling' redcurrants and sugar every time you wish to make a drink.

There are a number of techniques that can be used to introduce flavour to spirits or to create water-based infusions. Alcohol, by its very nature, does an excellent job of drawing out and suspending the volatile compounds of the ingredients it comes into contact with. Infusing and extracting these volatiles is the basis for the production of many flavoured spirits and liqueurs.

FUNDAMENTALS

In its simplest form, infusion of a liquid is affected by the size of the particle(s) to be infused, the weight of the particle(s) and the temperature, pressure and alcohol content.

It's generally accepted that chopping something to half its size will make it infuse four times faster. This not only has a huge effect on the time it takes to infuse a liquid, but also on the amount of spice, herb or fruit required. So long as the particles are not so small that you cannot filter them out afterwards, it is almost always better to chop or grind your ingredients as fine as you can.

Density and intensity are much harder to measure than size. A pink peppercorn is far more intense of flavour and dense in structure than a white tea leaf, for example. All ingredients are different and it would need a lot of pages to list the relevant infusion times and quantities for every single commonly used ingredient.

The aim is to infuse the ingredient at the right pressure and temperature for a length of time that best extracts all that is good about the ingredient, without extracting bad, astringent or bitter notes (unless bitterness is what you're after!).

Warm infusions speed up the extraction process of almost everything, as well as extracting solubles that are unobtainable at lower temperatures. In its simplest form, a warm infusion is a saucepan and a hob/stove. For many ingredients this is the quickest and most efficient infusion process, and excellent when making flavoured syrups and liqueurs because sugar can be dissolved whilst the solution is still warm. The downside of warm infusions is the potential for heat-based spoilage. Fruit zests begin to stew at sustained high temperatures, herbs release undesirable bitter chlorophyll notes, and the subtleties of flowers are overpowered by generic vegetal characteristics.

MACERATION

The most common form of infusion is simple maceration: adding herbs, spices, nuts or fruit to water (generally with sugar) or alcohol. Macerations can be either cold or warm, depending on the product that you're infusing, and can take anything from an hour to a month to get the best results.

Speak to any bartender and almost all will admit to their first foray into infusion including a bottle of vodka, a herb or fruit of some kind and a warm coffee machine, or glasswasher. Despite all the modern practices used for infusing flavours, a

bottle of liquor with some fruit or herbs chucked in still remains a very effective way of doing things (pictured above, left). This is partly due to the fact that the technique sucessfully 'contains' the infusion. Think about it – when a chef makes a tasty stock and fills the room with wonderful aroma, all that aroma is flavour that is lost from the stock itself. Keeping flavour sealed in is one of the key steps to a successful infusion.

SOUS VIDE

Sous vide, or 'under vacuum', is a controlled warm maceration. The process has two main benefits: the removal of air from the cooking process and the precise control of temperature. The ingredients are sealed into plastic pouches (pictured above, bottom right), then cooked in a waterbath (top right). The process is used a lot in modern kitchens as a way of precisely cooking meat and vegetables, but it can also be used for creating cocktail ingredients.

In a professional restaurant or bar, the infusion would be made by adding the ingredients to a heat-resistant plastic pouch, specifically designed for vacuum packing. The pouch and its contents are placed in a vacuum chamber, the air is removed and the bag sealed. Then the pouch is placed in a heated recirculating water bath, set to a precise temperature. The exact temperature will differ depending on what ingredients are being infused, and the level of extraction required, but will generally sit between 50–90°C/122–194°F. After a period of time, the infusion is removed, filtered and bottled.

There are distinct advantages to this approach: precise control of both the temperature and time of infusion; even radiation of heat throughout the infusion; no risk of overcooking or burning; little or no oxygen within the vacuum pouch, which avoids spoilage by oxidation; and a sealed package, meaning that no aromatics can escape.

At home, many of the same results can be achieved. You can buy inexpensive vaccum sealers from companies such as Sous Vide Supreme, or in place of a vacuum packer you can use ziplock bags – some of which can be purchased with hand-operated pumps to remove the air (just make sure you have a good seal on the bag or you'll find your precious infusion leaking into the water bath!). Sous Vide Supreme sell water baths for as little as £220/$340. One day 'water ovens' like these will be as commonplace in our homes as a microwave. Placing a saucepan filled with water in a low temperature oven is a cheaper way of doing things, but very hard to control.

For a long time I've considered the option of putting a sealed infusion through a dishwasher or washing machine cycle (set to 60°C/140°F). Certainly, the yield would be huge as the appliance could be filled with lots of infusions, but I'm yet to persuade my wife that the potential sacrifice of the machine is worth it!

See page 192 for my sous vide Lime Shrub recipe (using sherry vinegar), or page 105 for my sous vide Cranberry Consommé.

PRESSURE INFUSION

Infusing ingredients under pressure can speed up infusion time significantly. The most obvious way of doing this is with a pressure cooker.

A pressure cooker (pictured above) is essentially a large pot with a pressure-sealable lid. They are excellent for infusions that require a decent amount of heat in order to best extract flavours, because pressure cookers work by increasing the boiling point inside the cooker. (See page 166 for my pressure-cooked Brown Orgeat.)

Most pressure cookers have a gauge indicating the pressure inside the device. Add water and some hardy spices that enjoy high temperatures (burdock root, star anise, sarsaparilla), and at 15 psi of pressurethe water inside will boil at 120°C/248°F, extracting flavours that would be otherwise unobtainable without the increased temperature.

Warning: Never pressure cook alcohol-based infusions, since high temperatures and alcohol vapour are not safe together!

Another simple and inexpensive method that relies on pressure is 'nitrogen cavitation'. This requires a cream whipper gun (pictured right) that uses 8-g N_2O canisters (see Foams, Airs & Eggs, pages 48–49). Adding a liquid to the whipper followed by selected herbs or spices, then charging the cream whipper, results in a rapid infusion time.

The process is based on the nitrogen gas dissolving into the liquid, then forming explosive bubbles once the pressure is quickly released. These bubbles are powerful enough to break apart cell structures in some plant matter and it's this action that increases infusion speed. Repeating the process a few times can yield significant results in a matter of minutes.

One of the huge advantages of nitrogen cavitation is that the infusion doesn't require any heating and therefore ingredients aren't susceptible to temperature-based spoilage.

Pressure infusion can be very useful in the manufacture of bitters and tinctures that use dense ingredients like roots, barks and seeds.

DISTILLATION

Though not a method that is especially practical, distillation is nonetheless a very effective way of making infusions, with the added benefit of crystal-clear results. After all, the world's most popular infused spirit, gin, is made this way.

Small distillation setups can be purchased reasonably cheaply, but be aware that in many countries it is illegal to distil or redistil spirits without a licence.

HYDROCOLLOIDS
JELLIES, GUMS & GELLING AGENTS

Hydrocolloids are a family of compounds that can be used to thicken liquids, strengthen ice creams, create alcoholic jellies and jams, stabilize foams and airs, emulsify fats into aqueous (water-based) solutions and create fluid gels. Given the diversity of both the different types of hydrocolloid and their various applications, this section is an important part of the modern mixologist's repertoire.

Hydrocolloids work on the principle that dissolving tiny particles in a liquid causes the liquid to 'slow down' as the particles bump and rub into each other. In small quantities this results in a slight thickening; in larger doses it creates liquids with a purée-like texture, or even solid gels where the particles have been packed tightly enough so that they stick together, like a traditional jelly.

There are simply too many different types of thickening, stabilizing and solidifying agents to go into all of them in this book. They range from fruit- and plant-based hydrocolloids, such as pectin and tapioca, through to marine-originating compounds like agar, carrageenan and alginates. There are also various gums that have been used for centuries as thickeners and stabilizers – gum arabic, locust bean gum and guar gum. Finally, there are microbial-based hydrocolloids like gellan gum and xanthan gum, and modern cellulose-based hydrocolloids such as methyl-cellulose.

FUNDAMENTALS

With the exception of gelatine leaf, hydrocolloids tend to come in powder or flake form. Be sure to keep them that way by storing in a cool, dry place. Keep gelatine leaf dry and in a sealed container.

All hydrocolloids require some kind of dispersion and hydration. That is, they must be evenly and completely mixed into the liquid. In some cases this may require aggressive mixing (with a blender, for example), while in other instances a gentle stir may be enough. Ultimately, the aim is to surround each hydrocolloid molecule with water, thus creating a uniform solution.

Some hydrocolloids will only dissolve and disperse at certain temperatures (see the chart on page 37). Using a heated magnetic stirrer or a Thermomix (pictured left) makes this task a lot easier, but you can of course always rely on a whisk, pan, hob/stove and thermometer!

SUMMARY OF HYDROCOLLOID
APPLICATIONS

JELLY

Make jellies as edible garnishes/accompaniments, or as an entirely edible alcoholic drink. First, disperse the gelling agent into the liquid (using the recommended ratio), then heat to the necessary

temperature, cast into a mould, chill and serve. See my Royal Purl Stock Cube on page 82 for an example of use.

FLUID GEL

Useful for suspending particles in drinks, whilst still maintaing a 'liquid' mouth-feel. First, disperse the gelling agent into the liquid (using the recommended ratio) and heat to the necessary temperature. Chill, then shear using a whisk or blender. See my Hot & Iced Julep on pages 144–145 for an example of this.

THICKENING

Thickening, or altering the viscosity of a liquid is useful when floating different liquids, or for creating textural points of difference and extended flavour release. First, disperse the gelling agent into the liquid (using the recommended ratio), then heat to the necessary temperature, chill and shear until smooth.

FOAMING

Many types of hydrocolloid can be used to create foams; see pages 48–49 for more on this.

TYPES OF GELLING AGENT

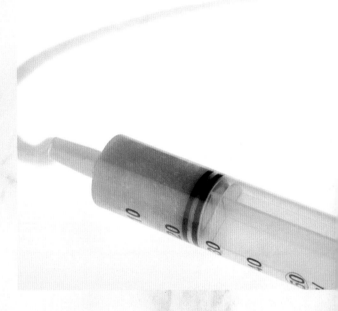

Each hydrocolloid has its own characteristics. Texture, melting point, cloudiness, alcohol and acid tolerance all vary according to the type of hydrocolloid you choose to use. Some are better suited to certain applications (see the table on page 37) and in some cases two hydrocolloids can be combined to better achieve a specific gelling goal. Of course, in other situations, combining two hydrocolloids – such as gelatine and methyl cellulose – can be disastrous.

AGAR-AGAR

Agar-agar (or agar) is a complex carbohydrate-based gelling agent that is extracted from red algae. It can be used to stabilize foams, thicken liquids and make fluid gels, and is also very useful for clarification (see pages 41–42). Agar produces a more temperature-stable jelly than gelatine that melts at around 85°C/185°F, and as such can be served warm, will not melt in the mouth and requires chewing in order to break it down.

GELATINE

Gelatine is a derivative of collagen protein that is usually extracted from animal skins, and is used to create traditional jellies that are non-heat resistant but have a traditional springy texture. It is capable of jellifying spirits, vermouths, wine and sherry, and can be used to great effect as an accompaniment to a drink. Along with agar-agar, gelatine can also be added to foams to create more stable, mousse-like toppings. Gelatine melts in the mouth, giving a soft, creamy texture. An alcohol content actually increases the strength of a gelatine, until it becomes 30–50% of the gel, at which stage it will cause the gel to precipitate into solid particles.

A number of fruits, including kiwi, pineapple and melon, are incapable of being made into gelatine gels as they contain certain enzymes that break down protein chains. This can be overcome by gently warming the juice to deactivate the enzymes.

Gelatine is usually sold in either granulated or sheet (leaf) form. Gelatine is graded by bloom strength, an expression of its gelling power. This number (which can be anything from 30–300) refers to the tenderness or brittleness of the resulting jelly, with 30 producing a very tender, almost liquid-like jelly, and 300 producing a very tough and brittle jelly.

Both granulated and leaf gelatine require presoaking in cold water before being added to the warm solution that you are preparing to be jellified. Hydrating the gelatine first is an excellent practice as direct submersion in warm liquid can cause the gelatine to become sticky and clump together.

GELLAN

Gellan is a carbohydrate-based gelling agent that is secreted by a bacterium. Gellan is available in two kinds: low-acyl and high-acyl.

Low-acyl gellan can form gels that melt at over 100°C/212°F, and is often used in the production of ice cream as a stabilizer that slows the melting process. High-acyl gellan is similar to low-acyl, but it forms opaque jellies that have a lower melting point (around 75°C/167°F). Gellan gum can be used in low concentrations to form excellent, heat-stable fluid gels.

GUM ARABIC

Gum arabic is derived from the sap of the acacia tree. It is traditionally used as an emulsifier in the manufacture of soft drinks due to its excellent ability to suspend oil particles in a liquid. See my CL 1900 on page 174 for an example of its uses.

METHYL-CELLULOSE

Methyl-cellulose (or methocel) is extracted from fibrous plant matter and behaves rather like the opposite of gelatine – it only remains jellified when hot and melts when cooled. Typically, the compound is hydrated in cold liquid, then once heated above 50°C/122°F it will begin to set into a jelly. The jelly will only precipitate if the temperature drops below 50°C/122°F and the process can be repeated.

Methyl-cellulose can be used to add effect to ice cream cocktails: by including 1–2% methocel in an ice cream batter, the frozen mixture can be dropped into boiling liquid and still retain its shape.

The result is ice cream that is both hot and cold! See my Hot & Cold Nitro Eggnog Ice Cream recipe on page 122 for an example of this.

SODIUM ALGINATE

Alginates are carbohydrates extracted from brown seaweed that only form jellies in the presence of calcium. Enterprising chefs of the past have profited from alginate's unusual feature by using it as a spherification tool. Spherification is the creation of edible liquid-filled balls that are held together by a thin outer film. When small they are reminiscent of caviar, while larger balls can look like olives or cherries.

The process works by adding sodium alginate to the liquid that you wish to spherify. The liquid is then drawn up into a syringe, or a dropper bottle. A vessel containing a weak calcium solution (usually calcium chloride or calcium lactate) is then used as a setting bath. Droplets of the alginate solution are carefully dispersed into the bath and the calcium acts as a catalyst for the setting of the alginate droplets. Removing the balls quickly results in a liquid-centred sphere that bursts under minimal pressure, releasing flavourful juice. (See the Bramble Redux on page 90 for my recipe for smashed blackberry liqueur pearls.)

If allowed to sit in the calcium bath for a while, the balls will eventually harden all the way through. Even if removed quickly from the bath, the balls will still harden over a period of time, though this can be avoided by heating them to 85°C/185°F for 10 minutes. Caviar spheres form more readily in higher concentrations of calcium, and you will also find that the solution remains quite viscous if it has a low pH. Alginate solutions will still form spheres even with an alcohol content of 20%.

Reverse spherification is, as the name suggests, the opposite way around. The bath contains the hydrocolloid (sodium alginate) and the calcium (calcium chloride or calcium lactate) is added to the liquid you want to be spherified. The major advantage of this approach, which is especially useful for larger balls, is that the gelling occurs on the outside surface of the ball, resulting in a kind of jelly shell. What this also means is that the ball will never harden all the way through, since there is no alginate present within the centre of the ball.

XANTHAN GUM

Xanthan gum is a by-product of microbial fermentation, and among the most versatile and commonly used hydrocolloids. It is a thickening agent that can be used to create alcoholic 'jam' and toothpaste, as well as providing ice creams with a firmer, elastic texture. Only tiny quantities of xanthan gum are needed to thicken liquids into a paste-like form; higher concentrations will yield firmer pastes. No heating or cooling is required for the process and it can be served at virtually any temperature. Xanthan gum pastes can even be achieved with neat (above 40% ABV) spirits and solutions of virtually any pH.

The chart below lists applications for each gelling agent, as well as typical hydration, gelling and melting temperatures, which can differ according to concentration, pH, ABV, salinity and the sugar content of the gel.

Agent	Application	Usage	Hydrates/Gels	Melts	Notes
Agar-agar	Fluid gel, brittle jelly	0.1–1%	95°C / 35°C 203°F / 95°F	85°C 185°F	High tolerance of acid, salt and alcohol and heat.
Gelatine	Soft/elastic jelly	1–5%	60°C / 10°C 140°F / 50°F	37°C 99°F	Tolerant of alcohol up to 30% ABV. Intolerant of pH below 5 and high salt content. Sugar increases gel strength.
Gellan gum (High-acyl)	Gel spirits	0.1–3%	85°C / 75°C 185°F / 167°F	75°C 167°F	Very high alcohol tolerance. Requires chewing to break down.
Gellan gum (Low-acyl)	Heat-stable fluid gel, slowing ice cream melt	0.1–1%	85°C / 20°C 185°F / 68°F	80–130°C 176–266°F	Very brittle when set, requires presence of minerals to set. Good for flammable alcohol jelly.
Gum arabic	Oil in water emulsion	5–20%	Any	N/A	Traditionally used for stabilizing flavours in soft drinks.
Methyl-cellulose	Hot gels, warm ice cream	0.1–3%	<40°C / 50–80°C <104°F / 122–176°F	<20–30°C <68–86°F	Highly tolerant of alcohol and extreme pH. Sets when hot, melts when cooled.
Sodium alginate	Spherification	0.5–2%	Any	N/A	Tolerant to 30% ABV. Won't gel below pH 4. Sugar aids gelling. Requires calcium to gel.
Xanthan gum	Thickening	0.05–2%	Any	N/A	Instant thickening. Highly tolerant of alcohol, extreme pH and salt.

JUICING, DRYING & DEHYDRATING

JUICING

Extracting juice from a fruit may seem like a simple thing. After all, in its most basic form it requires only a squeeze of the fingers to extract the complex nectar from an orange. But some fruits require specialist treatment, sometimes in an unconventional way, in order to best extract their essence, and not all juicing methods are equal!

Fresh fruit juice contains a cacophony of complex volatile oils, lipids, protein, acids and sugars. Retaining the best bits of the juice is vital in the quest for delicious drinks. Almost all of the techniques for achieving this require a not insubstantial level of violence. Breaking apart plant cells and stealing their inner goodness is not an easy thing to do, so let's take a look at some of the ways it can be done.

PRESS

A press can constitute anything from a hand-held citrus press (Mexican elbow) to a cast-iron, heavy (often bolted down) lever-operated press. The premise is simple: crush the fruit enough and the cells will rupture, releasing the juice to fall through a mesh or coarse filter to be collected below. These devices work well for citrus fruit.

JUICER

Juicers work a bit like a grater. The fruit is dropped down a chute and then violently shredded. A spinning surface then separates the pulp from the juice, sending the juice into one receptacle and the pulp into another. These machines work very well for drier ingredients (such as carrot, celery, apple) that would be impossible to juice in a press. The downside of a juicer is that often the pulp retains a lot of water and flavour.

FREEZE JUICING

It might seem counter-intuitive to freeze fruit in the pursuit of extracting juice from it, but the technique works very well indeed for soft fruit. Freezing a blackberry causes ice crystals to form in the cell structure of the fruit. The cells then rupture, and once the fruit is defrosted the juice will flow much more readily when processed through a juicer. Repeated freezing and defrosting will yield even better results.

ENZYMATIC JUICING

Chemistry can be an excellent assistant in the pursuit of free-running juice. Many of the proteins that make up the structures of fruit and vegetables also have 'anti-proteins' or enzymes that break apart the mortar that holds the plant together. The structure of an apple, for example, is held together largely by pectin (the same stuff that jam and marmalade makers use to harden conserves). Soaking the sliced fruit in a pectinase (the enzyme that breaks down pectin) solution will soften the fruit considerably, thus making extraction of juice that little bit easier.

OSMOTIC JUICING

If your goal is fruit juice for the production of a syrup or liqueur, osmotic juicing is for you! It works on the principle that water inside the fruit will always try to equalize with its surroundings, a process known as osmotic pressure. Sprinkling sugar over strawberries and allowing them to rest for a day or so will cause much of the juice to leech out as the moisture-rich interior of the fruit attempts to equalize with the dry surface of the fruit. Following that, simply juice as normal – the resulting juice will obviously be sweeter than without the sugar treatment.

DRYING

Drying ingredients might seem like a strange thing to do in the goal for tasty cocktails; after all, you can't drink something with no liquid in it! True as that may be, there is a place for dried and powdered ingredients in the creation of delicious drinks.

Drying food to preserve it is one of the oldest culinary techniques we know of. For millennia, humans have stored ingredients in low-humidity environments to encourage the desiccation of water and the preservation of the food. There are two reasons for this. Firstly, drying vastly extends the life span of the product, and secondly, it concentrates the flavour. Removing the water from a fresh apricot means that there is a higher concentration of all the flavourful compounds present within the fruit left behind. Dried food can then be used to infuse flavour, powdered down and turned into a sherbet, or simply used as a decorative garnish.

There are some very expensive ways to desiccate and dehydrate food, most of which are used in commercial applications such as the production of instant coffee or gravy granules. Some of these processes involve blasting thin jets of liquid with warm air; others involve slowly thawing frozen ingredients under low pressure. It's more likely that you would use an inexpensive cabinet dehydrator, or simply an oven or hairdryer!

Dehydrating ingredients by heating them with warm air works by evaporating the water in the product and lowering the humidity around the product. Let's use a slice of apple as an example: the heat causes the water on the outside of the apple to evaporate away, raising the ambient humidity. Constant airflow lowers the humidity, and moisture from within the apple migrates to the surface, continuing the evaporation cycle. Dehydrating with warm air typically takes place at 35–80°C/95–176°F; warmer air will usually dehydrate more quickly. The one caveat with this is the process of case-hardening, where the temperature is too high and the exterior of the product dries hard, preventing further evaporation of moisture. Case-hardening is exactly what happens when you bake bread. Low and slow is nearly always the best strategy for drying ingredients when complete desiccation is the goal.

POWDERED LIQUID

Since drying liquids into a powder is very difficult without expensive equipment, I have got around this by first mixing the liquid with sugar. Icing/confectioners' sugar works very well as it contains a small amount of cornstarch, which helps with thickening the liquid. Combine the liquid (spirit or otherwise) with icing/confectioners' sugar, then spread the paste onto perforated greaseproof/wax paper and place in the dehydrator (or a low oven) at 40°C/104°F for 12 hours and you'll be left with a thin sheet of flavoured sugar. Grind the sugar up with a pestle and mortar or through a coffee mill and the powder can be used for dusting drinks or flavoured-sugar glass rims. You can also try the same process with salt, which could result in some very interesting salt rims for Margaritas.

DEHYDRATED GARNISHES

Drying garnishes can result in stronger aroma, interesting visual appeal and powerful taste. Even something as simple as a slice of lemon can look amazing once dehydrated, the added bonus being that it will keep for many weeks afterwards in an airtight container. I have also found that dehydrated ingredients impart much more flavour to cocktails than their moist counterparts. For example, a dehydrated slice of banana in a Daiquiri will release much more flavour into a drink than a slice of fresh banana. This is because the dried product becomes more hydroscopic (absorbent) once dehydrated, which allows the flow of liquid in and out of the cracks and capillaries of the fruit, thus increasing infusion time significantly.

INFUSION

As with above, infusing flavour into your syrups, liqueurs and cordials is often a lot easier and economical with dried products. Moisture in fruit and vegetables acts as a protective layer, preventing access from the outside without crushing, cutting or heating. Remove the water and you then have unlimited access to the inner flavourful structure of the plant. It's also that a much lower weight of the product is required for a desirable outcome: infusing 10 g/⅓ oz. dried figs into vodka yields considerably more flavour than infusing 100 g/3½ oz. fresh figs.

CLARIFICATION

◆

Ridding a liquid of its opacity, cloudiness or colour can be very handy if your aim is a 'purer'-looking drink, or if you just want to confuse someone by making their Margarita look like water!

The molecules that make liquids look cloudy or that give them colour are thousands of times larger than the ones that register to us as taste or smell, so in most cases you need not worry that you're depriving a guest of too much flavour.

There are a whole bunch of ways to clarify liquids, covering a variety of budgets and levels of difficulty. With that in mind, I've separated the techniques in this section and ordered them in degrees of cost and difficulty.

EGG WHITE

An oldie, but a goodie. Egg whites have been traditionally used to filter impurities from liquids for centuries. The technique works under the principle that egg white contains long protein strands that trap impurities like a magnet. Try dropping an egg white into a simmering pan of brewed tea and watch it magically change colour as you spin the liquid around. Chefs use 'egg rafts' for clarifying a whole range of things, including consommés and stocks. Naturally, the technique has its limits, but even today it's surprisingly effective, especially for removing stubborn 'hazes' in semi-clarified solutions.

SIMPLE FILTERING

Sometimes a simple filter might be all that's required to reach the level of clarity you're after. Filters come in all sorts of different grades, from wire-mesh sieves/strainers, to fine laboratory-grade filters and muslin cheesecloth filters. Filters are capable of removing larger insoluble particles from a liquid and, if nothing else, provide a good first stage before moving on to more intensive

techniques. If the liquid that you are filtering has been heated, it's normally best to filter while it's still hot as the liquid will be more viscous. Also, check out the 'superbag' brand of filter, which are sold according to the micron aperture of the filter.

PECTIN ENZYME

Pectin is a gelling agent used a lot in the production of jams. It naturally occurs in plant cell walls and accounts for up to 2% of the composition of fresh fruits and vegetables. Essentially, it's part of the cement that holds a fruit together. For fruit and vegetable juices this is a useful thing to know, as there exists naturally occurring enzymes that break down pectin and therefore break down otherwise stabile juices and purées. Pectinase, pectin lyase and pectinesterase are some of the enzymes that have been branded and commercially packaged, and are available to buy online.

To use pectin enzyme, whisk around 2% pectin enzyme to cloudy apple juice and allow to sit for 12–24 hours. Clear liquid will float to the top and needs only to be carefully poured off. (The results are improved by centrifuging the liquid.) Pectin enzymes work best on fruits and vegetables with high pectin contents, especially apple and carrot juice. Apple juices with especially low pH or that have already had an acid added to them wouldn't work very well.

JELLY FILTRATION

Where enzymes break down the structure that suspends colourful particles in liquids, hydrocolloid (jelly) filtration aims to trap them, allowing only the clearer liquid to leach out. There is a variety of hydrocolloids that work, but the best is probably agar-agar. Extracted from red algae, agar-agar is a gelling agent not dissimilar to gelatine, but is quicker to use and vegetarian friendly.

Whereas gelatine gels need refrigerating to set, agar-agar sets at room temperature. Because of this it does need dissolving at a higher temperature than gelatine (see Hydrocolloids, page 35). Most of the time this method will be used to clarify fruit and vegetable juices, which has the slight drawback that the juice will need to be boiled in order to hydrate the agar-agar.

The best way around this is to boil only a small portion (20% of the total liquid for example), then add 2 g agar-agar per kg/2¼ lb. of total liquid. Whisk the agar-agar in, then temper the rest of the cool juice into the gel solution. Allow the solution to set in an ice bath and it should form a loose gel. Gently break up the gel using a whisk and transfer to a muslin cheesecloth suspended over a suitable container. The liquid that leaches out should be almost totally clear. Some agitation of the muslin may be required towards the end of the filtering, but don't get too aggressive as cloudy agar particles can squeeze through. If you have access to a centrifuge (who doesn't?!), it will do a much quicker and effective separation of the solids and liquid than a muslin cheesecloth.

Gelatine freeze clarification can achieve similar results to agar clarification, but is considerably more time consuming. This method requires you to make a refrigerated gelatine gel (5 g per kg/2¼ lb. liquid) that then goes into the freezer (or can be frozen immediately with liquid nitrogen – see page 44). Once frozen solid, the jelly returns to the fridge to defrost, sat on a suitable muslin cheesecloth filter. As the jelly defrosts, the structure fails and liquid leaches out, dripping through the cloth.

The only real benefit to this process is that the liquid doesn't need to be heated as much as with the agar method, but the effects of the heat are negligible and in my opinion the speed of the agar method vastly outweighs any slight negative effects of an additional 30°C/86°F heating.

CHARCOAL FILTERING AND CHILL FILTERING

Activated charcoal is carbon that has been treated with oxygen. It is unique and unrivalled in its surface area to mass ratio. The more surface area, the better the chance that large impure molecules adsorb onto the surface of the charcoal. Charcoal filtering is best used as a finishing process to remove final traces of cloudiness and colour.

This type of filtration has been employed to soften spirits for over two centuries. It's perhaps most famous for its use in the vodka production process, mostly due to brands boasting about the number of times their spirit is filtered. But charcoal filtration features in the production of many spirits as a way of softening harsh characteristics and ensuring consistency. A common household water filter contains activated charcoal.

Many whiskies are 'chill-filtered'. This process removes the haziness that can sometimes be caused by fatty acids and esters present within the aged liquid. As the name implies, the liquid is chilled to around -1°C/30°F, then filtered through a cellulose or metal filter. The chilling results in some of the molecules clumping together to become a larger mass of particles, thus making them easier to remove from the liquid.

BUON VINO PRESSURE FILTER

There exist pieces of equipment designed specifically to remove cloudiness and colour from liquids – the Buon Vino is one such piece of apparatus. The machine has two hoses, an in and an out. Submerse one hose in the liquid that you wish to filter and another in an empty container. Turn the pump of the machine on and it will draw up the liquid and push it through a filter plate within the machine, removing colour and expelling a liquid much clearer in colour. Simple.

VACUUM FILTERING

Less of a method in its own right and more a time-saving device. Vacuum pumps and some vacuum packers can be put to good use by sucking liquid through fine filters. They can be used in conjunction with hydrocolloid filtration and simple filtering to speed up processes, or with finer-grade filters where gravity simply will not suffice.

The process normally involves some kind of specialist flask with a filter attached. The vacuum pump creates a low-pressure environment, drawing in liquids fine enough to squeeze through the filter. It's a much quicker process and much more effective than gravity alone.

ABOVE *Agar Clarification:* **1.** *Gently breaking a lime gel* **2.** *Passing through a muslin* **3.** *The (almost) clarified results*

ROTARY EVAPORATION & DISTILLING

If you want to make a liquid perfectly clear and you're willing to sacrifice a bit of flavour, distilling is the way to go. Whether it be through a rotovap (see Rotary Evaporation, page 52) or a traditional still, the heating, evaporating and condensing of a liquid will result in a water-clear distillate.

Rotovaps have a slight advantage here, as very little direct heat is required, so heat damage can be kept to a minimum. The main problem with the process is that some (and sometimes a lot) of the flavour can be left behind in the evaporating flask. The process is more one of separation (of the distillable and non-distillable) than of clarification. Depending on the liquid that you're distilling and how you intend to use it, this might be acceptable, but using a rotovap as an everyday clarification method is probably a bit too time consuming and not the best use of this expensive piece of equipment's abilities.

CENTRIFUGAL SEPARATION

At the top of the food chain and probably the most expensive option is the centrifuge. Centrifuges work by spinning liquids at incredibly high speeds (some spin at up to 70,000 RPM), exerting a gravitational pull on the liquid that is known commonly as G-force. This huge pull on the liquid causes the components to separate based on their density: oils float on top, solid particles sink and the bulk of the liquid phase sits somewhere in the middle. The same processes take place under the Earth's normal gravitational pull, but a centrifuge makes it happen a lot quicker. Add the centrifuge's abilities to some of the techniques previously listed, such as enzymatic or jelly filtration, and you have a super-effective hybrid clarification process.

Centrifuges can be used for all manner of applications, from separating the water out of tomato juice to drawing a spirit back out of a pulpy infusion. They typically run for 5–50 minutes, depending on the density of the liquid and the degree of separation required.

DRY ICE & LIQUID NITROGEN

◆

It's hard to beat ice for some simple old-fashioned chilling, but deploying more extreme cooling methods can open up some wonderful time-saving techniques as well as service options that seem like the stuff of science fiction.

LIQUID NITROGEN

Nitrogen in its liquid form (also known as LN_2) is -196°C/-320°F and as such should be treated with great respect. It will burn your skin instantly on contact and can be particularly nasty if spilt onto loose clothing or shoes. Goggles, cryogenic gloves and a cryogenic apron are essential.

Liquid nitrogen must be stored in a specialist dewar – a purpose-built pressurized vessel that is capable of maintaining a constant liquid state. However, even when stored in an expensive nitrogen dewar, the liquid will continue to evaporate through valves placed on the unit. Attempting to store liquid nitrogen in anything other than a specialist dewar can be disastrous.

Nitrogen must be kept in a well-ventilated area. The nitrogen gas that is released from the dewar's valves is harmless, but when it bonds with oxygen atoms in the atmosphere it forms nitrous oxide. This gas is not harmful either, but the reaction does deplete the surrounding air of the oxygen and so can cause asphyxiation. Store outside or in a well-ventilated room.

When I'm using liquid nitrogen I generally dispense a small amount into a double-walled steel coffee pot or wine cooler. You can also get styrene baths designed specifically for the purpose, too.

Now on the fun stuff, what can liquid nitrogen be used for? The first and most obvious use is freezing things. Liquid nitrogen will freeze literally anything (with the exception of a couple of other elements), including spirits. Edible cocktail lollipops can be made with relative ease by submersing an ice lolly/popsicle mould into a bath of liquid nitrogen (see Cosmopops, page 105). Liquid nitrogen can also be used as a bath for stirring cocktails in. Stirring down a Martini in liquid nitrogen means that the drink can be served as low as -30°C/-22°F (very cold indeed). Most spirits of 40% ABV freeze at around -23°C/-9°F. You can also use liquid nitrogen to quickly chill glasses by pouring a splash into the glass and quickly swirling.

LN_2 can also be used to make ice creams. Production of alcoholic ice cream is very hard and laborious to do with a conventional freezer or with an ice cream maker, but with liquid nitrogen it's achievable in under a minute. Besides time, the other advantage to making LN_2 ice cream is that the speed of freezing forms smaller ice crystals, so the texture feels creamier.

Finally, you can also use LN_2 to quickly infuse spirits with fruit or herbs. Douse the ingredient in liquid nitrogen and, once it's frozen solid, smash it up with a muddler or anything heavy. Once the ingredient is powdered, pour spirit over and marvel as the flavour and colour quickly infuses.

DRY ICE

Dry ice is carbon dioxide in its solid state and its temperature is around -79°C/-110°F. Dry ice is a great tool for its unique sublimation properties (i.e. it evaporates to gas directly from solid, thus skipping its liquid phase). Dry ice easily burns the skin on contact and should therefore always be handled with gloves and the appropriate utensils. It should be stored in a suitable cool box that limits evaporation, as when left at room temperature it is prone to disappearing rather quickly.

When liquid is poured over dry ice pellets, the dry ice begins to evaporate very quickly, creating a visible plume of CO_2 gas. This is due to its sudden submersion in something much warmer than its freezing point. When hot liquids are poured over dry ice, the result is a quite violent bubbling reaction as the contrasting temperatures attempt to equilibrate. By pouring liquids that have intense aromas over the dry ice, you can produce an aromatic mist that adds great theatre to a drink and ticks a bunch of multi-sensory boxes. The Aviatrix does this with the Knize Ten Fog (see page 74).

Care must be taken not to add dry ice to liquids containing surfactants or foaming agents (most hydrocolloids). This is because the bubbles created by the sublimation of the dry ice are stabilized by the agent, and their failure to collapse will cause the liquid to foam and expand very quickly indeed!

It should also be mentioned that adding dry ice directly to a drink is dangerous and inadvisable – when swallowed, dry ice can be very harmful.

Dry ice can also be used to make effervescent alcoholic sorbets (see my Sparkling Daiquiri Sorbet, page 162). Because dry ice is carbon dioxide, it carbonates any liquid that it's mixed with and the liquid retains some of the gas even once it's frozen solid. Because dry ice is so cold, it never struggles to freeze high alcohol liquids either.

And one final benefit to using dry ice in place of normal ice to make a sorbet or granita is that it won't dilute the drink, which can be very desirable.

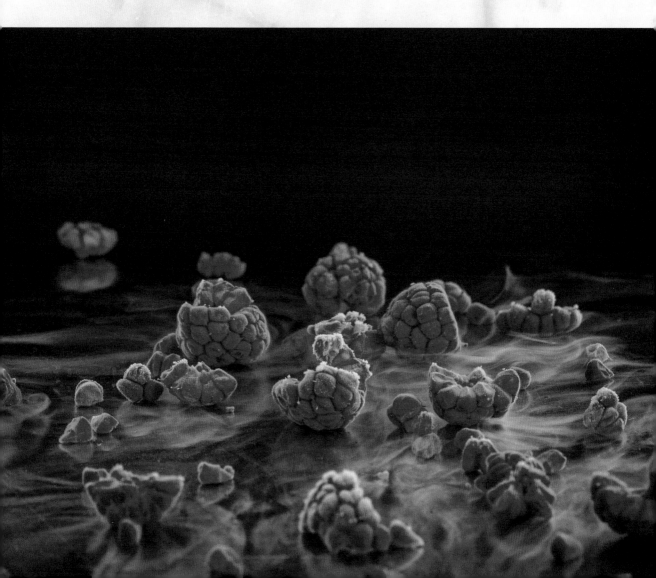

SMOKE

◆

The first person to ever serve me a smoked cocktail was my chef friend Tristan Welch. He presented me with a hand-held smoking device, fittingly called a 'smoking gun', and proceeded to pump apple-wood smoke onto the surface of a drink, then place a little glass lid on it. Over time, the smoke slipped into the fabric of the drink, and when the lid was released the effect was a fantastic smoke-infused liquid. Smoke is produced by burning wood. Below 300°C/572°F, most of the smoke produced by smouldering wood is a result of cellulose and hemicellulose breaking down. This kind of smoke can smell a bit nasty as it contains some of the more acrid and astringent compounds produced by burning wood. Most of the positive aromatic effects of smoke derive from the breaking down of the lignin present within the wood. Lignin is a compound that makes up around one quarter of the structure of wood (depending on the type), which, when it reaches temperatures of over 300°C/572°F, breaks down into complex aromatic molecules called carbonyls and phenols. It's these compounds that contribute the typical sweet and spicy aromatics to foods such as vanilla, caramel, and cloves. As the temperature of the wood reaches 400°C/752°F, the smoke becomes denser, almost liquid-like, and it's at this stage that it has the best flavours and the bulk of the aromatic compounds.

Creep too high, however, and there's a risk that the wood will catch on fire (if nothing else, smoking drinks is proof that there can be smoke without fire!). At this stage, the wood increases in temperature up to 1,000°C/1,832°F – bad for all those precious aromatics, which are combusted along with anything else in the vicinity.

The most affordable and easiest way to impart smoke into a drink is to use a hand-held smoking device. There are other brands, but I'm personally a big fan of the PolyScience smoking gun (pictured left), which costs around £60/$100. It's durable, reasonably easy to clean and very effective. The gun section has a steel crucible with a standard pipe filter. The wood is placed in the crucible, then ignited with a flame. A switch turns a fan on that draws the smoke into the device and then out through a flexible pipe. The smoke can be easily directed into a vessel, cloche, mixing beaker or glass. The draw of air through the crucible causes the smouldering wood to heat sufficiently without catching alight. If the temperature of the wood reaches 500°C/932°F there is a danger that the wood will spontaneously combust, but this can be controlled by restricting airflow into the crucible.

- Place the wood in the crucible of the smoking gun and switch on the motor.
- Ignite the wood with a flame or chef's blowtorch, blowing out the flame if necessary.
- Allow the smoke to build in colour and density for 5 seconds.
- Direct the flow of smoke.

Be sure to clean your smoker regularly as aromatic oils released by the burning of wood can build up inside the device. The repeated heating and cooling of these oils can result in them being broken down into foul-smelling compounds that will degrade smoke quality significantly.

The type of wood you use will have a bearing on the type of smoke that is produced. My favourite smoking woods are:

- **Hickory:** sweet, aromatic aroma, is typically used on a barbecue/outdoor grill
- **Apple:** lighter aromatic, but a pleasant fruity characteristic
- **Oak:** very bold and intense; use carefully so as not to overpower
- **Mesquite:** strong and rich aromatics

FOAMS, AIRS & EGGS

I often hear people scoff (not to be confused with quaff) at the idea of foams and airs in drinks, their argument being that they are a gimicky, modernist invention that bring little to the drinking experience. In some instances I would agree; foams and airs can seem like an afterthought or a futile attempt to make an average drink slightly more interesting.

But you only need to look around a bar to see that many of our most treasured beverages do in fact use foams and airs to great effect. Imagine a pint of Guinness without its creamy head, or a cappuccino without its light foamy consistency? Or even a Gin Fizz (see pages 60–61), with its thick creamy consistency. My advice is to not be too quick to discount the use of foams and airs – with the correct application, they can add a welcome textural point of difference, incredible visual appeal and interesting flavour release on the palate.

SCIENCE

Foams and airs both work in much the same way, the point of difference being that I'm classing airs as super-light foams – so light that they barely register a texture on the palate. Foam-bubble size typically ranges from 0.1–1 mm across, whereas 'air' bubbles can range from 3–10 mm.

Both foams and airs require the presence of either fat or a surfactant. Surfactants work by having a hydrophilic (water-loving) side and hydrophobic (water-hating) side, thus happily existing with gas on one side and water on the other. Without the sufactant, the bubbles will simply escape. This is known as a gas in water (g/w) emulsion, where the water is the continuous phase and the gas is the suspended phase. Foams can cover a large range of textures, from creamy mousse-like foams, to zero-gravity meringue pie-style fluffy foams. The formation of these different styles of foam and air is possible by using various surfactants aerated in different ways. The air or gas that makes up the volume of the foam or air can also affect the texture, stability and taste.

TOOLS

Whisks – like an Aerolatte, hand whisk or stand mixer – and blenders – such as a Thermomix or Blendtec – can be used to whip air into a liquid containing a surfactant. But by far the easiest and most effective way to create foams is to use a cream whipper. Cream whippers work by forcing nitrous oxide (N_2O) into the liquid to be whipped. First, the liquid is poured into the cream whipper and the lid is tightly screwed on. The vessel is then 'charged' using an 8-g N_2O cartridge. This increases the pressure inside the vessel to around 6 bar, forcing the nitrous oxide to dissolve into the liquid. When the liquid is dispensed through the nozzle, it suddenly reaches atmospheric pressure and the dissolved bubbles expand, creating a light, aerated foam. Cream whippers can be pre-prepared and chilled hours before they are used, and they also do a pretty good job of extending a liquid's life span.

STABILIZERS (SURFACTANTS)

Traditional ingredients like egg white and cream can be effectively used to create stable foams. Egg white creates protein-based foams. Powdered egg white (albumin) works even better, since fresh egg white is predominantly water and contributes to both volume and dilution. On the flip side, cream relies on fat globules to form a stable foam. Bizarrely, many foam stabilizers don't play nicely together as the fat present in cream actually inhibits the effect of the protein in egg whites (this is why getting fatty egg yolk in your soufflés is a bad idea).

Most hydrocolloids can be used as efficacious foam stabilizers as long as the liquid is within the

operating range of the hydrocolloid (i.e. acceptable pH, salinity, ABV – see pages 34–37).

Agar-agar, gelatine and gellan gum all work very well when combined with a cream whipper, but do require the liquid to be heated first so that the stabilizer can be dispersed. The flip side of this is that agar and gellan gum foams are reasonably heat stable, so can be placed on warm drinks and/or served warm themselves. Xanthan gum and albumin (egg white) powder do not require the liquid to be heated. Xanthan produces much larger bubbles than most other hydrocolloids, however.

Albumin powder is possibly the best all-rounder, since it produces nice, mousse-like foams without the need for heating (see the Aviatrix on page 74).

For airs, the best bet is lecithin. Lecithin is a lipid, or fatty substance, that is present in egg yolks. It is tolerant of high acidity and alcohol volume up to 30% at a ratio of around 1.5%. Lecithin produces very light foams when used in conjunction with a fish tank bubbler or Aerolatte milk frother. The result is similar to the texture of bubble bath. See the Green Fairy Sazerac on page 114 for an example of its use.

Agent	Application	Usage	Method	Notes
Agar-agar	Wet, sloppy foam	0.1–0.5%	Heat liquid to 85°C/185°F and disperse agar. Add to cream whipper, charge and chill.	Can be served warm.
Gelatine	Elastic, stable foam	3–5%	Heat liquid to 60°C/140°F and disperse gelatine. Add to cream whipper, charge and chill.	Great texture and no additional flavour from the gelatine.
Egg white	Stable mousse-like foam	3–15%	Whisk, or add to a cream whipper. Add to cream whipper, charge and chill.	No heating required.
Lecithin	Dry air	1.5%	Use a fish tank bubbler to aerate, or whisk with an Aerolatte.	Big bubbles.

49

ON EGGS

The use of eggs, egg yolks and egg whites in cocktails has a long history. Many old-fashioned drinks like Flips, possets and syllabubs require a whole egg for both a flavour and textural addition to a drink.

Lots of cocktails that emerged during the golden era, 1860–1930, also call for egg white in the drink. But some countries, like Japan, very rarely use raw egg in mixed drinks. So what is the purpose of the egg, and is it safe?

WHOLE EGGS

Texturally, whole eggs add a density, or thickness, to a drink, which especially aids in building an indulgent quality to a cocktail. We associate a thick, gloopy texture with foodstuffs rich in sugars, fat and protein (which these drinks tend to be), all necessary and sought-after components for survival. There is something rather primal and fundamental about sucking (the experience is more a combination of sipping and chewing) back a rich, gloopy cocktail, even though most of us can't manage more than a couple.

The egg adds flavour, too – 33% of an egg yolk is comprised of flavoursome fatty acids (the rest is made up mostly of water, 50%, and protein, 17%).

EGG WHITES

Egg whites assist in trapping air in a cocktail by creating a protein network throughout the drink. In some cases, this network fails quite quickly, causing most of the liquid to drain out of the protein structure, leaving a dry, fluffy foam on top of the drink. That's not to say that some air isn't trapped in the liquid portion of the cocktail; it is, but you'll also find that air gets trapped, to a certain extent, in drinks that don't contain egg white.

In some cases, however, when the other ingredients of the drink are conducive to a strong protein network, you may find that the egg white does a pretty good job of stabilizing the entire drink and emulsifying air bubbles with the liquid. Citrus juice and acids, for example, actually help in stabilizing and stiffening a cocktail containing egg white, since the acid denatures the protein in the egg white, allowing it to stiffen and hold firm.

HOW TO AERATE SUCCESSFULLY WITH EGG WHITES

The trick to dissolving tiny air bubbles into a drink containing egg white is to make them as small as possible. And the best way to do this is to combine the liquid, egg white and air as violently as possible. Drinks such as the Ramos Gin Fizz (see pages 60–61) attempted to do this by shaking the cocktail for minutes on end. That's one way to do it, but these days we have hand blenders and Aerolattes to help.

Many bartenders opt for a 'dry shake', which means shaking the cocktail first with no ice, then again afterwards with ice, the theory being that the ice somehow inhibits the emulsification of air and water in the drink. I have found this to be a wholly unsatisfactory solution to the problem, since any benefits gained by dry shaking first are negated by the subsequent shake with ice after. I did some trials in an attempt to uncover whether there was a better option out there and discovered that doing things the other way around (reverse dry shake) works a lot better.

Give the drink a regular shake with ice, then strain the drink, remove the ice from the shaker and shake the drink again, then pour into the glass.

An even better option is to shake with ice, then remove the ice and blitz with an Aerolatte. This creates huge amounts of aerated liquid and expends less energy in the process.

SAFETY

Both the UK's FSA (Food Standards Agency) and the US's FDA (Food and Drug Administration) advise cooking unpasteurized egg and egg-based products fully before use. Practically, this means that you should not consume or serve eggs that have not been cooked to a core temperature of at least 63°C/145°F for five minutes.

I should quickly dispel the myth that the alcohol in your cocktail will kill the dangerous bacteria in eggs. Most of the antibacterial cleaners that rely on alcohol for the killing of bacteria are a minimum of 70% ABV, much higher than all but the strongest spirits.

One way to avoid the risks of salmonella but still get the benefits of raw egg is to use pasteurized egg products in your cocktails. These are natural egg whites that have been precisely heated for a specific length of time in order to kill off any harmful bacteria. Packaged pasteurized egg whites are now commonly available in cartons.

You can also now buy eggs that are pasteurized in the shell. As with stand-alone egg whites, the whole eggs are heated at a controlled temperature for a set period of time until the risk of bacteria is sufficiently reduced.

The downside of pasteurized eggs is that the texture (and foaming ability) of the product is affected. If you have ever eaten a pasteurized boiled egg you'll have noticed that the texture is somewhat mushy, and likewise with cocktails, the foam is never as good as with fresh eggs – though less risky of course! So let's look at the risks of using raw, unpasteurized eggs in cocktails.

In the UK, the FSA conducted a survey between 2005 and 2007 on shell eggs purchased from 1,567 catering premises. They found from the 9,402 egg samples collected that only one had traces of *Salmonella Enteritidis* inside the egg itself, with a further five samples having traces on the external surface of the egg shell.

Contracting salmonella poisoning can be fatal, but it also often results in vomiting, sickness and diarrhoea symptoms, and in some cases it can simply pass through the system unnoticed. It's estimated by the FDA that less than 1 in 5,000 of the known cases (there may be many more mild or unreported cases) of salmonella poisoning from eggs proves to be fatal.

So in summary, if 1 in 10,000 eggs are infected with the bacteria, and you have a 1 in 5,000 chance of dying from the bacteria, that means there is a 1 in 50,000,000 chance of dying from salmonella poisoning from ingesting raw egg white. This is the same likelihood that the Large Hadron Collider at CERN would swallow up the entire universe, and five times less likely than you dying from falling aeroplane parts.

In the UK it's a good idea to buy eggs with lion stamps on them. The lion stamp guarantees that the producer has followed safety guidelines and codes of practice that aim to further reduce cases of salmonella in shell eggs. Another option is to use albumin (egg white powder – see page 48).

ROTARY EVAPORATION

A rotary evaporator (or rotovap, pictured below) is a laboratory-grade piece of vacuum distillation equipment. Lab technicians use rotovaps for precisely separating potentially dangerous compounds from solutions by means of meticulously controlled evaporation. From a bar's perspective, it can be used to create infusions, concentrations and hydrosols, and is also useful for clarification.

The premise is that the boiling point of any given liquid changes according to air pressure. At standard atmospheric pressure (1013 mbar), water boils at 100°C/212°F, but if you happen to be on top of Mount Everest (260 mbar), it will boil at a mere 69°C/156°F. This is the beauty of a rotovap. By lowering the pressure inside it (some will go down to 6 mbar), we also lower the boiling point of the liquid, and by doing so it's possible to avoid heat damaging (or cooking) liquids and ingredients that would normally be spoiled using a traditional still. Heat damage, you say? Yes. Ever tried drinking distilled orange juice? Probably not, but I can tell you it's not very tasty. Many of the flavour compounds within the juice, which turn out to be really quite fragile, are denatured when afflicted by

man's terrible fire. Heat damage is irreversible (you can't un-toast toast), so avoiding it altogether is a good idea. In a rotovap, the evaporation flask is clamped onto the rest of the system and semi-filled with a liquid, combination of liquids or even a combination of liquid and solids (such as fruits, herbs or spices). The whole system is then lowered and the flask submerged into a temperature-controlled water bath. Next, the flask is set to rotate within the water bath, ensuring that the temperature of the glass is as consistent as possible and increasing the surface area of the liquid inside. A greater surface area inside makes for a quicker evaporation. A faster rotation will also encourage a quicker evaporation, as it stretches the surface area of the liquid.

A vacuum pump and controller allows you to lower the pressure within the rotovap and carefully control the boiling point of the liquid in the evaporation flask. Drop the pressure too quickly and there's a risk of the liquid boiling over and flooding the whole system.

Lots of vapour and a nice low temperature are no use if you don't have a way of turning them back into a liquid. Some rotovaps use cold traps that can be filled with dry ice. But many rotovaps have a glass condensing coil that you can pump a mixture of ethylene glycol (antifreeze) and water through. The bigger the difference between the temperature of the water bath and the temperature of the condenser, the more efficient the distillation. To pump coolant, you need a recirculating chiller that's capable of chilling down to at least -10°C/ 14°F. Bigger is better, too.

Hydrosols (water-based infusions) can be made by adding solid ingredients into the evaporation flask with water. This is great for delicate ingredients such as herbs and flowers. Products such as orange blossom water are made in much the same way.

AGEING COCKTAILS

◆

This section acts as a primer for all kinds of cocktail and liqueur/spirit ageing. For examples of their use, please check out the drinks I reference here in the Cocktails section.

BARREL AGEING

During the early days of transatlantic voyages, it was common practice to store everything in barrels – from jellied eels to dead bodies. Oak barrels are robust, naturally antibacterial and reasonably inexpensive to make. Alcohol was also kept in casks, inexplicably mellowing harshness, adding spice, vanilla and nuttiness, as well as integrating flavours together. But despite the recognition of this, there would have been little understanding as to why.

These days, we have a much better insight into what goes on when oak and liquor interact, but there are still some elements that are a mystery and the art form can be difficult to control or predict. Master blenders – as the name suggests – are highly sought-after craftsmen, employed to wrangle the oak into giving its best, and understanding when the time is right to remove a spirit from the cask. Without these people we wouldn't have the joys of Scotch whisky, bourbon, Cognac and other aged spirits. Barrel ageing is probably the most complex ageing technique, since the wood itself becomes an ingredient, and an unpredictable one at that.

Barrels come in all sorts of sizes, types and ages. New oak casks will work quickly to impart flavour, whereas casks that are on their second or third fills will naturally have a decreased effect. You can acquire casks that have previously held other liquids – sherry, wine and bourbon, to name a few – as well as choose between differing char and toasting levels. The size of the cask affects the surface area to liquid ratio, with smaller casks imparting flavour much faster than larger ones. It's important to recognize that all of these factors, as well as time, will have distinct consequences on the drink that comes out of the barrel.

Chromatography reveals that a number of phenolic compounds and furanic aldehydes are produced as a result of barrel ageing. These compounds define what we recognize as key flavour identifiers of aged products – dry, vanilla, nutty, resinous, fruity, sweet and toasted characteristics, for example. We can break down the reactions that produce these flavours into three categories: infusion, oxidation and extraction.

INFUSION

Infusion refers to all the 'good stuff' that a spirit or cocktail will take directly from the wood. Think of a cask as a reverse tea bag, a highly compacted cylinder of flavour. The charring or toasting process that occurs on the inside surface of the cask breaks down the various structures of the wood into shorter chained sugars that infuse directly into the liquid.

Most of the 'wood' flavour that we are familiar with, such as vanilla, butter, caramel, banana and coconut, are formed as a result of the breakdown of lignin – a part of the secondary cell wall of the wood. Vanillin, responsible for the vanilla flavour, naturally occurs, unsurprisingly, most abundantly in vanilla (around 2% composition by weight) and is responsible for vanilla's claim to being the second most popular flavour in the world (chocolate is first, but it also contains vanillin, as does breast milk). The breakdown of lignin at higher levels can also provide toasty, smoky flavours, too.

All barrel-aged drinks will extract a certain amount of tannin from the wood. Tannin is more

prevalent in European casks than American, and contributes a great deal towards the colour of an aged spirit. On the palate it is apparent as a strange drying sensation, and if carefully integrated can add welcome structure and tactile balance to a drink.

OXIDATION

Oxidation is a crucial part of ageing some spirits and wines. It aids in the development and complexity of the liquid. The oxidation of ethanol (alcohol) converts to acetaldehyde, the compound responsible for sherry-like nutty, grassy notes. It is this oxidative effect that provides sherry and vermouth (vermouth also being partially oxidized during production) with their characteristic finish.

The subject of sherry actually has a great relevance to the barrel-ageing debate. Oloroso sherry is a marriage of wine and spirit that is aged in cask – in fact, the same ingredients (in principle) that are used to make a Martinez or a Manhattan: spirit, wine and bitters. On that basis, I think it's hard to dismiss the very concept of barrel ageing cocktails, as some do, when the same theory applies to such great effect in the production of sherries.

Continuing with acetaldehyde, it can, in turn, be oxidized itself, converting into acetic acid. Acetic acid in small quanities provides a 'bite' and 'fullness' to a cocktail, but in larger levels can add a harsh edge and so must be closely monitored.

EXTRACTION

Extraction is all about the softening of the drink. This process is understood to occur thanks to the presence of hemicellulose within the wood (around 15–25% of the total composition of oak). Hemicellulose reacts with acids present within the liquid and produces complex sugars. It is thought to be these sugars that slightly soften the drink, as well as giving the effect of integration and consistency. Interestingly, it's thought that a higher acidity will result in a greater softening effect, which is exactly why drinks containing vermouth work so well. For the particularly inspired among you, experimenting with bolstering the acid content of your cocktails before ageing may yield interesting results...

To see an example of Barrel Ageing, go to my Oaked Martinez on page 78.

BOTTLE AGEING

It might sound silly to suggest that putting a drink in a glass bottle, sealing it, then waiting for a while is likely to achieve anything other than a greater level of thirst.

It's generally accepted that spirits do not age in bottles, since the ABV is simply too high, but new research is now suggesting that this may not be entirely true. Over the course of years, vintage wines will mature, mellow and develop complexity whilst in the bottle. Since strong cocktails are generally about halfway between the ABV of wine and spirits (25–32% typically, once diluted), perhaps it isn't so crazy to suggest that some development may occur?

I have personally conducted triangular taste tests on aged cocktails versus fresh ones and there are indeed distinguishable differences – a harmony of flavours, a softening of alcohol – but it's hard to put a finger on exactly what it is. There is a bunch of theories that attempt to explain what happens when a cocktail, or spirit, is left in a bottle for a period of time, but at the time of writing, much of it is still conjecture.

One of my favourite explanations is that alcohol molecules and water molecules do not mix evenly at 20% ABV and above, and that ethanol molecules tend to cluster over time. It's possible that a newly mixed cocktail containing unaged spirits is more heterogeneously mixed and therefore harsher on the palate. As the cocktail rests, the alcohol molecules tightly cluster together, meaning that the drink slips down all the better!

For an example of bottle ageing, see the Champagne Gin Fizz on page 62.

STEEL AGEING

Steel ageing is an even greater mystery than bottle ageing, since it seems to work faster and have a more profound 'smoothing' effect on the cocktail. Best of all, it's very cheap and easy to have a go at steel ageing by purchasing steel drinking flasks.

See page 137 for my Industrial Revolution recipe, which has further comments on steel ageing.

GIN

VODKA

BRANDY & COGNAC

THE COCKTAILS

WHISKY & WHISKEY

RUM

TEQUILA

GIN

It's easy to overlook how unique a spirit gin is. For the most part, liquor is shaped by the product from which it's made (grain, grape, cane), the way in which it is produced (fermentation process, distillation, 'cutting') and in some cases the ageing process. Gin is different. Gin is a flavoured spirit. A gin producer starts with a neutral spirit, a blank canvas, vodka essentially. The distiller then adds 'botanicals' – herbs, fruits, barks, roots and spices – to the spirit and redistills it. The outcome is a clear liquor that holds within it all the volatile, distillable nuances of the botanicals used to flavour it.

I've tasted a gin that uses only two botanicals and I've tried a few with over 20. Some of my favourite gins use only four or five botanicals. The art of balancing just a handful of flavours, yet producing a complex spirit, really appeals to me.

Gin might be a British invention, but it is based on a much older Dutch drink called 'genever'. The word 'genever' is derived from the French word for juniper, and it's thought to have been around since the 16th century. Juniper is historically the primary flavour of both gin and genever. It is the ingredient that provides gin with both its fragrant pine aromatics, as well as its aromas of leather, cut grass and spice.

Genever was thought to have been used medicinally for a variety of ailments, including as a digestive aid, for the relief of kidney stones and for bowel infections. Thankfully, genever developed into being as much a social cure-all as it was a medicinal one. By the middle of the 17th century, the Dutch were drinking genever whenever possible. During the Thirty Years' War, English soldiers fought alongside troops from the Netherlands who took shots of 'Dutch courage' before battle. The English liked the idea of this, and so took the flavour of genever back home with them. London loved it, and both the production and consumption of 'gineva' swelled during the reign of the Dutch King, William

of Orange (1689–1702). Before long the drink was referred to as 'Dutch gin' and it was being sold from backstreets, pawn shops, street vendors and even through elaborately engineered pieces of guttering, down which the gin would be poured.

It was the middle of the 18th century and the gin craze was in full swing. It is thought that one in every four residences in the St. Giles district of central London was producing its own gin. Buying in cheap spirit and flavouring it 'in-house' was a common practice, but most of the time the ideal flavourings were unavailable, so less healthy substitutes such as turpentine were used.

Ultimately, the 'gin craze' wound down when strict acts came into effect, controlling the production and sale of the drink. This resulted in a handful of brands upping their game somewhat and producing gins of higher quality, with less sugar, resulting in the birth of 'London Dry' as a stand-alone style.

These days, London Dry can be made anywhere in the world, with the only real stipulation being that the flavour is primarily that of juniper. This rather vague requirement has, however, birthed a new style known as 'New Western', in which juniper is not necessarily the most dominant flavour. It would be unfair not to mention 'Plymouth gin', a stand-alone category of gin characterized by sweet botanicals and the fact that it has to be made in Plymouth, Devon, using water drawn from the hills of Dartmoor.

Gin has seen quite a resurgence in recent years. I put this down, partly, to its prevalence in classic cocktails. Over half of the drinks in *The Savoy Cocktail Book* (originally published in 1930) contain gin, and many of my favourite drinks are gin based. In this section, you will see some of those drinks in their classic form, followed by my modern interpretations, created using all of the means and resources available to me.

RAMOS GIN FIZZ

Here is a drink that breaks the first rule of mixology (along with quite a few of the other drinks in this book): keep it simple. The Ramos Gin Fizz combines a multitude of ingredients, including cream and lemon, and comes with instructions to shake for no less than 12 minutes. However, the result is a silky smooth pick-me-up that, when balanced correctly, rivals any drink for pure sipping pleasure.

The drink dates back to 1888 New Orleans and a gent named Henry Ramos. Due to the low cost of labour back then, Ramos would hire 'shaker boys' to pump out the cocktails, and they would stand in a line continuously shaking. All night.

Taking a look at the ingredients list, this drink strikes me as a classic case of trial and error prevailing. There are few, if any, other drinks that contain both lemon AND lime juice; who knows why, as they certainly both have a unique flavour. There are even fewer drinks that contain citrus and

cream together – that combo is pretty much universally accepted as a 'do not go there' throughout the bartending world. And then there is the addition of orange flower water, a unique ingredient that rarely appears in other mixed drinks. So surely the recipe must have been happened upon by chance? But what a day that must have been, as the finished product is an incredible achievement.

Expect to receive balanced refreshment and an oily consistency that slides down the gullet rather too easily. Sugar balances the sour as in a regular fizz, and the orange flower water adds a fragrant aromatic to accompany the gin. The first time I tasted a Ramos Gin Fizz, it immediately reminded me of my mum's lime cheesecake.

The shaking does a few things here: firstly, it cools and dilutes the drink. But after around a minute, the liquid reaches a plateau of temperature and dilution. The drink chills to around -2°C/28°F

50 ML/2 OZ. TANQUERAY GIN

25 ML/1 OZ. DOUBLE/HEAVY CREAM

½ EGG WHITE

15 ML/½ OZ. FRESH LIME JUICE

10 ML/⅓ OZ. FRESH LEMON JUICE

12.5 ML/½ OZ. SUGAR SYRUP (SEE PAGE 204)

3 ML ORANGE FLOWER WATER

A SLICE OF LEMON, TO GARNISH

Shake all the ingredients with cubed ice for no less than
12 minutes. Strain into a chilled highball glass and garnish
with a slice of lemon.

(depending on the ice used) and so the ice ceases to melt any more, but the drink will still stay cold. Minutes go by and not much changes at all. The other thing going on here is, of course, the mixing and emulsifying of the cream and egg. The egg acts as a surfactant, nicely combining the fat of the cream with the other ingredients into a silky smooth emulsion. To do this, the drink must be well mixed so that it doesn't split, although 12 minutes is probably a bit of overkill. This could, of course, be done prior to shaking with a blender, whisk or an ultrasonic probe, but hey, I guess it was cheaper to employ a bartender to do it back in 1888.

CHAMPAGNE GIN FIZZ

Back before I opened my second bar, The Worship Street Whistling Shop in East London, I worked with Ryan Chetiyawardana (the manager) on an interesting concept involving gin and yeast. Ryan had the idea of bottling a completed cocktail with yeast, allowing it to ferment, then serving the entire bottle at the table, complete with pop! The drink was titled Champagne Gin Fizz.

Development of the cocktail took a long time, as we had to wait for the yeast to go to work on each batch that we tested. Every alcoholic product in the world starts first with yeast, as it's this micro-organism that converts sugar into alcohol. In the case of Champagne and some bottled beers, yeast is used to 'prime' or carbonate the beverage after regular fermentation has taken place. Fresh yeast is added to the wine and sealed in a bottle for a length of time. The yeast then gets to work eating up residual sugars and converting them into carbon dioxide gas, providing Champagne with its unique style of fizz.

Ryan and I applied the same principles to a non-fizzy Gin Fizz (a Gin Flat?!). The aim was to not only carbonate the drink, but also to add the familiar Champagne 'biscuity' characteristics over the top of the usual Gin Fizz aromatics.

We started by testing various brands of Champagne yeast (Champagne uses a particular type of yeast to achieve its unique flavour). We tested them for speed, level of carbonation and contribution to flavour. We settled on the Lalvin brand EC-1118 as the fastest, most efficient yeast.

The next stage was to work out the exact specifications of the drink's ingredients. This would normally be a simple task, but in this instance the balance and flavour of the drink would be likely to change while the yeast goes to work. In addition to that, the sugar, acid and alcohol levels of the cocktail needed to be just right for the yeast to be as effective as possible. We set up various control tests and experiments with different sugar and acid contents to see which produced the best results. In some instances the drink failed to ferment at all, perhaps because the acidity was too high. In other cases we had bottles exploding, probably because the sugar level was too high. The trick was to store the primed bottles in a nice warm environment to encourage fermentation, then after a set period they would be transferred to a fridge, which halted the fermentation and left the yeast dormant. We also tested samples over different lengths of time to see if we could nail down an optimum fermentation period.

One thing that we learned throughout months of testing was that the effect of yeast is difficult to predict. Change one factor even slightly and the entire process can spiral out of control and result in something wholly undrinkable.

After getting through over a case of gin in the development process, we finally settled on an exact formula of ingredients, timings and temperatures. The next step was to label, batch and bottle enough of the product to keep us going... With over a week's preparation time, it was very important to keep healthy stock levels!

At the Whistling Shop we make this drink using Champagne bottles and a special corking device, but if you can get hold of some swing-top glass bottles, this drink is as easy to prepare at home as a loaf of bread.

CHAMPAGNE GIN FIZZ

◆

For the Lemon & Lime Gomme

50 G/2 OZ. LEMON ZEST • 40 G/1⅓ OZ. LIME ZEST

270 ML/9 OZ. WATER • 600 G/1 LB. 5 OZ. SUGAR

30 ML/1 OZ. VODKA • 3 G CITRIC ACID • 2 G MALIC ACID

•

SOUS VIDE the lemon and lime zest with the water at 60°C/140°F for 2 hours. Filter the liquid through MUSLIN CHEESECLOTH, then transfer it to a saucepan. Add the sugar, and heat until the sugar has dissolved, then add the vodka and acids. Bottle and refrigerate until required.

For the Champagne Gin Fizz

400 ML/13½ OZ. WATER

10 G/⅓ OZ. LALVIN EC-1118 CHAMPAGNE YEAST BRAND

170 ML/5¾ OZ. TANQUERAY LONDON DRY GIN

90 ML/3 OZ. 'LEMON & LIME GOMME'

ORANGE FLOWER WATER, TO SERVE

•

Makes 6 servings

Heat 100 ml/3⅓ oz. of the water to 35°C/95°F. Add the yeast, stir fast, then set aside for 5 minutes. Mix the gin, Lemon & Lime Gomme and remaining water in a large mixing bowl. Pour the yeast into the bowl and whisk vigorously to fully aerate the drink. Once fully mixed, transfer the mixture to a STERILIZED CHAMPAGNE BOTTLE and apply the CORK AND CAGE. Store at around 30°C/86°F for 9 days, then put in the fridge, standing up, for a further 2 days.

•

To serve, atomize (see page 202) chilled Champagne flutes with orange flower water and fill to the brim!

◆

MARTINI

50 ML/2 OZ. TANQUERAY NO. TEN GIN • 15 ML/½ OZ. MARTINI EXTRA DRY VERMOUTH

AN OLIVE OR A TWIST OF LEMON ZEST, TO GARNISH

Stir all the ingredients with cubed ice for 60 seconds. Strain into a chilled martini glass and garnish with an olive or a twist of lemon zest.

Tread carefully – you are in the presence of the undisputed king of the cocktail world. What is it that makes a Martini so iconic? Universally revered as the driving force behind cocktail culture itself and twisted and embellished to within an inch of its life, there's a good chance that the first cocktail you ever heard of was a Martini. How can one drink command such a huge share of the cocktail pie?

It's hard to place a finger on exactly what it is that makes a Martini so great. For many, it is likely to be the glass that it's served in. Officially named a 'cocktail glass', the iconic v-shaped bowl on a stem is inextricably connected to the drink itself, so much so that through the 1980s and 90s, virtually any drink served in a martini glass was called an '[insert flavour here] Martini'.

David A. Embury describes the Martini in *The Fine Art of Mixing Drinks* (1948) as 'the most perfect of aperitif cocktails', and it's certainly true that the botanical, bordering on medicinal, properties of the drink open up the palate in a way like no other.

If you really want to know what is so special about a Martini, take a seat in a grand hotel bar, the American Bar at the Savoy in London, or The NoMad Hotel in New York are both perfect, and order one. If you can't make it there, try making one from my recipe above.

For some folk the drink is surprisingly strong (it's nothing like the 'Apple Martini' that you were served by the wannabe cocktail bartender in the local pub when you were 18!), and it often takes a few attempts to really engage with it. But at one time or another, something special will happen: the drink will make perfect sense, the veil will be lifted and it will become incredibly appealing – suddenly the simple combination of only two ingredients will seem like the most obvious synergy of flavours in the world. It is perhaps the combination of simplicity and magic that makes the Martini such a holy sanctity amongst followers.

As for the origins of this drink, well, as you would expect from a cocktail as magical as this one, they are a matter of great contest. The facts are as follows… The 'Martini' pre-dates the 'Dry Martini' (more on the differences shortly). The Martini is probably based on the Martinez (see page 76), which in turn is more than likely based on the Manhattan (see page 134). Where the name 'Martini' came from is not fully known, but it's generally accepted that the Martini & Rossi (vermouth) company promoted a Martinez made with Martini vermouth; the name change promptly followed.

The earliest reference to a Martini Cocktail that I know of comes from Wehman's *Bartenders' Guide* (1891) by Henry J. Wehman:

(Use large bar glass) Fill the glass with ice, 2 or 3 dashes gum syrup, 2 or 3 dashes Bitters, 1 dash of curaçoa, ½ wine glassful of Old Tom Gin, ½ wine glassful of vermouth.

It sounds suspiciously like a Martinez, and so corroborates the link between the two drinks nicely. The Dry Martini took a few more years to come about, tastes changed perhaps, and in 1906 a drink that has strong similarities to the Dry Martini of today is published in *Louis' Mixed Drinks* by Jaques Louis Muckensturm:

> 2 liqueur glasses dry gin
> 1 liqueur glass French vermouth
> a dash of curaçao
> 2 dashes of orange bitters

There is much debate over the ratio of gin to vermouth in a Martini. It should always be made with dry vermouth (which is slightly sweet despite what the name suggests), so the 'dryness' of the Martini is dictated by how little vermouth goes into the drink. Winston Churchill liked his Martinis so dry that merely a glance across the room at the bottle of vermouth would suffice. Certainly, when my bartending career began, the trend was to make a Martini with a ratio of around 15:1 in favour of the gin – very dry indeed. These days, I personally like to drink a 3:1 Martini, which some would class as wet (heavy on the vermouth), but it works for me. A 3:1 ratio is far more reminiscent of the Martinis served in the 1920s and 30s.

Then there is the question of shaken or stirred? Well, we all know how James Bond preferred his, but is there a correct way to make a Martini? History certainly points to the stirred Martini, but in his 1948 book *The Hour*, Bernard DeVoto had this to say:

> Or take the superstition, for I cannot dignify it as a heresy, that the Martini must not be shaken. Nonsense. This perfect thing is made of gin and vermouth. They are self-reliant liquors, stable, of stout heart; we do not have to treat them as if they were plover's eggs. It does not matter in the least whether you shake a Martini or stir it. It does matter if splinters of ice get into the cocktail glass, and I suppose this small seed of fact is what grew into the absurdity that we must not 'bruise the gin'.

And I tend to agree. There are three main differences between a shaken Martini and a stirred one:

1. A shaken Martini can be made a lot quicker (sometimes essential!).

2. A shaken Martini will have a greater degree of aeration. Tiny bubbles of air become trapped within the folds of the liquid, which is also what gives it a slightly cloudy appearance. Aeration, in my experience, is very rarely a bad thing. It tends to make drinks feel lighter on the palate and usually gives a better flavour release (wine experts do this a lot with all that decanting and slurping).

3. A shaken Martini looks different. You might find that the cloudy appearance causes the drink to lose some of its 'mellow' and 'yellow' qualities. Despite the taste and aroma not being dramatically altered, sometimes a difference in clarity, colour and consistency can have just as much affect.

My experience has taught me that wetter Martinis prefer to be stirred and dry ones shaken. Whether this is to do with the lower ABV of a wet martini or the fact that it has more wine in it, I do not know.

Olive or twist? Now here is a highly subjective question and one that only you can answer. I have been known to indulge in either and, on occasion, both – only if I'm hungry. A brief warning about twists: don't zest half a lemon over the drink as it will taste, surprisingly, of lemon and only lemon. A small strip or circle (about the size of a postage stamp) of zest is all that is required to freshen the drink the required amount. In fact, I'd wager that far more damage can be done with a lemon zest than a shaker where a Dry Martini is concerned.

FIXED MARTINI

Meddling with a drink like the Martini is like taking a felt-tip pen to the *Mona Lisa*. It's simple and perfect, why mess with it? Well... because I can and it would be boring not to. If it ain't broke, make it better!

The primary function of a Dry Martini is to be an aperitif, so I think that's a good starting point for some positive modifications. The definition of an aperitif is 'an alcoholic drink taken before a meal to stimulate the appetite'. There are numerous different kinds of aperitif that do a similar trick. The Italians especially are famous for their amari and bitter aperitifs that liven up the palate and get the salivary glands working. Saliva helps carry flavour around the palate, keeps everything nice and moist and can be considered the first stage of digestion. The release of saliva kick-starts the stomach into releasing digestive juices that will later process all the food and drink you intake. A good aperitif before a meal can significantly aid the digestive process.

With that I mind, I think there's a little work to be done with the Martini, since despite all its harmonious brilliance and aromatic perfection, it doesn't harbour a huge amount of bitterness or other saliva stimulants.

Bitterness is relatively easy to come by: many common ingredients have strong bitter characteristics. The only problem is that cloves, cardamon and star anise also have strong aromatic qualities to them that will crush the subtle nuances of a Martini. If I'm going to add bitterness to the drink, it needs to be pronounced but subtle – integrated. As is often the case, the obvious choice is right under our noses: wormwood.

The word 'vermouth' comes from the German word for wormwood, *wermut*, the reason being that vermouth historically contains, amongst many other ingredients, wormwood. Wormwood is a perennial shrub, most famous for flavouring absinthe (wormwood in latin is *Artemesia absinthium*), toxic in large quantities but delightfully bitter in lower concentrations. These days, vermouths are somewhat on the safe side, with very little bitterness being detectable in the common brands. I'll aim to correct that by adding a touch of wormwood into my Super Dry Martini.

There exists a family of foodstuffs known as sialagogues that promote the production of saliva and therefore the digestive juices in the stomach. Some common sialagogues are ginger, blue iris and cayenne pepper. (If you don't believe me, try putting some cayenne pepper on your tongue and you'll find yourself swallowing back saliva for the next minute or so!) By bolstering the herbal element of the vermouth in the drink with a couple of choice ingredients, it might be possible to increase saliva production in the mouth, too.

The plan, then, is to create a mild herbal infusion, with selected ingredients that will aid in the preparation of the digestive system.

FIXED MARTINI

—————◆—————

For the Sialagogue Infusion

100 ML/3⅓ OZ. TANQUERAY GIN • 2 G FRESH GINGER, GRATED • 1 G GROUND CAYENNE PEPPER

1 G BLUE IRIS FLOWERS • 1 G MALIC ACID • 0.2 G WORMWOOD LEAVES

•

Put all the ingredients in a glass jar, seal and allow to infuse for 2 weeks.

For the Fixed Martini

50 ML/2 OZ. TANQUERAY NO. TEN GIN • 15 ML/½ OZ. MARTINI EXTRA DRY VERMOUTH • 5 ML 'SIALAGOGUE INFUSION'

2 DROPS OF GRAPEFRUIT BITTERS • AN OLIVE, TO GARNISH

•

Stir all the ingredients together with cubed ice and strain into a chilled coupe glass. Garnish with an olive.

—————◆—————

NEGRONI

◆

25 ML/1 OZ. TANQUERAY NO. TEN GIN

25 ML/1 OZ. CAMPARI

25 ML/1 OZ. MARTINI ROSSO VERMOUTH

A SLICE OF LEMON (OR GRAPEFRUIT), TO GARNISH

•

Stir all the ingredients over cubed ice for 60 seconds, then
strain into a chilled rocks glass with cubed ice (or use a large
hand-cracked piece of ice). Garnish with a slice of lemon.

◆

Ask any cocktail bartender what their favourite drink is and they'll probably beat about the bush suggesting different drinks for different times of the day, or simply say 'a beer'. Ask them what their second favourite drink is and they'll quite possibly tell you that it's a Negroni.

Here is a drink that ingeniously combines herbal aromatics, a bitter-sweet balance as addictive as crack and a decent backbone of booze to make the whole thing worthwhile. The gin provides the bulk of the alcohol content, along with a dry, earthy quality. The vermouth gives a little bit of dilution, some sweetness and a decent herbal flourish. Finally, Campari gives a huge spiced bitter orange sting and a decent glug of sugar to boot.

The commonly accepted story of the Negroni's creation takes us back to 1920s' Florence, and a man named Count Camillo Negroni. He orders an Americano (Campari, Italian vermouth and soda), but with gin in place of soda. The truth is a little more muddy and a matter of some contention. In fact, the debate has raged on enough to have now involved members of the Negroni family and Italian historians. My best understanding comes from the book *Sulle Tracce del Conte* ('On the Trail of the Count', 2002) by Luca Picchi, which,

backed up by a considerable amount of historical documentation, intimates that the drink is named after [deep breath] Cammillo Luigi Manfredo Maria Negroni, who originally asked Fosco Scarselli, bartender at Cafe Casoni, to fortify his Americano with gin. This happened at some time in either 1919 and 1920. One of the ways in which the story is qualified is by a letter sent from Frances Harper of London to [the evidently unwell] Negroni on 13th October 1920: 'You say you can drink, smoke and I am sure laugh, just as much as ever. I feel you are not much to be pitied! You must not take more than 20 Negronis in one day!' Clearly the Count was fond of his own drink!

Even though the history is not all that clear, making a Negroni is very easy indeed. You might prefer to go slightly heavier on the gin, or drop the Campari down a touch, but the recipe above is widely accepted as the proper way. The garnish can have a big impact on this drink – an orange twist is common, but I also like a grapefruit twist and have been known to put a slice of cucumber in there too. In the US, the Negroni is more often served straight up (in a martini glass), but in Europe we still serve it on the rocks.

FAIRGROUND NEGRONI

I must confess that this drink is at least partly inspired by a cocktail served to me by my friend Paul Tvaroh of Lounge Bohemia in Shoreditch, London. Paul created a unique take on the classic Campari and Soda by serving a simple glass of soda accompanied by a stick of Campari candyfloss/cotton candy. I was instructed to eat the candyfloss/cotton candy while sipping on the soda. The result was an intense bitter-sweet hit, counteracted by effervescent soda. Brilliant.

The drink got me thinking how cool it would be to re-create 'all the fun of the fair' in a cocktail. Each of the three usual Negroni ingredients will be deconstructed into an edible treat and served together for the ultimate fairground experience. There's a lot of work to do, so let's get started!

For the Campari candyfloss/cotton candy I need sugar. Candyfloss/cotton candy is made by heating and spinning sugar until liquid strands are shot through tiny holes. The tiny threads of sugar are reasonably stable, so can be wound up together to form big clumps of cotton wool-textured sugar. Campari actually has a lot of sugar in it, around 22 brix (22% sugar), and it's this sugar we need to make the candyfloss/cotton candy.

To make the Campari sugar, I gently reduce a bottle of Campari down in a saucepan along with 10 drops of pink food colouring, over a very low heat for 3 hours, evaporating off as much of the water and alcohol as I possibly can. Many of the aromatics and, crucially, the bitterness are left in the pan along with all the sugar, and what I am left with is a syrup with the texture of thick honey.

I spread the syrup out on a sheet of greaseproof/ wax paper and leave it to dry out in a low oven, or in a dehydrator for 8 hours. Every hour or so, I break up the resin into smaller pieces and ensure that all surfaces get a decent amount of warm air over them. What I am left with is an intensely bitter crystallized sugar. I add 1 teaspoon dry Campari sugar to a candyfloss/cotton candy machine, and following the instructions, form a stick of Campari candyfloss.

I'm now going to make marshmallows out of both the gin and the vermouth. The end result will be the classic contrasting pink and white soft sweets, but with the flavour of gin and vermouth. Marshmallows are reasonably easy to make as they are basically a type of jellied meringue. Because I'm using gelatine to make my marshmallows, it means that they will be stable, even with a bit of alcohol in there.

To make the gin marshmallows, I put 225 g/8 oz. (caster) sugar in a saucepan along with 5 ml liquid glucose and 50 ml/2 oz. water, and heat the mixture to 127°C/260°F exactly using a temperature probe or confectioners' thermometer. I stir in 5 gelatine sheets that have been softened in a little water first, until they dissolve.

In a mixing bowl, I whisk 1 egg white to stiff peaks with an electric hand whisk, then continue whisking while slowly pouring in the hot sugar mixture and 35 ml/1¼ oz. Tanqueray gin. I continue whisking for about 3 minutes more until the mixture is glossy and firm – the more air, the lighter the marshmallows will be. Once firm, the mixture is transferred to a suitable mould (such as a bread pan), which has been greased and dusted with 50/50 mix of icing/confectioners' sugar and cornflour/cornstarch. The gooey mixture is left to set for an hour or two. Once set, the marshmallows are turned out of the mould and chopped into cubes using a hot knife.

To make the sweet vermouth marshmallows, I follow the same method and use the same ingredient ratios, simply substituting the 50 ml/2 oz. water and the Tanqueray for 100 ml/3⅓ oz. Martini Rosso.

I'm also going to garnish the drink with vermouth-flavoured popping candy. You will probably remember this stuff from your childhood sweet shop. It looks a lot like sugar, but when you put it in your mouth it pops and cracks, which is both amazing and a little

disconcerting! It came as a surprise to me to discover that the process used to create popping candy is both patented and very dangerous. My version is more simple and more of a 'fizzing candy' than popping.

To make the fizzing candy, I start by dusting a sheet of baking parchment with a little sugar and 30 g/1 oz. citric acid powder.

In a saucepan, I combine 260 g/9 oz. granulated sugar, 60 g/2 oz. glucose (or corn) syrup, 2 drops of red food colouring and 15 ml/½ oz. Martini Rosso concentrate, which I have made by reducing Martini Rosso gently on the hob/stove for 4 hours until I am left with a syrup.

Using a temperature probe, the mixture is heated to 150°C/300°F, being careful to keep it moving so that sugar crystals are not able to form on the side of the pan. Once heated, I take the pan off the heat and add 5 g bicarbonate of soda/baking soda and quickly whisk the mixture until it is dissolved. The sugar mixture is quickly poured onto the baking parchment, then I sprinkle a further 30 g/1 oz. citric acid powder evenly on top. I allow the sugar to cool, then smash it up into little pieces so that it resembles shards of popping candy.

Last but not least, I'll finish the ensemble with a gin-flavoured ice cream, dusted with Campari sugar (the same that is used to create the candy floss).

I put 500 ml/17 oz. whole milk in a saucepan with 4 g juniper berries and heat them to 65°C/150°F. The milk is then strained to remove the berries.

In a stand mixer, I beat the 120 g/4 oz. egg yolks with 250 g/9 oz. sugar and 5 g sodium alginate (this is optional, but improves the firmness of the ice cream) for 5 minutes. I continue mixing while slowly pouring in the warm juniper-infused milk. Once everything is mixed, I return the mixture to the pan, heat it to 70°C/160°F, and hold the temperature for 10 minutes, to pasteurize. The mixture is then allowed to cool, before it is refrigerated for a minimum of 12 hours.

Once the mixture has been chilled, I stir in 350 g/12 oz. sour cream and 100 ml/3⅓ oz. gin, then freeze the ice cream, either in an ice cream maker or using liquid nitrogen or dry ice.

To serve, I simply assemble all of the components!

AVIATION

The first reference I can find for the Aviation cocktail is in the 1916 book *Recipes for Mixed Drinks* by Hugo R. Ensslin. This places the likely creation date of the drink slap-bang in the middle of the golden era of aviation. It's easy to forget, given the mundane commercialization of air travel today, that once upon a time aviators were the rock stars of the world. While the legendary aviator Howard Hughes was still in short trousers, the aviators of the early 19th century were literally armed with nothing more than a pair of flying goggles, a cigarette and a healthy dose of determination, all in the quest for gravity defiance.

Since their conceptions, cocktails have consistently reflected the trends, fashion and icons of their times in both ingredients and titles (the Sidecar, Mary Pickford and Flaming Lamborghini are all examples of this). So it comes as no surprise that a cocktail should be named after the lofty

endeavours of the aviator. And not just any cocktail; this one contains gin, traditionally the preferred tipple of flying men, and is even the colour of a morning blue sky. Besides all of that though, it tastes absolutely fantastic in my opinion and ranks highly as one of the best twists on a Sour out there.

When I first tested my mettle behind the stick, the Aviation was commonly recognized to be a Gin Sour with maraschino liqueur in place of sugar. Simple, right? That particular recipe was taken from Harry Craddock's *The Savoy Cocktail Book* (1930). Undoubtedly this is a tasty version of the drink, but it's not the original version, or the best...

To find the original, we must travel back to 1916, and the aforementioned *Recipes for Mixed Drinks* by Ensslin. In this book, we find the original recipe, which has less maraschino than the Savoy version and includes an extra ingredient – crème

50 ML/2 OZ. TANQUERAY GIN

25 ML/1 OZ. FRESH LEMON JUICE

5 ML MARASCHINO LIQUEUR

5 ML CRÈME DE VIOLETTE

•

Shake all the ingredients together and strain into a chilled
coupe glass. There's no garnish, but you may choose to
perform a salute to your relevant country of origin.

de violette. This liqueur is flavoured, as the name suggests, with the violet flower. The taste is like that of the little blue candy that you sucked on as a child; floral, sweet and entirely unique. Now this is not a flavour to lead off with – put too much crème de violette in any drink and all you're likely to taste is sickly, grandmother's potpourri, floral assault bomb. Use a couple of dashes like a seasoning, though, and you get a wonderful floral aromatic to accompany the other flavours in the drink, and that's exactly how an Aviation works.

AVIATRIX

I guess I should first explain the name of this drink. An aviatirx is a female aviator. Amelia Earhart was one of the first women to be dubbed an aviatrix, in part due to her successful attempt to fly over the Atlantic Ocean in the 1920s. It seems fitting to me that this drink should be named after the female aviators out there, since it has many qualities desirable to the fairer sex.

How good an Aviation cocktail is depends largely on the quality of the crème de violette. One of the main reasons that, up until recently, everyone omitted the crème de violette was because no-one was actually manufacturing it. Now there are around half a dozen brands of crème de violette available, and some of them are very good (Bitter Truth and Briottet are my two favourites).

There is, of course, nothing to stop you making your own crème de violette with real violet flowers. One of the main benefits of doing this is that you get a very natural violet flavour – a far cry from some of the organically synthesized violet flavourings out there. I've experimented a lot with making floral liqueurs. Flowers are difficult to work with since they are very delicate and their aromatics are highly volatile – part of the reason why they smell so good! Any kind of heat is likely to damage the flowers irreparably, so I'm using a cold infusion of violet flowers into gin. Although, there's nothing to stop you trying a nitrogen cavitation infusion or sous vide (see pages 31–32).

Other than my perfected violet liqueur, I'm going to leave the Aviatrix more or less true to the Aviation. But one other piece of creative license I will allow myself is the incorporation of a visible aroma to accompany the drink.

A few years back, I attended a seminar on historical perfumery conducted by the aptly named Odette Toilette – I don't think it's her real name mind you. The seminar took a tour of the last 100 years through the medium of perfume. Just like cocktails, the scents and smells that we appreciate or find alluring have changed and developed according to the times. The smell of lavender might have been great in the 1920s, but in the 30s it was 'sooo last decade' – you get the idea. In the 1920s, aviation was a seriously hot topic; 'those magnificent men in their flying machines' were the superstars of their time – men wanted to be them and women wanted to be with them. Perfume houses jumped on this straight away and many scents were marketed as a one-way ticket to loop-da-loop heroics. These perfumes exhibited characteristics of rough leather, tobacco smoke and even a touch of engine grease or petroleum. It sounds less than appealing, but when paired with traditional scents the aromas can be very evocative.

One such perfume was the masculine Knize Ten, by Knize. It's dry and leathery with lots of civet (musk) lurking underneath. There's aromas of rough rope, burnt rubber and hay. It literally smells like you're suiting up back at the base ready for daredevil sortie (whatever a sortie is). I'm going to use this scent as visible cloud-like accompaniment to my drink. Chocks away!

AVIATRIX

◆

For the Violet Liqueur
700 ML/23²/₃ OZ. TANQUERAY GIN

10 G VIOLET FLOWERS • 2 G VIOLET LEAVES

2 G ROSE PETALS • 0.2 G VANILLA SEEDS

400 G/14 OZ. SUGAR

•

To make the violet liqueur, combine all the ingredients (except the sugar) in a glass jar and allow to infuse at room temperature for 10 days.

•

Warm 200 ml/6¾ oz. of the infusion in a saucepan and add the sugar. Allow the sugar to dissolve completely, then mix the syrup with the remaining violet infusion. Store the Violet Liqueur in the fridge for up to 6 months.

For the Aviatrix
5 ML 'VIOLET LIQUEUR' • 50 ML/2 OZ. TANQUERAY GIN

20 ML/²/₃ OZ. FRESH LEMON JUICE

5 ML MARASCHINO LIQUEUR

1 G ALBUMIN (EGG WHITE POWDER)

•

Shake all the ingredients together with cubed ice and strain into a chilled coupe glass.

For the Knize Ten Fog
2 G KNIZE TEN • 100 ML/3¹/₃ OZ. WARM WATER

DRY ICE

•

Mix together the Knize Ten and warm water, then pour over dry ice.

◆

MARTINEZ

This is the grandaddy of gin cocktails and the missing link between the dark spirited cocktails of the 19th century and the gin boom of the early 20th. The Martinez is a combination of gin, vermouth and bitters, usually with a splash of maraschino liqueur or orange curaçao. Now if that sounds a bit vague, it's because this is a vague drink and the bare-bones information I've just given you is about all we are certain of! The truth is that Martinez recipes vary wildly over the years, but it's partly the elusive nature of the drink that makes it so attractive – every time I drink one I wonder if this is the Martinez, or simply another variation of the concept.

The first thing that we can be sure of is that the Martinez and Martini are lookalike siblings. Born a few years apart in the late 1800s, the first-known reference to a Dry Martini is strikingly similar to that of a Martinez.

The first reference to a Martinez in a cocktail book comes from O. H. Bryon's *The Modern Bartenders' Guide* (1884). Byron rather vaguely describes a Martinez as: 'Same as a Manhattan, only you substitute gin for whisky'. This wouldn't be too much of a problem if Byron hadn't listed two different Manhattan recipes in the same book and failed to mention which to use as a reference point. Both Manhattans are the same except one uses sweet vermouth instead of dry vermouth, which leads us nicely on to the crux of the matter.

Should a Martinez be made with sweet or dry vermouth? The two cocktails are very different: dry vermouth creates, well, quite a dry cocktail, whereas a sweet vermouth Martinez is far bolder as the whisky and wine do battle in the glass.

Let's consider that question while move on to the next reference to see if further light can be shed on the matter. Jerry Thomas's revised edition

50 ML/2 OZ. TANQUERAY GIN

25 ML/1 OZ. MARTINI ROSSO VERMOUTH

5 ML MARASCHINO LIQUEUR

3 DASHES OF DR. ADAM ELMEGIRAB'S BOKER'S BITTERS

A TWIST OF ORANGE OR LEMON ZEST OR A CHERRY, TO GARNISH

•

Stir the ingredients with cubed ice for 75 seconds, then strain
into a chilled coupe glass and garnish, as prefered.

---

of *The Bon Vivant's Companion* was published in 1887 with a Martinez recipe comprising of:

> *Take 1 dash of Boker's Bitters*
> *2 dashes of Maraschino*
> *1 pony Old Tom Gin*
> *1 wine glass vermouth*
> *2 small lumps of ice*

> *Shake up thoroughly, and strain into a large cocktail glass. Put a quarter of a slice of lemon in the glass, and serve. If the guest prefers it very sweet, add 2 dashes of the gum syrup.*

Incredibly, this recipe for a Martinez is also vague on the vermouth front, leaving the style up to your imagination. Fortunately, we are aware that in late 19th-century America, Italian (sweet) vermouth was far more common than French (dry) style.

Also, the drink is shaken, which goes against the modern practice of making a Martinez, but it's not too much of a big deal.

The obscurity continues into the third (*Stuart's Fancy Drinks*, 1896) and fourth (*Consolidated Library of Modern Cooking and Household Recipes*, 1905) historical recipes for the drink – with the third recipe being taken directly from the pages of O. H. Bryon, and the fourth plagiarizing Jerry Thomas's book!

After around a decade's gap in recipes for the Martinez, the cascade of Prohibition-era cocktail books begin listing the drink once again. But this time there is a strong shift towards dry vermouth and a ratio of ingredients in greater favour of the gin. All in all this seems to point towards a style of Martinez moving towards that of the Dry Martini.

So there we have it, inconclusive evidence on what exactly a Martinez is. The recipe I'm listing above is my personal favourite Martinez, and as the original recipe suggests, it's based entirely on a sweet Manhattan. Feel free to play around with it, invert the gin and vermouth, try dry vermouth, change up the bitters or stick an umbrella in it if you think it'll make it right for you!

OAKED MARTINEZ

Ageing cocktails is not a new thing. The current trend for putting drinks in barrels, letting them sit for a while, then selling them – often with a marked-up price – might seem a recent invention, but both barrel ageing of spirits and cocktails has been going on for rather a long time. (For more on aging drinks, see pages 53–55)

It's not surprising, then, that some bright spark thought it might be interesting to age a completed cocktail. It might seem odd to further develop a finished drink through the medium of oak – kind of like making a cup of coffee, then putting a tea bag in it – but certainly it would be shameful not to give it a try, right? At the turn of the 20th century, bottled drinks, be it cocktails or sodas, were all the rage. The Heublein company were selling and advertising 'wood aged' cocktails by 1906 (conceivably earlier, too) and continued to do so right through to the 1930s. One advert from *Theatre Magazine* in July 1906 read:

A delicious cocktail that's always ready for you or your guest – and better than any made by guesswork effort can be. Club Cocktails are scientifically blended of fine old liquors and aged in wood to exquisite aroma and smoothnesss.

Seemingly, the 'club cocktails' were a selection of popular drinks from the era, including familiar names such as the Martini and Manhattan.

Since the Martinez has something in common with both the Martini and the Manhattan – if you ask me it's the missing link between them – I'm selecting it as a great candidate for ageing. While I am not against the idea of ageing a cocktail that already contains an aged ingredient – a Manhattan or Rob Roy for example – I do get a little more pleasure out of ageing a drink that his little or no aged components already in it.

OAKED MARTINEZ

---◆---

2 LITRES/2 QUARTS TANQUERAY LONDON DRY GIN

2.5 LITRES/2.5 QUARTS MARTINI ROSSO VERMOUTH

1 LITRE/1 QUART WATER

100 ML/3⅓ OZ. MARASCHINO LIQUEUR

100 ML/3⅓ OZ. ORANGE CURAÇAO

10 ML/⅓ OZ. DR. ADAM ELMEGIRAB'S BOKER'S BITTERS

•

Makes about 40 servings.
(The volume can be scaled back for a smaller barrel, but the ageing time may need to be reduced.)

•

Add all the ingredients to an **8 OR 10 LITRE/2.5 GALLON MEDIUM-TOASTED EUROPEAN OAK CASK** (I personally prefer the colour and flavour of European oak over American oak). The optimum resting time will depend on the exact conditions under which the cask is stored. Aim to keep it in an area where the temperature fluctuates (goes up and down) every day, as this encourages the expansion and contraction of the wood, which speeds things up considerably. It is possible to emulate this by using a **HEAD BAND** (used for home brewing) strapped around the cask. Rotating the barrel also aids with interaction, as does a quick shake from time to time.

•

Taste the contents regularly and keep some back to compare weekly. Extract all of the liquid once you deem it ready. I would expect this to be somewhere between 3 and 6 weeks. Remember not to over-age the cocktail – hints of gin, orange and wine should be accompanied by the oak character of the cask.

•

To serve, stir the ingredients with cubed ice for 30 seconds, then strain into a chilled coupe glass.

---◆---

PURL

◆

1 LITRE/1 QUART BITTER (BRITISH ALE) • 200 ML/6¾ OZ. HENDRICK'S GIN • 150 G/5 OZ. (CASTER) SUGAR

50 G/2 OZ. HONEY • 5 G AMARILLLO (PREFERABLY, OR OTHER) HOPS • 2 G DRIED WORMWOOD LEAVES

3 CLOVES • A 15-CM/6-INCH PIECE OF CINNAMON STICK • ZEST OF A GRAPEFRUIT

•

Makes about 6 servings

•

Combine all the ingredients in a saucepan and heat gently to around 70°C/158°F, but do not boil.
Keep the pan covered and ladle into heatproof mugs or cups for each guest.

◆

It should come as no surprise that the Purl is a drink very close to my heart. After all, it's the name of the first cocktail bar that I opened!

It was my colleague Thomas Aske that came up with the name Purl for our bar – at the time, I had no idea what it was. Thomas had been reading Charles Dickens' *Sketches by Boz*, a collection of short stories depicting life in Victorian London. One section describes the actions of Londoners leaving the threatre:

One o'clock! Parties returning from the different theatres foot it through the muddy streets (...) retire to their watering houses, to solace themselves with the creature comforts of pipes and purl.

Further research dug up a reference to Purl in Dickens' *The Old Curiosity Shop*:

Presently, he returned, followed by the boy from the public house, who bore in one hand a plate of bread and beef, and in the other a great pot, filled with some very fragrant compound, which sent forth a grateful steam, and was indeed choice purl, made after a particular recipe.

Little did we know, however, that Purl had been around long before Dickens' time. Even as far back as the 17th century, in fact, when Samuel Pepys mentions Purl in one of his famous diary entries; he writes, 'Thence forth to Mr. Harper's to drink a draft of purle, whither by appointment Monsieur L'Impertinent...'

So what exactly is Purl? Well, it happens to be, in my eyes at least, one of the greatest warm winter pick-me-ups ever to grace a bar top. Choice spices and herbs combine with malty beer, bitter wormword and the botanical aromatics of gin to form a delicious concoction similar to mulled wine.

To create our bar's namesake, we set about trying various recipes, based on references in fictional works and other texts. However, I should say that not once, despite days of research, did I manage to find an actual recipe for Purl. Still hunting! So the recipe above is based on my own findings of how the ingredients combine and what spices best complement the beer and gin. The only certain rule that I could determine was that it had to contain beer, gin and wormwood – which, if you think about it, tenuously places the drink within the Martini family of cocktails.

ROYAL PURL STOCK CUBE

◆

I love presenting drinks in new and interesting ways. There's something about serving a drink to a guest and allowing them to mentally work through a ritual and discover something special about it.

The idea for this drink came from the common stock cube. Stock cubes are basically concentrated ingredients that have been dried or turned into a jelly. When hot water is poured over them, they either melt (jelly) or dissolve/hydrate (dried cube). If you can pack all that salt, meat and vegetable flavour into a little cube of jelly, why not combine the flavours of a cocktail into a cube? The benefits are undeniable: imagine making 100 cocktail cubes that only need hot water adding to form a tasty drink? In just a few hours you could make enough to see you through the entire winter season!

I know what you're thinking – what about the alcohol? Well fear not, using the correct gelling agent (see pages 34–37) it is possible to retain nearly all the alcohol within the cube. But this is not a simple process. To end up with a 'normal' cup of Purl, I need to remove almost all the water from the concentrate, retain as much flavour as possible and lose none of the alcohol. Time to get scientific...

Gelatine-based gels cope quite well with alcohol and only begin to fall apart when alcohol takes up more than 40% of the total gel volume (that's why it's so easy to make alcoholic 'jello-shots'). A quick bit of maths should determine how big and how strong my purl stock cube needs to be to hold sufficient alcohol for the drink.

I'm assuming that the total volume of the finished drink will be 180 ml/6 oz. and that a typical cup of Purl will be 10% ABV. The maximum strength my stock cube can realistically be without being unstable is 35%

ABCV, so to make a 180 ml/6 oz. drink at 10% ABV, I will need a cube with a volume of 50 ml/2 oz. at 35% ABV and 130 ml/4½ oz. water to melt it.

Gin makes up roughly 15% of a cup of Purl, beer is responsible for a further 75% and the remaining 10% is sugar and flavourings. I now need to juggle flavour, alcohol and water in my cube to reach the same kind of ratio of ingredients. The only possible way of achieving this is by using a malt (beer) concentrate. Over 70% of my cube needs to be gin in order to get the necessary alcohol strength, and a further 20% sugar, which leaves only 10% for beer flavour. There is a wide variety of malt syrups and concentrates available from home-brewing stores and websites. Some are sweeter than others, but since I'll be using such a small amount I don't expect it to significantly affect the final sweetness of the drink.

To make the stock cubes (this recipe makes about 40), in a large jug/pitcher, I combine 1 litre/1 quart Tanqueray Malacca gin, 100 g/3⅓ oz. barley malt syrup, 70 ml/2⅓ oz. apple juice, 150 g/5 oz. honey, 150 g/5 oz. (caster) sugar, 15 g/½ oz. grapefruit zest, 2 g dried wormwood, 1 g cloves (about 5) and 2 ml Angostura bitters and leave them to infuse for 48 hours, then the mixture is filtered and transferred to a saucepan.

I hydrate 25 g/1 oz. leaf gelatine in cold water, then add it to the infusion in the pan and gently warm the liquid to 60°C/140°F, whisking until everything is fully dissolved. The mixture is set aside to cool, then poured into 50 ml/2 oz. moulds and refrigerated for 5 hours until the jelly has set completely.

To make the drink itself, I place a jelly stock cube in a teacup along with gold leaf, a slice of dehydrated orange, a strip of cinnamon bark and some juniper berries and top up with hot water.

SINGAPORE SLING

◆

35 ML/1¼ OZ. TANQUERAY GIN • 15 ML/½ OZ. CHERRY HEERING LIQUEUR • 5 ML BENEDICTINE DOM

15 ML/½ OZ. FRESH LEMON JUICE • 2 DASHES OF ANGOSTURA BITTERS • A SPLASH OF SODA, TO TOP UP

A SLICE OF LEMON, TO GARNISH

•

Build the ingredients into a chilled highball (or sling) glass filled with cubed ice, then give it a quick stir and top with a splash of soda. Garnish with a slice of lemon.

◆

My Chinese-Singaporean friends find it highly amusing that some of the world's worst Singapore Slings are served in Singapore. It's true that globally many folks class the Singapore Sling as a total abomination of a cocktail – a slaughtering of gin by sweet liqueurs, pineapple juice and toxic red syrups. Of course, many people's only experience of drinking a Singapore Sling is in Singapore airport, or in a flair cocktail bar when they were 18. I personally believe the Singapore Sling to be, at its best, a well-balanced refreshing cocktail with sweetness to balance a drying medicinal backbone. Let's dig deeper...

The drink was supposedly invented in the Long Bar at Raffles Hotel at some time between 1900 and 1920 (broad, I know), by a Hainanese-Chinese bartender called Ngiam Tong Boon. Raffles include the following line on their cocktail list in the Long Bar:

Originally, the Singapore Sling was meant as a woman's drink, hence the attractive pink colour. Today, it is very definitely a drink enjoyed by all, without which any visit to Raffles Hotel is incomplete.

The term 'sling' had been applied to a mixed drink at least 100 years before that, but one of the earliest references to 'slings' in Singapore appeared in the Singapore newspaper *The Straits Times* on 2nd October 1903, in reference to drinks served at a moning send off for celebrity horse trainer, 'Daddy Abrams' on his voyage to Australia, where included on the menu was 'fizzy wine [and] pink slings for pale people'.

Now, despite knowing that the early Singapore Sling was pink, a definitive Singapore Sling recipe from that time is not the easiest thing to come by. What we know for sure is that it contains gin, lemon, soda and ice. It probably contained bitters. It likely had cherry brandy in it. It possibly had a touch of Bénédictine DOM liqueur in it, too. The main reason we believe all this stuff is down to a recipe for a 'Straits Sling' published in Robert Vermeire's 1922 book, *Cocktails and How to Mix Them*, which goes as follows:

This well-known Singapore drink, thoroughly iced and shaken, contains:

2 dashes of orange bitters,
2 dashes of Angostura bitters,
the juice of half a lemon
⅛ gill of Bénédictine
⅛ gill of dry cherry brandy / ½ gill of gin

Pour into a tumbler and fill up with cold soda water.

Is it possible that the Singapore Sling was originally called a Straits Sling? Perhaps the name was later altered as a result of the drink's popularity in Singapore and at Raffles Hotel. Who knows?

Raffles Hotel themselves have admitted to having lost the original recipe for their Singapore Sling at some time during the 1950s, so now serve a drink based on the original Singapore Sling, developed by none other than the nephew of Ngiam Tong Boon. Given the similarities between the current commonly accepted Singapore Sling formula and Vermeire's 1922 version, it's possible that Ngiam Tong Boon's nephew simply took the earliest sling recipe he could find.

DISCO SLING

For my twist on a Singapore Sling, I'm going to leave the ingredients relatively untouched, just tweak them slightly. What I will be changing is the garnish, with the aim of presenting the drink with all the cheesy 1980s disco flamboyance possible.

Cocktail garnishes in the 80s covered anything from the tame cocktail umbrella, through to exotic fruits, silly straws and outrageous glassware. So, for my drink I'm going to have to come up with something even more absurd. Of course, the classic 'don't even go there' garnish is the citrus wheel. Perch a circular slice of lemon on the rim of a glass and you'll immediately knock 20% off its sale value. But I have an idea that we could take the citrus wheel to the next level and make it a genuine feature of the drink.

Around three years ago, I was made aware of an enzyme called transglutaminase – you may know it better by its street name 'meat glue'. Meat glue is commonly used in commercial food manufacture for moulding meat into sticks, balls or letters of the alphabet. While some of this food may be questionable in its quality, transglutaminase is a naturally occuring enzyme that is flavourless, colourless and no more harmful or morally questionable then gelatine. It works by binding together proteins to form bonds that are as strong as if the meat was simply [ahem] born that way.

So you might be wondering where all this is going – 'Surely he's not going to glue meat to the drink?!' Well, whilst meat glue does only work on products with protein in them (meat, fish, dairy), it can be made to work with fruit and vegetables by impregnating them with gelatine (which is derived from collagen, a protein) first.

What I am attempting to do is create a hybrid citrus fruit – one that is made from equal parts lemon, lime and orange. The steps required to achieve this are a little more complicated than simply injecting the fruit with gelatine, but worth it for the visual effect.

DISCO SLING

◆

For the Hybrid Citrus Wheel

1 LEMON, 1 ORANGE AND 1 LIME, ALL OF NEAR EQUAL SIZE

12 G/½ OZ. GELATINE • 300 ML/10 OZ. WATER

ABOUT 5 G TRANSGLUTAMINASE

•

Soak the gelatine in the water for 5 minutes. Heat the water to at least 65°C/149°F to dissolve the gelatine, then allow to cool in a small bowl.

•

Slice the citrus fruits into 3 lengthways and submerge in the gelatine water. Place the bowl in a VACUUM PACKER and pull a vacuum 3 times so that the fruit absorbs some of the gelatine/water solution.

•

Remove the fruit from the bowl and, whilst still damp, dust the cut edges of the fruit with the transglutaminase, ensuring that all the surfaces are evenly covered. Reassemble the fruits, using a wedge of each different citrus fruit, and wrap tightly with clingfilm/plastic wrap, then refrigerate for at least 12 hours to set.

•

Once set, simply peel off the cling film/plastic wrap and slice the fruit into wheels.

◆

For the Disco Sling

35 ML/1¼ OZ. TANQUERAY GIN

10 ML/⅓ OZ. CHERRY HEERING LIQUEUR

5 ML BENEDICTINE DOM • 5 ML FRESH LEMON JUICE

5 ML FRESH LIME JUICE • 5 ML FRESH ORANGE JUICE

5 ML PRESSED PINEAPPLE JUICE

2 DASHES OF ANGOSTURA BITTERS

A 'HYBRID CITRUS WHEEL', TO GARNISH

Shake all the ingredients with cubed ice for 10 seconds, then strain into a chilled highball glass. Garnish with the Hybrid Citrus Wheel.

BRAMBLE

◆

40 ML/1⅓ OZ. TANQUERAY GIN

20 ML/⅔ OZ. FRESH LEMON JUICE

10 ML/⅓ OZ. SUGAR SYRUP (SEE PAGE 204)

15 ML/½ OZ. CREME DE MURE

BLACKBERRIES (OR RASPBERRIES), TO GARNISH

•

Build the first three ingredients over crushed ice in a chilled rocks glass, then pour the crème de mure over the top so that it 'bleeds' down through the ice. Garnish with two blackberries and a slice of lemon.

•

NB: For my personal tastes, this recipe is a touch on the sweet side, but it comes straight from the man himself, so who am I to argue? If you want it a little drier, try taking 5 ml sugar syrup out and adding 5 ml extra lemon juice.

◆

One of the best drinks to emerge from the cocktail car crash that was the 1980s is the Bramble. The drink was invented by legendary London-based liquid guru, Dick Bradsell. At the time, Dick was working in Fred's Club in Soho, a venue that schooled many of the future stars of the London bar scene. Dick based the drink on a Singapore Sling recipe, replacing the Bénédictine and cherry brandy with crème de mure.

But of course it's not. There has to be something special about a cocktail that is so renowned and yet relies on such a simple formula: a gin sour with a dash of blackberry liqueur. Why not strawberry liqueur, or coffee liqueur? Well, I personally think that something special is down to a clever combination of ingredients and a name that ingeniously describes it.

It's simple when you think about it. A bramble is a typically British prickly shrub, just as gin is a traditionally British product. Blackberry is the base of crème de mure, but wild blackberries don't just smell of blackberries, they also take in the smells of all the natural surroundings of the countryside – the earthiness of dried tree bark, the spice of a fallen pine cone or the sweet freshness of wild honeysuckle. These wonderfully nostalgic aromas are present in a lot of gins too: while juniper provides earthiness and pine-like flavours, coriander gives a citrusy spice and angelica introduces the deep, resinous woody notes.

The combination of gin and crème de mure is genius, and couple that with a name that no other word in the English language could better describe, and you have a winning drink.

BRAMBLE REDUX

◆

The aim of my Bramble Redux is simple – to bring to life the British countryside in the drink. I wanted the drink to evoke the feeling of blackberry picking in early autumn, with a crunchy forest floor and the heady taste of ripe juicy fruit.

I decided to serve both blackberries and raspberries in the glass, in two fantastic ways. Both fruits have a peculiar make-up: they are like a collection of juice-filled balls, huddled together to form a berry. Each ball is like a piece of fruit in its own right, and I'm going to promote this fact in the drink.

First, I'll take a handful of raspberries. The aim will be to break the raspberry up into its component balls, and to use those balls to decorate the drink. The problem is that attempting to deconstruct a raspberry with only a pair of tweezers is very difficult – fortunately, I have a short cut! Liquid nitrogen (see page 44) has a great many uses, but one of the best is cold embrittlement. Liquid nitrogen freezes nearly anything, and when used to freeze fruit, the water in the fruit freezes solid and becomes brittle, like glass. You can then use a mallet or hammer to break the fruit apart, making pieces split apart where the bonds are weakest. In the case of fruits like raspberries, this is where the tiny balls connect to the plant. The end result is a collection of tiny raspberry pearls that look amazing on a drink.

For the blackberry (crème de cassis) component, I spherify the crème de cassis into tiny balls of a similar size to the raspberry ones. The result is dark-coloured balls that look similar to the raspberry ones (made from real raspberry), except the blackberry balls are actually filled with an intense alcoholic blackberry liqueur!

To do this, I blend 50 ml/2 oz. low calcium water with 1 g sodium alginate using a stick blender. Once the sodium alginate is fully dissolved I mix in 50 ml/ 2 oz. crème de cassis, then transfer the mixture to a syringe or dropper bottle. If air bubbles are present, I allow the mixture to sit for an hour or two for them to disperse, as these will cause the balls to float in the calcium chloride solution (see below).

To form the balls, I mix 400 ml/14 oz. water with 2 g calcium chloride and fill another container with fresh clean water for rinsing. Using the syringe, I expel droplets of the blackberry mixture into the calcium chloride bath one by one. After a minute or so, I strain the balls out of the bath and rinse them in the fresh water.

To make the drink, I build 50 ml/2 oz. Tanqueray gin, 10 ml/⅓ oz. fresh lemon juice, 7 ml sugar syrup and 5 ml malic acid solution at pH 3.0 over crushed ice. (I chose to use a touch of malic acid, since it is naturally present in blackberries and adds a clean freshness different to that of citric acid). I garnish the drink with the raspberry balls, spherified blackberry pearls and some fresh oregano leaves, which add an amazing warm woodland aroma.

VODKA

Poor old vodka. Here is a spirit that had been minding its own business for 400 years, confined to the cold depths of Eastern Europe and Asia, then along came the 20th century.

Global trading, experimental consumers and hardened drinkers with a desire for something as strong as whisky but a little less noticeable on the post-working-day palate all took an interest. Vodka became the modern man's drink; with its neutral odour and excellent mixability, it donned boardroom back bars in the 1950s and 60s, and by the 1980s vodka was the go-to liquid in the mixologist's speed-rail. Why? Well, it would mix with anything, which was hardly surprising since it didn't really taste of anything! But nonetheless, we continued to combine popular ingredients with vodka, showing genuine surprise when the drink tasted exactly of that ingredient. But all good parties must come to an end, and as the 21st century approached, this particular party took a nosedive – and the hangover was not pretty. Vodka was shunned from cocktail lists, declared insipid, characterless and without honour among such upstanding individuals as gin, Cognac, whisky and rum.

That was ten years ago. Today, the vodka resurgence is gathering pace, as its producers endeavour to create more interesting flavoursome liquids that focus on quality of ingredients, honest production information, traceability and, most importantly, great flavour. Instead of boasting about how many times the product has been filtered, brands now preach about the variety of grain they use and how it translates into the complex flavour profile in the glass. Sure, vodka will never be as powerfully expressive as a Scotch or a Cognac, but there is much more to shout about than ever before.

The origin of vodka is a matter of great contest between Russia and Poland. I have independently asked Polish and Russian vodka experts to tell me (in confidence) who they truly believe invented

vodka, and both sides were patriotic to the extreme.

Both countries make a strong case, but one thing we do know is that the first-known written reference to vodka is from a single Polish text dating back to 1405. The Russians have a number of references to spirits ('bread wine') dating from 1429 onwards. The Russians undoubtedly rule the roost when it comes to consumption of spirits, necking back 3 billion litres (25 litres per person) of duty-paid vodka in 2011.

The nation that came up with the name (from the word *voda*, translating to 'little water') or first began producing vodka is kind of irrelevant anyway, since any products more than 200 years old would be drastically different from the carefully crafted liquor of today.

Most vodka is made from grain, usually rye, wheat or barley, but some are made from potato. The product is fermented into a type of beer, then distilled in large column stills that pump out a liquid of at least 96% ABV. This spirit is then cut back with water and sometimes filtered to remove certain undesirable flavours. How the vodka is distilled and how many times it is distilled, plus the level of filtration (if any), are important factors that determine how well the flavour of the product from which it is made is expressed. Many vodkas still pride themselves on their cleanliness and neutrality of flavour (usually achieved through multiple distillations and aggressive filtering), while other brands will be keen to inform you that their vodka is less tampered with and altogether more characterful.

I consistently refer to the Polish vodka Belvedere and more recently Belvedere Unfiltered as excellent examples of characterful, well-balanced products that are perfect for mixing most cocktails. Other notable brands include Vestal, Polish potato and rye vodkas with a focus on vintages, and Chase, which is made on a farm in Herefordshire, England.

ESPRESSO MARTINI

50 ML/2 OZ. BELVEDERE VODKA

20 ML/²⁄₃ OZ. ESPRESSO

10 ML/¹⁄₃ OZ. SUGAR SYRUP (SEE PAGE 204)

•

Shake the ingredients together with cubed ice and single
strain into a chilled martini glass.

Back when I first cut my teeth as a cocktail bartender, when bigger cocktail lists were better and flaming an orange twist was regarded as innovative, the Espresso Martini was the height of cool. Caffeine, alcohol, sugar. Everything the body needs for a good night out, and all held together by our 1980s superhero, the martini glass.

The Espresso Martini is based on a drink created by the UK's crown prince of cocktails, Dick Bradsell while he was working at the Soho Brasserie. The story goes (and it does vary depending on who you ask) that an attractive female model approached the bar where Dick was working and asked him for a drink that would 'pick me up, then fuck me up' – if only all drink requests came with such exact requirements. Dick eyed the bar's shiny new espresso machine and promptly mixed vodka, espresso and sugar

together, then served it in a martini glass. The Espresso Martini was born.

The growing popularity of espresso coffee in the 1980s and 90s made the Espresso Martini an inevitability. The espresso in the drink achieves three things at once: first, it masks the alcohol in the vodka; second, it gives a caffeine kick to the receiver; and third, it turns the drink a stunning opaque brown. Also, if you use a good-quality coffee and extract the espresso correctly, you'll be rewarded with a pale foamy head, produced by the CO_2 bubbles dissolved in brewed coffee. Serve an Espresso Martini in a half-pint glass and it really does look like a Guinness!

IMPROVED COFFEE COCKTAIL

I am a massive coffee geek. The vast majority of this book was written under the effects of coffee's

magical motivational qualities. So it is with regret that I admit to a very well-considered belief – coffee and alcohol don't mix very well. Actually, it's not that they don't have the potential to mix well, it's just that most coffee-based cocktails break the first law of cocktail making – the drink must taste at least as good as its best ingredient.

Many years ago, when I was still a fresh-faced bar-rookie, a guest asked me for the best Irish coffee I could make with the ingredients I had to hand. I extracted a perfect Americano using coffee beans roasted two weeks previously, mixed it with Bushmills 12-year-old whiskey, added some sugar and whipped up some fresh cream to go on top. The ingredients were near enough perfect, so it should have been an excellent drink, but the truth is that it was average at best. Both the whiskey and coffee cancelled out all the subtleties and nuances of each other. It would have been far better to serve the coffee and whiskey side by side.

With this drink, I set about to change this by using top-quality coffee to make my own coffee liqueur. To do this, I called upon my friend James Hoffmann, owner of Square Mile Coffee roasters in London, and a man who happens to be one of the foremost authorities on coffee the world over. Over the course of a few months, James and I experimented with a variety of different coffees, infused and distilled into vodka using various methods. Everything from the grind size, brew ratio and the exact infusion time were analysed. The goal was to create a lightly sweetened coffee infusion that could hold its own as a sipping liquid, but also make an awesome cocktail ingredient. Most importantly of all, we wanted the liqueur to exhibit all the brilliant characteristics of the coffee and not fall into the trap of being another generic coffee-flavoured syrup.

This recipe will provide you with a simplified version of our coffee liqueur, but be aware that the quality and freshness of the coffee that you use is the most important factor in the equation.

This is a great cocktail, but you can also use the liqueur for other mixed drinks such as a White Russian, or try it simply with coke (it tastes great, trust me). It's also wonderful as a base for an ice cream – try adding a splash to my Hot & Cold Nitro Eggnog Ice cream (see page 122).

IMPROVED COFFEE COCKTAIL

◆

100 G/3½ OZ. ESPRESSO COFFEE BEANS
330 ML/11 OZ. BELVEDERE VODKA
SUGAR SYRUP (SEE PAGE 204)

•

Makes enough for 5 servings

•

Finely grind the coffee beans (if the coffee is already ground, it isn't fresh enough!).

•

Add the ground coffee and vodka to a **CREAM WHIPPER**, shake, and pressurize with two 8-g N₂O cartridges (see page 32). Leave to sit for 10 minutes. Depressurize quickly, unscrew the lid and filter the contents through a **PAPER COFFEE FILTER**.

•

Stir the sugar syrup into the filtered infusion at a ratio of about 12 ml/½ oz. per 100 ml/3⅓ oz. (adjust the sweetness to taste).

•

Stir the liqueur over cubed ice for 90 seconds, then serve in chilled mini liqueur glasses.

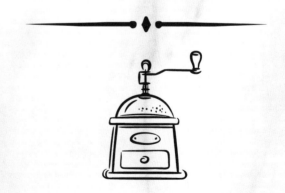

MOSCOW MULE

These days, it's 'the done thing' for a new brand of liquor to promote a selection of cocktails that best communicates the product's identity and flavour – a way of best utilizing the product, if you like. But it wasn't always that way. Go back 50 or so years and a new product would often find it very difficult to establish a foothold in a marketplace dominated by age-old, tried and tested brands. Launching a new spirit category was an even greater challenge, but that was what John G. Martin did with the Smirnoff brand back in the 1940s.

It's hard to imagine a cocktail bar that doesn't stock vodka, but that's what it was like before the 1940s. *The Savoy Cocktail Book*, originally published in 1930, lists only two cocktails containing vodka out of around 800 drinks. Sure, people had heard of it, especially those seeking asylum from Russia after the revolution, but it was not a commonplace product. By the 1980s, everyone was drinking

vodka, and every bar was serving it – so what the hell happened?

Rudolf Kunnett was a Russian-born businessman, living in Paris, who acquired a dying vodka brand from one Vladimir Smirnov. After failing to make a go of it, he sold the rights to John G. Martin of the Heublein spirits company in the US for $14,000. It was 1938. Heublein marketed the product as 'White Whiskey' – apparently after a mistake made when corking the bottles – and the slogan 'It leaves you breathless' was born, cleverly promoting the clean flavour of the product along with reassurance that your spouse won't smell it on you after a daytime session [ahem].

Sales weren't great to begin with, as apparently daytime drinkers hadn't taken to the product quite as planned. But in 1946, John Martin found himself in the Cock 'n Bull pub on Sunset Boulevard, chatting to the proprietor who had made a similarly

50 ML/2 OZ. SMIRNOFF BLACK VODKA

25 ML/1 OZ. FRESH LIME JUICE

10 ML/⅓ OZ. GOMME

100 ML/3⅓ OZ. GINGER BEER

A SPRIG OF FRESH MINT, TO GARNISH

Build the drink straight into a **COPPER MUG** with cubed ice and garnish with a sprig of mint.

poor investment in ginger beer. John and Jack mixed the vodka with the ginger beer and capped it off with a squeeze of lime, then sourced copper mugs to serve it in (allegedly from another failed business-person), and the Moscow Mule was born.

Shortly after, the pair acquired one of the first-ever Polaroid cameras and went from bar to bar photographing bartenders posing with bottles of Smirnoff vodka and copper mugs of Moscow Mule. They would show the Polaroid photographs to bar owners who didn't sell the product as a means of sealing the deal. Customers went nuts for the stuff and the vodka revolution had begun.

The drink was, for a very short time, called a Little Moscow, and the first 500 mugs were stamped as such. I own an original unopened bottle of Cock 'n Bull ginger beer and dream of mixing it with a 1940s bottle of Smirnoff in an original copper mug. One day.

BARREL CART MULE

There's no greater example of combining history with science (in a drink) than that of fermented beverages. The practice of carbonating drinks through anaerobic fermentation has been around for millennia, dating back as far as 7000 BC and it's still being used today in the manufacture of many beers, soft drinks and, of course, Champagne.

Until 1767, all drinks would be carbonated this way, through a process of yeast converting sugar into carbon dioxide (and alcohol). That was until Joseph Priestley discovered a method of directly infusing water with carbon dioxide. That discovery put an end to the businesses of many of the craft soda water and ginger beer sellers that dotted the streets of London at the time. The manufacture of soft drinks became much more of an industrial process, rather than the craft movement it had previously been.

If you ever try a proper bottle of fermented ginger beer, you will recognize a huge difference between the traditional product and the flavoured, forcefully carbonated brands of the modern day. But a traditional technique such as this is not without its pitfalls: the science of yeast is complex and often hard to predict.

The idea for this drink was first conceived by Thomas Aske, one of the co-founders of Fluid Movement. He suggested barrel fermenting a Moscow Mule, in the style of a traditional cart trader of 18th- and 19th-century London. Thomas researched a few recipes, and the culmination of his efforts was presented to an audience of around 300 at an annual London bar show. When Thomas attempted to extract some of the liquid to taste for the first time, the barrel obliged by firing a stream of liquid into the front row of the audience with not insubstantial force! The moral of the story is, yeast and fermentation are difficult to work with!

For my Barrel Cart Mule, I'm taking inspiration from a recipe published in the 1852 book *London Labour and the London Poor*. One section of the book discussed the transition from traditional street-trade ginger beer to that of the soda-fountain ginger beer. It also lists a recipe for a classic fermented ginger beer:

The streetsellers who 'brew their own beer' generally prepare half a gross (six dozen) at a time. For a good quality or the 'penny bottle' trade, the following are the ingredients and the mode of preparation: 3 gallons of water; 1 lb. ginger; lemon acid; essence of cloves; yeast and 1 lb. raw sugar. This admixture, the yeast being the last ingredient introduced, stands 24 hours and is then ready for bottling.

I set about combining these ingredients with the addition of vodka, then barrelled it for 48 hours. Given enough headspace (space inside the barrel that isn't liquid), this is long enough to get the yeast working, then I transferred the drink to bottles for the remaining fermentation. The trick is for the sugar level to be just right in the mixture; too much and the bottle might explode; too little and the ginger beer will be flat. After a few attempts, I settled on the recipe here.

BARREL CART MULE

❖

4 LITRES/4¼ QUARTS MINERAL WATER

10 G/⅓ OZ. SALT • 140 G/5 OZ. GRATED ROOT GINGER

20 G/⅔ OZ. CREAM OF TARTAR • 6 CLOVES

1 LEMONGRASS STALK, SHREDDED

10 PINK PEPPERCORNS • 140 G/5 OZ. SUGAR

1 BOTTLE (700 ML) BELEVEDERE UNFILTERED VODKA

5 G DRIED BAKER'S YEAST

•

Makes enough for 30 servings

•

SOUS VIDE 1 litre/1 quart of the water with the salt, ginger, cream of tartar, cloves, lemongrass and peppercorns at 65°C/150°F for 3 hours. Strain the liquid through a **MUSLIN CHEESECLOTH**, then while the liquid is still warm, add the rest of the water, the sugar and the entire bottle of vodka. Whisk in the yeast until fully hydrated.

•

Transfer the liquid to a suitable **BARREL OF AT LEAST 6 LITRES/6⅓ QUARTS** in size, then seal for 48 hours. After resting, remove the liquid and transfer to **STERILIZED FLIP-TOP GLASS BOTTLES** for conditioning. Rest for at least 2 weeks at room temperature, then transfer to a fridge to chill before opening.

❖

COSMOPOLITAN

◆

40 ML/1⅓ OZ. BELVEDERE CITRUS VODKA • 20 ML/⅔ OZ. COINTREAU • 15 ML/½ OZ. FRESH LIME JUICE

15 ML/½ OZ. CRANBERRY JUICE • A STRIP OF ORANGE ZEST, TO FINISH

•

Shake all the ingredients together with cubed ice until ice cold,
then double strain into a chilled martini glass.

•

To finish, take a strip of orange zest peeled from pole to pole. Hold it upright between your thumb and
middle finger, aiming at the drink's surface. Hold a flame on the zest for no more than 2 seconds, then
squeeze hard. The zest should fold outwards, releasing a jet of flaming oil right on top of the drink.

◆

The Cosmopolitan really was the poster boy of the cocktail revival during the 1980s and 90s. It's iconic pale pink hue rested in a long-stemmed martini glass defines an entire era of cocktail culture and enjoyment of mixed drinks.

How has this drink remained on the tip of everyone's tongue for so long? Well, this might come as a shock, so brace yourselves – it's really very tasty. That is, when it's made correctly. The genius of a Cosmopolitan is that it combines all three of the major citrus fruits into one balanced drink. This fact is often overlooked, mainly due to the colour of the liquid, which would have you believe that it's raspberry, strawberry or cranberry flavoured.

'But it is cranberry flavoured!' I hear you cry. No. It's cranberry coloured, that's all. A properly mixed Cosmo should contain only a small splash of cranberry, for a little colour and dilution. It's the other ingredients that are doing the heavy lifting here – citrus vodka, orange curaçao, lime juice.

Of course, the balanced flavour is not the draw for everyone, but it may well be the reason for repeat ordering. The fact that it shares its name with a popular fashion mag has done it no harm over the years. Neither has its seductive, oh-so-pink colour (ranging from salmon through to electric).

Back in the 80s, guests would order a Martini, just so they could hold a drink in a martini glass. Cheryl Cook, a bartender from Florida, recognised this in 1986, so created an approachable drink loosely based on a Cape Codder (vodka and cranberry), but with the addition of Rose's Lime Cordial and a splash of triple sec. Crucially, it was served in a martini glass. The drink was a big hit, but when Toby Cecchini, a New York-based bartender, got a hold of it, he tweaked it into the drink we recognise today. Lime cordial was removed and replaced with lime juice, the triple sec was upped and the cranberry reduced until the drink was a soft pale pink.

But the story doesn't end there. Toby chose to garnish his Cosmo with a twist of lemon. These days we usually garnish with a flamed orange zest and it's Dale DeGroff that we have to thank for that. Dale has never revealed exactly where the idea came to him from, but the act of igniting oils from the surface of the orange skin and firing them on to the top of the cocktail turned the Cosmo into more than just a cocktail – now it was theatre.

The original cocktail was made with newly released Absolut Citron, but I much prefer the naturally macerated flavour of Belvedere Citrus.

COSMOPOPS

◆

I am a child of the 1980s, so whilst Cheryl, Toby and Dale were perfecting the finer points of the Cosmopolitan, I was learning to tie my shoelaces and sucking on ice lollies/popsicles. So it seems quite fitting that it's this drink out of all the drinks in this book that I choose to turn into a nitro-frozen ice lolly/popsicle. But it's not for nostalgic reasons alone; on a fundamental level, the Cosmopolitan lends itself well to being frozen and presented on a stick. It's a drink designed to be served very cold, it's pink in colour and has a surprising sourness on the palate. An alcoholic frozen treat on a stick is also a great representation of the late 80s/early 90s 'style before substance' approach to food and drink. I'm using a simple ice lolly/popsicle mould that can be purchased online or in homeware stores to make 16 Cosmopops.

I've adjusted the recipe slightly, upping the sweetness a little, as I've found that the tongue is less forgiving to intensely sour food when that food is also very cold. Strangely, the same phenomenon exists in reverse: when serving a normally chilled drink warm, I usually find a touch more sugar is required. This is probably not so much a genetic human trait, but more down to the association we have with cold things being sweet (ice cream) and hot things also being generally sweet, too (milky coffee, sweetened tea). With that in mind, the temperature that we serve drinks and the corresponding sweet/sour/bitter balance is likely to (and does) differ between different countries and cultures. Useful to remember when I'm bartending abroad!

To make the cranberry consommé base for the Cosmopops, I vacuum seal 300 g/10 oz. frozen cranberries and 100 g/3½ oz. sugar together in a plastic pouch and heat in a 80°C/175°F water bath for 3 hours. Once heated, the consommé is passed through a fine sieve/strainer and refrigerated until needed. This makes around 250 g/9 oz. consommé, enough for over 50 Cosmopops.

In a jug/pitcher, I combine 200 ml/¾ oz. Belvedere Citrus vodka, 100 ml/3⅓ oz. Grand Marnier, 75 ml/2½ oz. fresh lime juice, 10 ml/⅓ oz. orange bitters, 15 ml/½ oz. grenadine and 10 ml/⅓ oz. glycerine, along with 50 ml/2 oz. of the cranberry consommé. The glycerine thickens the liquid and gives an unctuous texture, which helps from both a taste and tactile point of view, improving the mouth-feel as the Cosmopop melts.

The mould is filled and ice lolly/popsicle sticks are placed in the holes, then I put it in the freezer for a minimum of 3 hours. The Cosmopops are too high in ABV to set properly in the freezer alone. Chilling them in the freezer first is important, however, as it stops the nitrogen from freezing them too quickly resulting in a better-shaped ice lolly/popsicle. It also lessens the amount of nitrogen required to freeze the Cosmopops.

I transfer the filled mould to a double-walled or insulated stainless steel bath and submerse in liquid nitrogen for 1 minute. Any remaining nitrogen is poured away and I carefully prize the mould apart to reveal the cosmopops.

All that remains is to wait for the Cosmopop to warm up for 5 minutes before enjoying them, as they tend to stick to your tongue when freshly removed from the liquid nitrogen!

BLOODY MARY

The exact origins of the Bloody Mary are cause for much dispute. It's generally accepted that Fernand Petiot created the drink back in the 1920s while working at Harry's Bar in Paris. But it seems highly unlikely that the drink would have contained vodka, and probably would have been made with gin instead.

Which takes us to 1940s New York, where Petiot was working at the St. Regis Hotel. Allegedly, the manager of the hotel, Serge Obolensky, asked Petiot to spice up a vodka and tomato juice (comedian George Jessel popularized the unspiced version during the 1940s). Petiot added Worcestershire sauce, salt and pepper and a twist of lemon.

Of course, there's a solid argument in the fact that a Bloody Mary is simply spiced tomato soup sold cold and with vodka. The practice of vodka accompanying or featuring in savoury food is not a new one after all, with the most obvious being

Russian borscht soup, made from seasoned beetroot/beets and sour cream. Pepper, spice and fresh acidity somehow greatly complement the neutral grainy backbone of vodka.

It's in the realm of the hangover cure that the Bloody Mary has made it's home – hey, it all but rules the realm! Taking a look at the key components, it's easy to see why it's such an obvious go-to. Vitamin C, salt, capsaicin and palate-coating viscosity. Most of my friends make funny noises when I offer them a Bloody Mary, but it's hard to prize them away from one when they're caught in the throws of a nasty morning after.

The greenery was, allegedly, a later addition to the concoction, when at the Ambassador Hotel in Chicago a bartender spied a patron stirring her Bloody Mary with a stick of celery. Visually, the green/red combination gives the drink an altogether natural – it grew out of the ground like

50 ML/2 OZ. BELVEDERE VODKA

**150 ML/5 OZ. OF THE BEST-QUALITY TOMATO JUICE
YOU CAN LAY YOUR HANDS ON**

10 ML/⅓ OZ. FRESH LEMON JUICE

7 ML WORCESTERSHIRE SAUCE (ABOUT 3 DASHES)

3 ML TABASCO (ABOUT 3 DASHES)

1 G SALT (1 LARGE PINCH)

1 G GROUND BLACK PEPPER (1 LARGE PINCH)

A CELERY STICK AND A SLICE OF LEMON, TO GARNISH

Shake (I like it that way) all the ingredients together with cubed ice, then strain into a chilled highball glass. Garnish with a celery stick and a slice of lemon.

that – look about it, and sometimes that's all you need to make you feel human again.

One final note on making the drink. There is some debate around whether the mixture should be shaken, stirred, thrown or rolled. At some point in time a bright spark (second only to the person who said a similar thing about shaken gin Martinis) came up with the idea that commercially available tomato juice might in some way be 'bruised' by the action of shaking. Clearly they chose to ignore the fact that the tomato had already been picked, squashed, blended, filtered, heat concentrated, then rehydrated. And they must have concluded that tomatoes are the only fruit that can be bruised, since it's still ok to shake berries, citrus and pretty much anything else that grows on a tree or bush. Needless to say, tomato juice cannot be bruised, but the method of preparation CAN make a difference to the temperature, dilution and final

viscosity of the drink, which are all important elements.

One of the ingredients that is all to often omitted from the melange is the lemon juice, yet it plays a crucial role in freshening up the (more than likely) bland cartoned tomato juice. Of course, you can press your own tomato juice, but it's a bit of a hassle, and actually produces a very different drink.

One final tip - if you're really struggling for good tomato juice and can't be bothered to make your own (see page 108), try using a fresh carton of chilled gazpacho soup instead.

ULTIMATE BLOODY MARY

I have made a lot of Bloody Marys in my time. I have tasted quite a lot too, not to mention judged a few dedicated Bloody Mary competitions over the years. This drink is a culmination of the best bits from all those drinks. This drink is not the easiest

ULITMATE BLOODY MARY

❖

For the Tomato Vine Vodka

700 ML/23²/₃ OZ. BELVEDERE UNFILTERED VODKA • 20 G/²/₃ OZ. FRESH HORSERADISH

20 G/³/₄ OZ. TOMATO VINE LEAVES

•

Add all the ingredients to a blender and blitz until everything is well mixed. Transfer to a bottle and allow everything to rest for 5–7 days, then carefully pour the vodka through a COFFEE FILTER to strain out the bits.

For the Spiced Tomato Water

2 KG/4½ LB. RIPE TOMATOES • 35 ML/1¼ OZ. FRESH LEMON JUICE • 15 ML/½ OZ. SHERRY VINEGAR

25 ML/1 OZ. SUGAR SYRUP (SEE PAGE 204) • 8 G SALT • 3 G POWDERED MSG (SEE PAGE 29)

• 5 G POMEGRANATE MOLASSES • 1 G TABASCO • 3 G WORCESTERSHIRE SAUCE

•

Blanch the tomatoes in boiling water for 1 minute, then quickly remove them and transfer to an ICE BATH – the skins should crack and become easy to peel. Once peeled, process the tomatoes through a JUICE EXTRACTOR, or blend them and filter through MUSLIN CHEESECLOTH. (The typical yield should be around 1 litre/quart, but this may differ based on the water content of your tomatoes. If you have more than this, adjust the recipe accordingly. Add all the remaining ingredients and stir together, then check the seasoning and adjust to taste.

For the Celery Foam

300 ML/10 OZ. CELERY JUICE (USE A JUICE EXTRACTOR) • 1 G SALT • 2 G SUGAR • 3 G LECITHIN

•

In a stand mixer or stainless steel bowl, blend all the ingredients together until foamy.

For the Ultimate Bloody Mary

50 ML/2 OZ. 'TOMATO VINE VODKA' • 150 ML/5 OZ. 'SPICED TOMATO WATER'

5 ML TIO PEPE FINO SHERRY • 'CELERY FOAM' • A CELERY LEAF, TO GARNISH

•

Shake the vodka, tomato water and sherry together with cubed ice, then strain into a chilled highball glass. Scoop the celery foam on top and garnish with a celery leaf.

❖

drink to make – especially if you have a hangover… In fact, don't even attempt it if you have a hangover – but it is completely worth it.

First, let us tackle the tomato juice, since it is clearly a very important part of the drink. The type of tomato you use is not critical because we will be adjusting the flavour with sugar and acids to compensate for any lack of natural sweetness (tomatoes can range anywhere from 2–5% sugar by weight) or freshness. Just make sure you use ripe tomatoes as the juice flows more readily. Briefly blanching them in boiling water helps too. Along with sugar, salt and lemon juice, we're also going to bolster the flavour of the tomato with MSG (monosodium glutamate) an amino acid that occurs in abundance in tomatoes and provides the delicious umami (savoury) flavour.

I'm also going to be using tomato leaves, which provide the most amazing sweet tomato aroma that transports you to a greenhouse filled with tomato vines. Traditionally, tomato leaves were thought to be poisonous. But as with many food superstitions, it transpires that the belief was most likely based on superstition rather than actual scientific fact. The reason for the fuss was that tomato leaves were thought to contain the dangerous alkaloid solanine, which also makes green potatoes poisonous. But as Harold McGee, undisputed king of food science

(and author of the seminal piece *On Food and Cooking*), unearthed in his 2010 *New York Times* article, it transpires that there is no such chemical found in tomato leaves after all. What is present (as well as the commonly consumed green tomatoes) is an alkaloid aptly named tomatine, which is toxic in very high quantities (one study estimated you would need to consume a whole pound of leaves to feel any effect and that the 'hazard in most situations is low'). Since I plan on using less than a gram of leaves for a single serving I think that we can be assured of the drink's safety.

Many of the most elaborate Bloody Marys that I have tried favour using freshly muddled chilli or a complex combination of spices to provide the essential heat. I find this a little baffling, since it's difficult to gauge how hot any chilli actually is, and very hard to balance spices when mixing a drink on the fly. One way around this is to bottle your own spiced mixture, which works nicely, but I am opting to stick with the classic combination of Tabasco and Worcestershire Sauce, with the addition of a touch of horseradish.

For acidity, I'll be using both lemon juice and sherry vinegar. Sweetness will come from both sugar and a touch of pomegranate molasses.

Finally, in place of a celery stick, I'll be serving a seasoned 'celery foam' on top of the drink.

BRANDY & COGNAC

Ask any bartender what their preferred base spirit for classic cocktails is and it's highly unlikely that brandy will be their top choice. In recent years, brandy and Cognac have managed to traverse a fine line between the overweight, flushed-faced aristocratic man, and the long-with-lemonade hip-hop nightclub. And despite every bar and home bar having a bottle of brandy, we've seen that bottle steadily migrate towards the back of the shelf in recent years.

This is a strange and ironic thing, however. Cognac was the first global spirit and the first to create a 'super-premium' category. Many landmark cocktails are based on brandy and Cognac. Long before vodka, tequila and even gin became serious mixological ingredients, brandy was the obvious choice for the pioneering bartenders of the day.

Let's start by clarifying one thing: Cognac is a regionally specific brandy that is protected by law. 'Brandy' comes from the Dutch word *brandewijn* (burnt wine), can be made anywhere in the world, and in many countries doesn't even have to be made from grapes (though it usually is), whereas Cognac is controlled much more strictly.

Cognac came about as a result of geography. The Charante River is navigable to Cognac, and therefore the town is of critical strategic importance. From the 12th century the town traded salt, and by the 16th century Cognac's vineyards were becoming famous for their white wines. Distillation came next, and in 1549 *eau de vie* (wine distillate) was shipped from La Rochelle. Export was a critical part of Cognac's growth as a global product – even today, very little Cognac is consumed in France in comparison to Armagnac (another regionally specific French brandy), which is produced in a fraction of the volume.

During the 17th century, 'Cognac brandy' became famous in its own right and was achieving a premium price. It was in the 18th century, however,

when Cognac really got a grip on global trade. At one time, Dutch merchants were buying around half of all the Cognac produced and using it to make liqueurs. It was also around this time that the now ubiquitous Cognac houses emerged – Remy Martin, Hennessy, Martell, Courvoisier and Hine. Each house had its own style of product and as we moved into the 19th century they sat among the most famous brand names in the world.

In 1877, disaster struck and the phylloxera bug devastated the vineyards of Cognac, all but eradicating the entire industry. It took 25 years to rebuild it, during which time the world had moved on. Whisky, rum and gin had invaded the cocktail books and back bars, and hijacked many of the Cognac cocktails. When Cognac re-emerged it was a changed product. Pre-phylloxera, Cognac was dominated by the richer and more powerful Folle Blanche grape, whereas the new breed of Cognac was composed mostly of the lighter Ugni Blanc, with a new disease-resistant Folle Blanche taking a supporting role. The six different regions of Cognac were reclassified too, based on the chalk and clay content of the terroir, which duly affected the finesse of the final product.

These days, most Cognac producers don't produce their own eau de vie, but buy it from the open market based on its grape, terroir and distillation. It's the ageing and blending of the eau de vie that various Cognac houses take great pride in. There is a constant active involvement in the spirit through its lifetime, from the initial influence of new European oak, to blending, finishing, then marrying again in glass. I've heard it said that there is no other spirit category so in tune with the development of their product as Cognac.

V.S. (Very Special) Cognac is aged for between two and four years; V.S.O.P. (Very Superior Old Pale) is aged for four to six years; X.O. (Extra Old) is aged for over six years.

SAZERAC

For most of my 'cocktail adolescence', I was led to believe that the Sazerac was the first cocktail; the Jesus drink, if you like. At some point it dawned on me that mixed drinks had been around a lot longer than the Sazerac, but it was only once I reached my late 'cocktail teens' that I discovered that the term 'cocktail' also pre-dates this drink by a good 50 years.

Nonetheless, the Sazerac is an old drink, still dating back to 1850s New Orleans, where the Absinthe and Cognac of the French inhabitants combined with sugar and medicinal bitters to form one of the kings of classic cocktails.

The story goes something like this. It's the 1850s in New Orleans and a gent named Sewell E. Taylor begins importing Cognac to New Orleans, Louisiana. The brand is Sazerac de Forge et Fils. Coincidentally, or not, at around the same time, the Sazerac House bar opens in New Orleans, and

they begin selling the Sazerac cocktail. The drink contained Sazerac de Forge et Fils Cognac and absinthe, which at that time, across the Atlantic, was doing a great job of increasing France's artistic creativity and alcoholism (much to its eventual demise). The drink was also rumoured to use bitters produced at a local pharmacy that was owned by a druggist called Antoine Peychaud. Today Peychaud's bitter's remain an essential requirement for any great Sazerac. In fact, the brand probably only survives today as a result of the Sazerac, since it is called for in only a handful of other cocktails.

There is some historical reference to suggest that Peychaud served his own version of the drink from a French egg cup called a *coquitier*. It's this egg cup that has led some people to believe that the word cocktail was originally derived from Peychaud's Sazerac. It might seem strange that a

10 ML/⅓ OZ. LA CLANDESTINE ABSINTHE

1 WHITE SUGAR CUBE

5 DASHES OF PEYCHAUD'S BITTERS

50 ML/2 OZ. HENNESSY FINE DE COGNAC OR 'GOOD WHISKY'

A TWIST OF LEMON ZEST, TO GARNISH

•

Grab 2 old fashioned glasses. Fill one with crushed ice and add the absinthe. Stir. In the other glass, crush the sugar cube with the bitters until dissolved, then add the Cognac and some cubed ice and stir for 30 seconds.

•

Chuck away the contents of the absinthe glass, ensuring you remove all fragments of the ice. (This might seem wasteful, but the absinthe will be entirely noticeable in the final drink.) Finally, strain the mixture into the empty absinthe-washed rocks glass. Garnish with a little twist of lemon zest.

---

drugstore would sell you a (strong) alcoholic drink, but this was the era in which medicine became a recreational thing of beauty and the line between health and well-being was very much blurred.

Despite the Sazerac being invented in the mid 19th century, its first appearance in a cocktail book wasn't until William 'Cocktail' Boothby's *The World's Drinks and How to Mix Them* (1908). The recipe was apparently given to Boothby by Thomas Handy, a later proprietor of the Sazerac House in New Orleans. Interestingly, the directions listed it with 'good whisky' instead of Cognac. This omission of Cognac is almost certainly due to the outbreak of the phylloxera bug in the late 19th century, which caused nothing short of a complete collapse of the French wine industry. Wine and Cognac became largely unavailable, so Boothby replaced the Cognac with whisky in his book. Ironically, a brand of rye whiskey now exists called, you guessed it, 'Sazerac'.

GREEN FAIRY SAZERAC

One of the best and worst things about this drink is the absinthe. Don't get me wrong, I'm a strong practitioner of 'the green hour' (the tradition of drinking absinthe at 5 pm), but in the Sazerac the absinthe is kind of there, yet also not there. I hate the way that it gets discarded and that it's merely a suggestion, rather than being a fully fledged member of the family. If it wasn't for the presence of bitters, I would suggest that the absinthe is being used as a bitters. However, in this show the absinthe is indeed an aromatic modifier – a very small one, but of critical importance. I love the way that the absinthe twists this drink into being an entirely different beast to a regular Old Fashioned. In my ideal, Sazerac the absinthe adds the familiar vegetal, aniseed/anise and bitter wormwood qualities, like a vibrant supporting actress outshining her male lead in pursuit of Oscar glory.

When I created the Green Fairy Sazerac, I wanted to play off some of the edgy, psychoactive connotations applied to asbinthe (despite them being largely codswallop). So I removed the absinthe 'rinse' and instead placed the absinthe on top of the final drink, in the form of a light and fluffy 'air' (see pages 48–49). There was something magical about a green-tinged bubble bath floating on top of the cocktail, as it seemed to award a certain 'lime-light' (excuse the pun) to my favourite character. It also gives a certain nod to the mythical 'Green Fairy', who was said to seduce those who became heavily inebriated through absinthe consumption; she pops up in a lot of Impressionist art from the late 19th century.

And then there was the glass. It was too great a temptation not to use Peychaud's *coquitier* to serve the drink. I managed to find a silver-plated egg cup that came with a kind of 'cosy' to keep the egg warm. When inverted, the cosy sat perfectly in the cup and provided the ideal-sized drinking vessel. The silver of the egg cup has a profound effect on the appreciation of this cocktail, evoking a sense of expense, quality and refinement. And I love how you have to sip through the Absinthe Air to reach the Cognac mixture underneath. Divine.

GREEN FAIRY SAZERAC

◆

For the Absinthe Air

1.5 G LECITHIN • 50 ML/2 OZ. ABSINTHE • 10 ML/⅓ OZ. SUGAR SYRUP (SEE PAGE 204)

50 ML/2 OZ. WATER

•

For the Absinthe Air, combine the lecithin, absinthe, sugar syrup and water. Transfer to a blender to blitz it up, then use a FISH TANK BUBBLER submersed in the solution (see page 49) to generate a lovely light air.

For the Green Fairy Sazerac

50 ML/2 OZ. HENNESSY X.O. • 4 DASHES OF PEYCHAUD'S BITTERS • 7.5 ML SUGAR SYRUP

(SEE PAGE 204) • A PIECE OF LEMON ZEST, PLUS AN EXTRA PIECE TO FINISH • 'ABSINTHE AIR'

•

Add the Cognac, bitters, sugar syrup and one piece of lemon zest to a mixing beaker filled with cubed ice. Stir for 45 seconds, then strain into the chilled egg cup. Pile the Absinthe Air on top and finish with a final fresh twist of lemon zest, then discard.

◆

SIDECAR

40 ML/1⅓ OZ. HENNESSY FINE DE COGNAC

20 ML/⅔ OZ. COINTREAU

20 ML/⅔ OZ. FRESH LEMON JUICE

•

Shake all the ingredients together with cubed ice, then fine
strain into a chilled coupe glass. That's it!

The Sidecar is surely one of the most iconic yet under-ordered cocktails around. It is pretty much the only half-decent drink to come out of the 1920s Prohibition period, an era in which American bartenders were forced to ply their trade across Europe. This cocktail opitimizes a time in Europe when drinks were made to be savoured, glasses were designed to be sipped and men and women alike ordered expertly prepared cocktails that got straight to the point. Brandy and orange liqueur could easily fool you into thinking that this is an after-dinner drink, but the citrus freshens the ensemble, focusing high notes from both the Cognac and the liqueur. This is a man's aperitif.

Despite the exact origins of the Sidecar still being in question, the drink was unquestionably made famous by Harry MacElhone, one of a number of different Harrys who contributed towards making 'Harry' the first and foremost name in historical bartending. When MacElhone published *Harry's ABC of Mixing Cocktails* (1922) while working at The Ritz, he listed the Sidecar as equal parts Cognac, triple sec and lemon juice. Shortly after, he opened Harry's New York Bar in Paris. The bar still stands today; always busy, it reminds me of an American sport's bar installed in an old English tavern. The drinks are pricey, but it ticks all the boxes for nostalgia.

One of the etymological theories for the Sidecar comes from the story of an American army captain during World War I. After being chauffeured around by motorcycle sidecar between his base and (presumably) the bar, he required a drink that whetted his appetite for food while simultaneously warming his bones; a Sidecar would be a great fit.

Both Harry MacElhone and Robert Vermeire, who also printed an early version of the drink in *Cocktails and How to Mix Them* (1922), direct the bartender to use equal parts of Cognac, triple sec and lemon. I personally think that this creates a very dry and rather 'flabby' juice-driven cocktail that really isn't suited to modern tastes. Harry Craddock's *Savoy Cocktail Book* (1930) version has stood the test of time, using two parts of Cognac to one part of lemon and one part of triple sec. The balance of this drink seems to be much better, so that is the recipe I have listed here.

It's worth noting that this drink is often served with a sugared rim. This was a trend that reared its less-than-beautiful head in the 1930s. To this day, it's still questionable whether the sugar rim is necessary or not, and for me it simply blurs the line between the Sidecar and the Brandy Crusta (see page 128).

SIDE CARESS

Despite waxing lyrical about the pre-dinner benefits of this drink, I do still have some issues with it. My main problem with it is the lemon juice. I like the freshness and drying effect that it has on the palate, but I'm not a fan of the generic lemon flavour, which overpowers the subtleties and nuances of the Cognac. If the lemon kills off the Cognac, it's a waste of good Cognac, in my opinion.

One way around this is to use another type of acid in the drink. This retains the sweet-sour balance, but removes the flabby lemon flavour from the equation. I experimented with various acids when developing the Side Caress, but settled on tartaric. Tartaric acid is the predominant acid found in grape juice. It adds a sharp and long bite to the cocktail, but suits this drink all the better because Cognac is made from grapes.

That leaves us with the triple sec. There is quite an array of triple secs and orange liqueurs on the market. All, as you would expect, have a bitter-sweet orange note running through their core, but some exhibit more of an orange blossom, mandarin, almost peachy note, while others are deep, heavy and spicy. Because we are already working towards a goal in which the Cognac's nuances are carefully amplified, I have chosen to use Pierre Ferrand Dry Curaçao, which is slightly sweeter than most triple

secs and does a great job of lifting the fruit flavours out of the Cognac.

I've chosen to stir the drink instead of shaking. Cocktails with citrus juice in them are almost always shaken, as the fine particles tend to visibly separate when not combined with vigour. Without the citrus juice, we can stir the drink and retain some of the clarity and colour of the Cognac.

Finally, since this is an aperitif we are talking about, some kind of nibble must be made available. Thinking back to our English captain cruising the winter streets of Paris in his sidecar, what better snack to serve the gentleman with his early evening tipple than some salty French fries?

SIDE CARESS

For the Tartaric Acid Solution

5 G TARTARIC ACID

100 ML/3⅓ OZ. WATER

•

Dissolve the tartaric acid in the water. If you have **PH STRIPS OR A DIGITAL READER**, you should be aiming for pH 3.0. Store in a sealed glass bottle.

For the Side Caress

40 ML/1⅓ OZ. HENNESSY V.S. COGNAC

15 ML/½ OZ. PIERRE FERRAND DRY CURAÇAO

10 ML/⅓ OZ. 'TARTARIC ACID SOLUTION'

FRENCH FRIES, TO SERVE

•

Briskly stir all the ingredients together over cubed ice and strain into a chilled coupe glass. Add one of the ice cubes to the glass, too, and serve with a side of French fries.

EGGNOG

If it's nutritional value you seek, I urge you to look elsewhere. Eggnog will not be winning awards for its health benefits any time soon. Eggnog is, for all practical purposes, alcoholic custard, or, as I like to look at it, ice cream batter.

Eggnog has existed under various guises for at least 500 years. A very early English version, known as a posset, dates right back to the Middle Ages. It combined boiled milk with spices and ale or mead. Later, in the 16th century, recipes included the addition of eggs, and the drink would be served from a specially designed posset pot. The posset is so old, in fact, that it is one of the only mixed drinks that can lay claim to appearing in a Shakespeare play – Lady Macbeth 'drugg'd their possets' to put her husband's guards to sleep.

The etymology of eggnog is not entirely clear. One explanation is the combination of 'egg' and 'grog'. Even though 'grog' is usually associated with seafarers and rum rations, it has also been widely used as a generic term for both rum and alcohol. Another possible reason for the name 'eggnog' originates from the small English wooden cups called noggins. It's ironic that a drink that has such a strong connection with the festive period in the US possibly has the English to thank for both its name and recipe.

You only need to see the list of ingredients to understand why eggnog and its predecessors have become an essential winter libation. Alcohol warms the blood, sugar provides energy, eggs supply protein and the fat from the milk and cream gives the drinker the necessary 'layers' to survive the winter season. And, of course, traditionally it's served warm. Wholesome indulgence doesn't get much better than this. This classic recipe for warm eggnog will result in a creamy, booze-fuelled custard that is as bad for you as it tastes good!

2 EGGS, SEPARATED

75 G/2½ OZ. SUGAR

150 ML/5 OZ. HENNESSY FINE DE COGNAC

100 ML/3½ OZ. WHOLE MILK

50 ML/2 OZ. DOUBLE/HEAVY CREAM

GRATED NUTMEG, TO GARNISH

•

Makes 4 servings

•

Begin by whisking the egg whites to soft peaks in a heatproof bowl and with an electric hand mixer, or in a stand mixer.

•

Bring half a saucepan of water up to the boil and place a stainless steel bowl on top. (Make sure the bowl doesn't touch the water – it needs to be warmed by the steam only.) Add the egg yolks and sugar to the bowl and give them a good whisk until the sugar is dissolved.

•

Add the Cognac and continue to whisk – it's really important that you don't allow the liquid to boil, that is unless you like alcoholic scrambled eggs! Next, add the milk and cream and stir everything together. Check the temperature with a **THERMOMETER OR PROBE**, it should be around 60°C/140°F.

•

Pour the warm mixture into the egg whites, whisking as you go. Pour into glass mugs and grate some nutmeg over the top to serve.

THE CURIOUS
Mixology Impossible
BARTENDER

HOT & COLD NITRO EGGNOG ICE CREAM

If something can be turned into ice cream, it should be turned into ice cream. In the case of eggnog, most of the work is already done for us. The main components of an eggnog batter are the same, and in similar proportions to, an ice cream mix. That was too easy, so I'm going to take it to the next level and fit the needs of both warm and chilled eggnog lovers, by making this ice cream both hot and cold.

Good ice cream is a balancing act between sugar, fat, milk solids and texture. Fat tempers flavour intensity, but improves stability and lengthens flavour release. Milk solids (not fat) provide depth of flavour and density. Emulsifiers (such as lecithin) and stabilizers (like sodium alginate) can also be used to provide elasticity and creaminess in the final article. Couple this with the fact that we will be adding alcohol (which affects the melting point) to this particular ice cream, and it's a complicated balancing act.

I played around with quite a few different formulas to create my ultimate eggnog ice cream recipe, and settled on this one. The flavour release of the Cognac is amazing – it really places emphasis on the spiced fruit finish of the brandy.

To create the 'hot and cold' effect, I used a hydrocolloid (gelling agent) called methyl-cellulose (or methocel). This stuff works in the opposite way to gelatine: it stays solid when it's hot and softens when it gets too cold. It's brilliant when you put it in your ice cream mix, because when a scoop is dropped into boiling water, the methocel sets, retaining the shape of the ice cream ball. So the ice cream stays solid while the water heats it up. If you take the scoop out at the right time the ice cream will be hot on the outside and fully frozen on the inside!

To start, I add (in this order) 100 g/3½ oz. egg yolks, 5 g methyl-cellulose, 5 g lecithin and 100 g/3½ oz. sugar to a stainless steel stand mixer set to high speed. I leave these to mix for a couple of minutes before turning the speed down to medium and adding 150 ml/5 oz. Hennessy Fine de Cognac, 40 g/1⅓ oz. milk powder, 350 ml/12 oz. whole milk and 50 ml/2 oz. cream. (This will be enough for 4 servings.) Once everything is mixed to a smooth batter, add sufficient liquid nitrogen (see page 44) to freeze the ice cream into a solid, creamy mass. You can use an ice cream maker for this, but it will take a bit longer and tend to produce softer results due to the presence of the alcohol in the batter. Liquid nitrogen won't struggle to make the ice cream cold enough, and because of the quick freezing process, it forms smaller water crystals and results in a smoother ice cream.

I need the ice cream to be quite firm for the next bit, so leave it to set hard in the freezer overnight. The next day, I set a pan of water to simmer, then scoop a ball of the ice cream and gently lower it into the pan using a slotted spoon. I spin the ball of ice cream quickly for around 30 seconds, then scoop the ball from the water and place it in a cone. I garnish with a cinnamon stick – a nod to the British Cadbury's 99 Flake, an ice cream cone typically served in the summer – and dust with cocoa powder.

CORPSE REVIVER

'Corpse revivers' are thought to have once been a family of cocktails all to themselves, with references going back as far as the 1870s. Engineered to assist in the survival of the morning after the night before, many of these hangover cures have been lost to time and only a few still exist today, including #1. Whether it is a viable cure for a hangover still remains to be seen, but when made correctly, this is a pretty good option for the middle of the evening.

In stark contrast to the more popular Corpse Reviver #2, this drink relies on dark spirits to pack a pretty serious right hook. To put it simply, we are talking about a Cognac- and Calvados-based Manhattan (see page 134) with the bitters held back. In many books, the drink is listed as two parts Cognac to one part Calvados and one part sweet vermouth. This leaves very little space for the booze to hide, resulting in one of the strongest tasting cocktails I can think of.

Frank Meier was thought to have invented #1 at some point in the 1920s while working at The Ritz in Paris. In his *Artistry of Mixing Drinks* (1934), he lists the drink as equal parts Cognac, Calvados and sweet vermouth, shaken and strained. However, the drink also appears in Harry Craddock's *The Savoy Cocktail Book* (1930) as a stirred drink with twice the dose of Cognac. Harry states that it is: 'To be taken before 11 am, or whenever steam and energy are needed'. For the classic, I use Meier's proportions and Craddock's technique.

CORPSE REVIVER 1.1 BETA

With a name like Corpse Reviver, it's all too easy for someone like me to get carried away with crazy necromantic-themed service ware, mummified ice cubes and zombie garnishes.

As tempting as those ideas are, it's important to recognize the primary function of this drink –

corpse revival. It needs to be potent, uplifting, pungent. It also needs to be on hand and ready to administer in an emergency (we've all been there). The last thing I feel like doing, having fallen foul to the side effects of imbibition, is mixing myself a cocktail. My suggestion is to prepare a set of these, prior to inebriation, and store them in your fridge until the following day's 'hour of need'. For the keenest of hangover doctors, all this storing-cocktails-in-glass opens up the experimental realms of 'bottle ageing' (see pages 53–55), too.

Now let's look at tweaking the ingredients to assist further with the hangover. Intoxication results in dehydration, metabolism of alcohol (into acetaldehyde) and the depletion of a number of important vitamins and minerals, including A, B, B6, C and salt. Despite the obvious negative effect of drinking more alcohol with a hangover (ignoring the 'lift' it may or may not provide), I'm adding some of these missing vitamins into the Corpse Reviver 1.1 Beta in an attempt to assist the body in the recovery process.

We will start by adding a little extra sugar to the drink. This will place emphasis on the fruit flavours as well as giving the drinker a slight energy boost. I'm also adding a pinch of salt; in small quantities, salt will improve the flavour of almost anything without making it taste noticeably salty, it will also help with replenishing the salt that has been lost through 'alcohol-based activities'. We are also going to add a touch of chilli, because it kick-starts the senses and coats the palate, and because it's a great source of B vitamins. I'm putting a whole clove in there too. The flavour couples nicely with that of apple brandy, it has mild anasthetic properties and the bitterness will help settle the stomach. Finally, a caffeine tablet dissolved into the drink prior to bottling (always

IN THE EVENT OF AN EMERGENCY follow instructions closely:

REMOVE FROM CHILLER

FLIP QUICK-RELEASE CAP

TRANSFER IN TO GLASS

DRAIN   REVIVE

read the instructions on the packet) will secure the extra boost required to make it through the morning. This mixture certainly contains the 'steam and energy' that Craddock alluded to.

It's worth noting that caffeine is a double-edged sword when duelling with a hangover. Despite its apparent instant benefits, it is in fact a diuretic (like alcohol), so handle with care.

The trick with this cocktail is to resist the temptation to use the hottest chilli available, as it will ruin what is otherwise quite a tasty and well-balanced drink – somewhere between 500 and 2,000 on the Scoville scale would be about perfect. You can use store-bought chilli sauce, but it's unlikely to provide the same level of all-important B vitamins – you want to feel better, right?

CORPSE REVIVER 1.1 BETA

— ◆ —

½ RED CHILLI, WASHED AND DESEEDED

1 CLOVE

1 CAFFEINE TABLET

A PINCH OF SALT

25 ML/1 OZ. HENNESSY V.S. COGNAC

25 ML/1 OZ. SOMERSET 12-YEAR-OLD CIDER BRANDY
(I'M ENGLISH)

25 ML/1 OZ. ANTICA FORMULA VERMOUTH

5 ML SUGAR SYRUP (SEE PAGE 204)

100 ML/3½ OZ. WATER

A WHOLE APPLE, TO SERVE

•

Place the chilli in a suitable clean glass bottle with the clove.

•

Crush the caffeine tablet and salt in a mixing beaker, then add all the other ingredients (except the apple). Stir until everything is dissolved, then strain into the bottle, shake and seal.

•

Serve the drink with a whole apple (for vitamin C) and drink directly from the bottle in one fluid motion.

— ◆ —

BRANDY CRUSTA

---

1 LEMON • FINE SUGAR, FOR COATING THE GLASS

50 ML/2 OZ. HENNESSY FINE DE COGNAC • 5 ML GRAND MARNIER

5 ML MARASCHINO LIQUEUR • 5 ML SUGAR SYRUP (SEE PAGE 204)

2 DASHES OF DR. ADAM ELMEGIRAB'S BOKER'S BITTERS

•

First, zest the lemon. Use a sharp potato peeler and start at one end, winding down to the other end in a spiral fashion.

•

Take your zested lemon and cut it in half. Save one half for its juice (see below) and use the other half of the lemon to wet the rim of a small wine glass, Once moistened, 'crust' the rim by dipping it in a saucer of fine sugar, making every effort to avoid getting it on the inside of the glass.

•

Put all the liquid ingredients in a mixing beaker, add 5 ml of the lemon juice and stir with cubed ice for 40 seconds. Strain into the prepared glass and spiral the lemon zest up the inside.

Quite simply, the Crusta represents the pinnacle of 19th-century bartending.

It's 1840 in New Orleans and 'Cock-Tails', as they were known, have been around for some 40 years. A 'Cock-Tail' at that time consisted of a spirit (any), some bitters, a lump of sugar and some water, all stirred up. That's about as exciting as it got. A man named Joseph Santini was appointed to manage the New Orlean's City Exchange bar and restaurant. Santini went all Dr. Jekyll, messing with Mother Nature's plans and using all the techniques available to him to heinously fiddle with 'Cock-Tail' DNA. The result, no bullshit, was Cocktail 2.0.

His first move was to use ice instead of water. Insulated ice boxes had become available in the US around ten years previously. The use of ice to dilute and chill a drink would decrease the perception of alcohol in the cocktail and therefore reduce the amount of water needed, which dilutes flavour. People won't want lumps of ice in their drink though, so Santini used a mixing glass and strainer to transfer the finished drink into the glass.

SHERBET CRUSTA

For the Lemon Sherbet Glass

100 G/3½ OZ. ICING/CONFECTIONERS' SUGAR

25 G/1 OZ. LEMON POWDER (SEE PAGE 203)
(adjust according to strength of the powder)

10 G/⅓ OZ. BICARBONATE OF SODA/BAKING SODA

10 G/⅓ OZ. CITRIC ACID

10 G/⅓ OZ. TARTARIC ACID

2 G SALT

GLUCOSE SYRUP (FOR PAINTING THE GLASS)

◆

Mix all of the powders and salt together thoroughly. Lightly paint glucose syrup onto the outside of a coupe glass, then liberally dust the sherbet mixture over the glass using a fine sieve/strainer. Use a **HAIRDRYER** to gently dry the sherbet and form a dense crust.

For the Sherbet Crusta

50 ML/2 OZ. HENNESSY FINE DE COGNAC

5 ML GRAND MARNIER

5 ML MARASCHINO LIQUEUR

20 ML/⅔ OZ. WATER

2 DASHES OF DR. ADAM ELMEGIRAB'S BOKER'S BITTERS

A TWIST OF LEMON ZEST, TO GARNISH

◆

Stir together the liquid ingredients for 1 minute with cubed ice, then strain into the prepared glass. Add a single lump of ice to the glass, too, to help hold the temperature. Garnish the stem of the glass with a twist of lemon zest.

◆

Lick and sip!

Crushing up sugar is time consuming and often ineffective, so Santini turned it into a viscous syrup that could be poured and measured into the drink. He also added a rim (or crust) of sugar to the glass, to trigger textural change on the palate and to add little surprise pockets of sweetness to the experience.

How about using some of those new-fangled fancy European liqueurs to facilitate a subtle tweak of the flavour of the Cognac? We'll use maraschino to enhance the sweet soft fruit characteristics, and triple sec to add a dry, zesty finish. Lovely.

But now it's a bit sweet. Damn. We need to balance all that sugar and liqueur with something... But what? Any modern-day bartender would gesture towards the fruit bowl without a second thought, but when Santini reached for a lemon he was pioneering an all-new mixological territory. A couple of barspoons of lemon juice would balance the sweetness and plump up the fruitiness of the drink.

To finish (as if he hasn't done enough already), we'll place the zest of an entire lemon in the glass, just to show off.

And there you have it, the godfather of fancy drinks, a cocktail that by the 19th-century's standards was so complicated and fiddly that it's questionable if anyone would even attempt to make it. But its genius had not faltered by the end of the century, when it was featured in books by every one of the big-ball bartenders of the day: Jerry Thomas, William Schmidt and Harry Johnson, no less.

SHERBET CRUSTA

While it's tempting to pull out all the stops and create a drink using a bunch of different modernist techniques, it seems somehow sacrilegious to meddle with a cocktail that had already achieved so much in its time. So I'm going to leave the

ingredients relatively untouched and focus more closely on the 'crust'.

As beautiful as the crust looks on the classic cocktail, it isn't the easiest of drinks to consume. The lemon falls into the glass and the iconic image of the drink is ruined almost immediately. I wanted to overcome this by somehow integrating the lemon zest flavour into the sugar and by increasing the amount of sugar in the 'crust' so that the drink became part cocktail, part lollipop!

I settled on the idea of replacing the sugar with a lemon sherbet. The drinker can alternate between sipping the liquid and licking off the sherbet from the side of the glass. To create the sherbet, I used a combination of citric and tartaric acids (see pages 27–29), combined with bicarbonate of soda/baking soda, icing/confectioner's sugar and lemon powder. The bicarbonate of soda/baking soda is an alkaline, and when combined with the

acid and moisture (i.e. your tongue), the two produce an exothermic reaction, which produces the intense fizzing sensation. The lemon should link the sherbet with the drink nicely and the sweetness balances out the acidity.

I had also considered taking the cocktail a step further and adding orange and cherry sherbet (to match the curaçao and maraschino liqueurs) to the glass too, so that the drinker could try the drink alongside three composite sherbets.

I took the decision to remove the lemon juice and extra sugar from the drink, since it does muffle the Cognac a little and I now have a bright acidity provided by my sherbet instead. I've also added a good splash of water in there. This extra dilution really aids in bringing out some of the aromatics of the Cognac and the liqueurs, plus it helps to soften the onslaught of fizzing lemon sherbet and high-strength alcohol!

✳ WHISKY & WHISKEY ✳

In a bold move, this section combines cocktails made from whisk(e)y in its various guises. Hopefully, the act of denying American whiskey, Irish whiskey and Scotch whisky their own categories doesn't dilute the overall significance of these spirits within the cocktail world.

It's highly likely that whiskey originated from Ireland, not Scotland as is commonly believed. By the beginning of the 14th century, the art of distillation had reached Irish shores, spread by the teachings of travelling monks. Established latin-speaking alchemists named the distilled liquor *aqua vitae*, 'water of life', but the Irish and Scottish called it by its Gaelic name, *uisce beatha*. Over time, the term evolved into the name we know today – whisky.

Meanwhile, across the pond, rum had been the choice liquor of North America for over 100 years. However, once America gained its independence, Irish and Scottish immigrants set about making the spirit of rebellion – whisky.

Grain was cheap, abundant and generally a more attractive proposition than buying rum or molasses off the British. In 1785, Bourbon County was founded – named after the French General Lafayette, who was descended from the royal house of Bourbon. During this time, whiskey production across the US accelerated, but Bourbon County became famous for its particular style of predominantly corn – as opposed to rye – liquor.

The spelling deviation between the smorgasbord of different whisky and whiskey out there comes down to quality. During the 19th century, Irish and American distillers felt the need to differentiate themselves from the – at the time – inferior Scottish product. They did so by adding an 'e' to their whisky.

Irish whiskey is usually distilled three times in a combination of pot and column stills. It is commonly made from unpeated malted barley and so, in conjunction with the distilling process, usually results in a lighter, more delicate distillate than Scotch.

Like Irish whiskey, Scotch must be aged for a minimum of three years and distilled a minimum of two times. Scotch is famed for its diverse style, with each of the 100 or so distilleries in Scotland presenting a unique fingerprint, based on their location, use of peat (smoke drying), distillation process and ageing programme. Lowland whisky is light, grassy and delicate. Highland whisky is robust, resinous and fruity. Whisky from Speyside (the highest concentration of Scotch distilleries) is fragrant, aromatic and complex. And whisky from the island of Islay and its nearby islands is smoky, powerful and salty. Single malts are made entirely from malted barley and the product of one distillery, and blended whisky is a mixture of any number of single malt whiskies with grain whisky (a much lighter whisky distilled from unmalted barley).

American whiskey is a spirit made from grains and cereals in the US. The most commonplace of these whiskeys are rye, bourbon and Tennessee, all of which must be aged in new-American oak barrels. Rye whiskey must be made from a 'mash' comprising of a minimum of 51% rye. Bourbon and Tennessee whiskey need to be a minimum of 51% corn. Bourbon can legally be produced anywhere in the US (though it is most strongly associated with the state of Kentucky), has no minimum age restrictions and is permitted to have flavours and colour added. However, to be classed as 'straight bourbon', it must be aged for a minimum of two years and have nothing but water added to it after distillation and ageing. Almost all of the bourbons you'll find in your local bar are Kentucky straight bourbon. Tennessee whiskey, the most famous of which is Jack Daniel's, is a straight bourbon that must be produced in the state of Tennessee.

Different approaches to cask ageing usually result in a sweeter, buttery and more spicy product in US whiskey, as opposed to the cereal, fruit, grassy and honeyed notes of Scotch and Irish whisk(e)y.

MANHATTAN

◆

50 ML/2 OZ. WOODFORD RESERVE BOURBON

25 ML/1 OZ. MARTINI ROSSO VERMOUTH

2 DASHES OF BOB'S ABBOTTS BITTERS

A MARASCA CHERRY (OR TWIST OF ORANGE ZEST), TO GARNISH

•

Stir all the ingredients together with cubed ice for 60 seconds,
then strain into a chilled coupe glass. Garnish with a Marasca
cherry (not one of those radioactive red things!) or a small
twist of orange zest, if you prefer.

◆

There are a few reasons why the Manhattan can claim to be one of the most iconic cocktails in the world, the most obvious being that it is named after one of the world's most famous metropolitan islands. Another reason is that it has placed itself in the same social circle as the golden girl herself, the Martini. In fact, some might say the Manhattan is to Ken as the Martini is to Barbie. The final, and most important reason of all, is that it tastes absolutely fantastic!

The Manhattan is my go-to drink, a get-out-of jail-free card when decision making seems too much like hard work and all I really want is something familiar and tasty – a comfort blanket of corn and wine.

There is a popular story associated with the creation of the Manhattan that is more than likely untrue. But the story is such a good one that I'll tell it anyway, since, and I think you'll agree, it really ought to be true! The story goes that one Dr. Ian Marshall invented the drink in 1874. Apparently, he was attending a banquet hosted by Jennie Jerome (aka Lady Randolph Churchill – Winston Churchill's mother) at the Manhattan Club in NYC. The banquet was being held to honour presidential candidate Samuel J. Tilden. Allegedly, the drink was a great success and as word spread guests in other bars began ordering the cocktail made famous at the Manhattan Club.

Sadly, there is a big problem with that story. On the date of the supposed banquet, Lady Randolph Churchill was actually in Blenheim, England, christening her newly born son, Winston – a factual inconvenience, since it would be fitting that such a great drinker was linked to such a great drink.

It is a strange thing that you can take virtually any spirit, mix two parts of it with one part sweet vermouth, add a dash of bitters and be confident in the knowledge that it'll probably taste pretty damn good. With Cognac it's called a Harvard, with Gin it's a Martinez (see pages 76–77), with Scotch it's a Rob Roy (see page 150) and so on. Perhaps none work so well as the Manhattan, though.

Some folks believe that a Manhattan should be made with rye in place of bourbon. I have listed the latter, since its more readily available, but it really comes down to personal choice, with the rye being a little more spicy and a little more 'man-ly'.

INDUSTRIAL REVOLUTION

My variation on the Manhattan is inspired by the island of Manhattan itself. Arguably the world's first megalopolis, the island is famous for its iconic skyline of steel, concrete and glass. During the late 19th and early 20th centuries, Manhattan underwent significant economical, industrial and architectural growth. At the heart of this growth was steel – a strong carbon/iron alloy – and it's steel that I will be using to make my Industrial Revolution.

I was first drawn to the benefits of steel ageing by my friend Craig Harper, a big Scot with a strange penchant for blue cocktails and a head full of old drinking references. Craig mixed a few Manhattans, then aged them for around six weeks in steel, glass and wood (oak). He presented them during London Cocktail Week in 2011 and I got a chance to taste them alongside a freshly made Manhattan. The steel-aged sample was the most exciting drink for me. The flavour had not been significantly altered in any one direction, but the ingredients showed a hugely increased degree of integration. The drink no longer seemed a collection of parts, but rather a complete product – like it was born that way. In other words, steel had achieved, in a short space of time, exactly what every bartender aims to achieve every time they pick up a pair of bottles – integration.

I tried to research what was going on. How could a cheap, relatively inert material like steel do such a magical job of integrating ingredients? The problem is, there are virtually no research papers or studies on this subject, despite the fact that nearly all wine and spirit producers use steel to rest their products.

Craig and I decided to conduct further sensory tests on steel-aged Manhattans to see if we could uncover exactly what was going on. We used low-cost stainless steel flasks designed for hiking and climbing. If you're going to attempt this, be sure that your flask is steel not aluminum, and the cheaper the better, as the more expensive options tend to be coated with other materials. We systematically rested four Manhattan samples, all made to the same specifications and all with the same amount of headspace (air) in the flask. Three of the samples were already diluted with an appropriate quantity of water, so only required chilling once ready to drink. The one remaining sample was not diluted, so needed stirring down with ice to construct the finished drink. We wanted to see how the ABV of the liquid affected the ageing process.

Sadly, the results were highly inconclusive. One thing we did learn, however, is that steel ageing certainly has a profound effect on the cocktail. When compared to a freshly made Manhattan of identical proportions, the 10-week-old post-diluted sample tasted very well integrated, but somehow flat and lifeless. The pre-diluted sample of the same age, by contrast, was more rounded, spicy and fuller bodied. Perhaps diluting prior to ageing is the best practice?

Our eight-week-old pre-diluted sample was very under-whelming, soft and gutless. Finally, our six-week-old pre-diluted sample tasted great, full of flavour, with a cherry-like sweetness and just enough alcohol burn to add structure.

Further trials are needed, but for the moment, this is my favourite steel-aged Manhattan recipe.

INDUSTRIAL REVOLUTION

◆

300 ML/10 OZ. RITTENHOUSE RYE WHISKEY

150 ML/5 OZ. MARTINI ROSSO VERMOUTH

15 ML/½ OZ. MARASCHINO LIQUEUR

10 DASHES OF DR. ADAM ELMEGIRAB'S BOKER'S BITTERS

•

Makes enough for 5 servings

•

Combine all the ingredients in a **STEEL FLASK** and leave to rest for 6 weeks.

•

To serve, measure 95 ml/3¼ oz. for each glass and stir over cubed ice for 30 seconds. Strain into a chilled coupe glass.

◆

WHISKY SOUR

◆

50 ML/2 OZ. SCOTCH WHISKY • 25 ML/1 OZ. FRESH LEMON JUICE

12.5 ML/½ OZ. SUGAR SYRUP (SEE PAGE 204)

½ EGG WHITE (OPTIONAL)

A FRESH CHERRY AND A SLICE OF LEMON, TO GARNISH

•

Shake all the ingredients together with cubed ice. Strain into
a beaker and blitz briefly with a stick blender or AEROLATTE. Pour
into a rocks glass and garnish with a cherry and a slice
of lemon.

◆

Most recipes for a sour with whisky in them would include the letter 'e' in whisk(e)y, denoting the origin of the liquor to be American (bourbon and rye) or Irish. Scotch whisky is not the norm for a sour, but not wholly unheard of either. I've chosen to use Scotch for one simple reason – it tastes really good. That's not to say that this drink doesn't work well with bourbon, rye, Irish, Indian, Welsh, English or Japanese whiskey, too – or in fact virtually any other spirit – but the Scotch sour deserves a bit of recognition in my opinion.

The Sour is one of the staple cocktail families – not particularly exciting in itself, but an essential part of the cocktail demographic. Sours are the basis for other families of drink, such as Fizzes (a Sour shaken and topped with soda), Collins (a Sour stirred with soda), Rickeys (a lime Sour topped with soda) and the family that the Sidecar, Cosmopolitan and White Lady belong to. They are simple, dependable creatures that there is no shame enjoying from time to time.

Jerry Thomas's 1862 *How to Mix Drinks or the Bon Vivant's Companion* was the first cocktail book to publish a Sour recipe, five in fact, including the Whiskey Sour (with bourbon), Gin Sour, Brandy Sour, Egg Sour (with brandy and curaçao) and Santa Cruz Sour (with rum). The Whiskey Sour reads:

Take 1 large teaspoonful of powdered white sugar, dissolved in a little seltzer or Apollinaris water. The juice of half a small lemon. 1 wine glass of bourbon or rye whiskey.

Fill the glass full of shaved ice, shake up and strain into a claret glass. Ornament with berries.

This formula has remained almost untouched over the last 150 years and there's a very good reason for that – it works. Thomas's recipe calls for the reader to mix a water/sugar solution on the fly, but these days we use sugar syrup or gomme. The combination of spirit, lemon juice and sugar syrup in a 4:2:1 ratio results in a balanced drink most of the time, every time.

Why Scotch? Well, Scotch and lemon juice have as strong an affinity as any two ingredients I can think of (see exhibit A – the Hot Toddy), there's something medicinal abut the pairing. I also

love the way the malt and peaty (if applicable) notes shine through, softened by the sweet and sour balance, but still more than apparent. In fact, I've found that a Whisky Sour is an excellent tool for initiating non-Scotch drinkers into the balmy folds of malt whisky appreciation.

PANACEA

This drink is a variation on the Panacea cocktail that has been served at my bar, The Worship Street Whistling Shop, for over two years. When we first opened, much to our surprise, this Scotch whisky-based cocktail was the most popular drink on the menu and especially a hit with the ladies.

Ryan Chetiyawardana (our Bar Manager) came up with the concept of the original drink, which combined ingredients that have all been used medicinally in the past – hence the name. We make a honey and lavender shrub by sous vide cooking cider vinegar, honey and lavender together for a few hours. The infusion is then shaken with lemon juice, Scotch and egg white, then finished with a touch of sage 'dust' on top. It's divine, perfectly combining a lot of flavours that are perceivable in Scotch for a medicinal, warming cocktail.

The recipe opposite uses the same ingredients, but I'm combining them in layers. Just as with food, it's sometimes nice to have components of a drink separated, so that each sip is a slightly different experience. My foam will be flavoured with smoky single malt whisky and lavender. The liquid part of the drink underneath will consist of a lighter Speyside malt, with lemon juice, cider vinegar and honey. The idea is that the drink will appear to be a regular Sour cocktail, with a nice white foam on top. But once sipped on, it will become clear that the foam has a contrasting and complementary flavour to the liquid underneath.

PANACEA

For the Smoky Foam

150 ML/5 OZ. ARDBEG WHISKY • 150 ML/5 OZ. WATER • 10 ML/⅓ OZ. FILTERED LEMON JUICE

15 ML/½ OZ. SUGAR SYRUP (SEE PAGE 204) • 5 G DRIED LAVENDER FLOWERS

50 G/2 OZ. EGG WHITE

•

Add all the ingredients except the egg white to a CREAM WHIPPER and charge with two 8-g N₂O cartridges (see page 32). Shake the cream whipper vigorously for a minute, then allow to sit for a further 2 minutes. Depressurize the cream whipper by holding it upright and quickly squeezing the lever down, passing the contents through a mesh sieve/strainer into a bowl or beaker as you go. Clean the cream whipper of any lavender particles.

•

Pour the filtered liquid back into the cream whipper, along with the egg white. Shake well, then charge with a single 8-g N₂O cartridge. Refrigerate for at least 2 hours until ready to use. The foam should easily be enough for a dozen drinks and keep happily in the fridge for up to 10 days.

For the Sage Garnish

10 G/⅓ OZ. FRESH SAGE LEAVES

•

Place the fresh sage leaves on a baking sheet and put in a low oven for 2 hours to dry out (or use a DEHYDRATOR). Once dried, grind up the leaves.

For the Panacea

50 ML/2 OZ. GLENMORANGIE 12 WHISKY • 10 ML/⅓ OZ. FRESH LEMON JUICE • 5 ML CIDER VINEGAR • 15 ML/½ OZ. HONEY WATER (50:50 MIXTURE OF CLEAR RUNNY HONEY AND WATER)

'SMOKY FOAM' • A SPRINKLING OF 'SAGE GARNISH'

•

Shake the whisky, lemon juice, cider vinegar and honey water together with cubed ice, then strain into a chilled coupe glass. Gently dispense the Smoky Foam on top. Garnish with the ground dehydrated sage.

JULEP

———◆———

50 ML/2 OZ. BOURBON WHISKEY

5 G FRESH MINT LEAVES (ABOUT 12), PLUS MINT SPRIGS TO GARNISH

7 ML SUGAR SYRUP (SEE PAGE 204)

•

Add all the ingredients to the base of the **JULEP CUP** and stir for 1 minute. Chuck in a big scoop of crushed ice and churn everything together. Sit a **JULEP STRAINER** on top and garnish with mint sprigs.

———◆———

For our US compatriots, the Julep is synonymous with the Kentucky Derby, an annual thoroughbred horse race held in Louisville, Kentucky. Over the course of the Kentucky Derby weekend, the Churchill Downs race track makes an estimated 120,000 Mint Juleps for spectators – 'das a whole lotta mint!'

The drink itself is basically an Old Fashioned with mint in place of bitters, traditionally served in a (fittingly named) 'Julep cup' – a shiny steel, pewter or silver goblet. The drink also lends its name to the 'Julep strainer', a staple of the mixologist's bar kit bag that is commonly used for holding the ice back when straining a drink from mixing beaker to glass. The original intended use for a Julep strainer, however, was to sit on top of a Julep and stop pesky bits of mint and crushed ice making their way into your gob. Nowadays, we usually serve Juleps with thin straws that you could barely hope to breathe through, never mind fit a piece of mint up.

The first reference to a Julep dates way back to 1803 when it was described as 'a dram of spirituous liquor that has mint steeped in it, taken by Virginians of a morning'.

I like to make up a 'Julep mix', consisting of mint-infused bourbon and sugar. This is a bit more economical on the mint front, and sits quite happily in a bottle in my home spirits cabinet, requiring only a quick stir with crushed ice to be finished off. The recipe above was given to me by my bourbon-loving friend Jon Lister.

HOT & ICED JULEP

This recipe is inspired by Heston Blumenthal's 'Hot & Cold Iced Tea', served at The Fat Duck restaurant in Bray, England.

The idea of floating one drink on top of another (vertical float) is not a new one. There are entire books dedicated to shots, shooters, drops and the like that are popular in part because of the visual appeal of one drink sitting on top of another. Creating a drink with a horizontal float, however, is much more difficult. It seems impossible in fact – how can two liquids sit side by side and not mix together, especially if one is hot and the other cold?

Well, it is entirely possible and it was achieved by The Fat Duck back in 2005, with a side-by-side float of hot tea and iced tea. When you sip on the liquid, there is the most bizarre sensation of experiencing warm and cold at the same time, a bit like when you get one of those taps/faucets on a sink that instead of giving you warm water simultaneously dispenses both scalding and freezing cold water in unmixed form. The effect is achieved by making highly viscous (free-flowing) fluid gels.

We come across fluid gels a lot in everyday life; condiments like tomato ketchup and many shower gels are fluid gels, as they have a low viscosity, but still behave like flowing liquids. Imagine taking a bottle of brown sauce and a bottle of ketchup and squeezing them simultaneously into the base of a glass. As the glass begins to fill, the sauces won't mix; they'll simply sit side by side, the low viscosity caused by the gel structure being enough to prevent them from flowing into each other. However, horizontal floats are still achievable with liquids that are much more viscous than the stuff you put on your fries. I'm going to make fluid gels for my Julep that are viscous enough to feel like a liquid, but stable enough to prevent mixing.

This is, without doubt, one of the most forward-thinking cocktails that I have ever attempted to make, and one of the biggest challenges that I need to overcome is the incredible piece of evolutionary engineering that is the human tongue.

Our tongues and mouths are unrivalled in their ability to detect minute textural changes. A baby will try to put every object they can get their hands on in their mouth in an effort to understand its texture. Fooling the tongue is incredibly difficult, and getting the viscosity of my fluid gel right will be a crucial part of making this drink work.

The Julep is the perfect cocktail to attempt this with, since it is delicious both as a cold and a hot drink. It also gives me a chance to play with one of mint's unique properties, the fact that it can be both spicy and cooling at the same time. By bolstering some of the natural flavour compounds already present in mint, I can take my Julep to the extreme.

The cooling sensation of mint can come from a variety of compounds, but menthol is probably the one we associate it with the most. These cooling compounds trigger nerve endings in our mouths that are responsible for detecting when things are cold. The spiciness or pepperiness of peppermint comes from the compound caryophyllene. This compound is also found in cloves, some types of basil, some types of cinnamon and most predominately in West African black pepper. Like menthol, caryophyllene directly interacts with nerve endings responsible for detecting heat. Using these compounds, I'm going to adjust the coolness and spiciness of the two halves of my drink to further fool the palate.

I prepare the two halves of the drink separately, then combine them in the cup by pouring them in simultaneously. The measurements here need to be very precise – even the mineral content of the water you use can upset the balance if you're not careful.

To make the Julep infusion, I freeze 15 g/½ oz. mint with liquid nitrogen (see page 44), then break the leaves into a powder using a muddler or rolling pin. Next, I douse the mint with 200 ml/6¾ oz.

Woodford Reserve Bourbon and 25 g/1 oz. sugar syrup. The infusion is stirred briskly for 1 minute, then strained through a coffee filter or muslin cheesecloth to remove the fine mint particles.

To make the hot Julep, I put 100 ml/3⅓ oz. water in a saucepan along with 0.3 g agar-agar, 0.2 g citric acid and 1 g finely ground West African black pepper. I bring the mixture to the boil and ensure that all the agar is dissolved, then remove from the heat, strain, and whisk in 100 ml/3½ oz. of the Julep infusion.

To make the cold Julep, I put 100 ml/3⅓ oz. water into a saucepan along with 0.3 g agar-agar, 0.6 g citric acid, a postage stamp-sized slice of lemon zest and 1.5 g menthol crystals (nasal decongestant). I bring the mixture to the boil and ensure that all the agar is dissolved, then remove from the heat, strain, and whisk in 100 ml/3⅓ oz. of the Julep infusion.

I cool both mixtures separately in an ice bath and, once chilled, pass them through a fine-mesh sieve/strainer. The mixtures are both then bottled and reserved until required.

To serve the drink, I heat the warm Julep to 65°C/150°F in a water bath and simultaneously cool the cold Julep in an ice bath, or fridge. I have created a custom-made vessel to serve my hot and cold Juleps in: a metal tea cup with a secure-fitting plastic insert that can slide into the middle of the cup and acts as a partition between the two liquids when they are poured.

When the liquids are at the correct temperature, I carefully pour the liquids in either side of the partitioned cup at a steady rate, then remove the insert, cross my fingers and serve.

The drink must be consumed quite quickly, because the temperatures of the two halves quickly equilibrate when they are left to sit for more than a few minutes.

MIXOLOGY IMPOSSIBLE

OLD FASHIONED

I once asked a friend of mine what he thought was so special about the Old Fashioned cocktail. He told me: 'An Old Fashioned is all about savouring the moment; it's the curve on the corner of the ice cubes from minutes of melting, it's the undissolved granules of sugar that sway around in the current at the bottom of the glass and it's the unique clinking sound of ice on thick glass that can only resonate from an Old Fashioned.'

And of course it's true; an Old Fashioned is not a drink, it's a ritual, a moment in time to contemplate politics and classical music, accompanied by a cigar and a suitably old leather armchair. When we drink an Old Fashioned, it feels like we are drinking history. And it's not just the name; there's something time-honoured, weathered and worldly wise about savouring a well-made Old Fashioned.

It's fitting, then, that the Old Fashioned should define the original definition of a cocktail – spirit, sugar, water and bitters (see pages 14–15 for more on this). The act of adding a bitter-sweet edge to a normal glass of bourbon transforms the libation into something far more palatable, which awakens the senses and fortifies the mind in a way that neat spirit simply cannot. This is as gloriously simple as it gets, folks; the drink equivalent of seasoning a sirloin steak with salt and pepper, grilling it for a couple of minutes, then eating the whole thing with a hunting knife.

The oldest reference to an 'Old Fashioned Whiskey Cocktail' in a cocktail book is in George J. Kappeler's *Modern American Drinks* (1895); he writes:

Dissolve a small lump of sugar with a little water in a whiskey glass; add 2 dashes Angostura bitters, a small piece ice, a piece lemon peel, one jigger whiskey. Mix with small barspoon and serve, leaving spoon in glass.

A 5-CM/2-INCH PIECE OF ORANGE ZEST

A BROWN SUGAR CUBE

5 ML SUGAR SYRUP (SEE PAGE 204)

2 DASHES OF BOB'S ABBOTTS BITTERS

60 ML/2 OZ. WOODFORD RESERVE BOURBON WHISKEY

•

Take a heavy rocks glass and put the orange zest in the bottom, followed by the sugar cube, sugar syrup and bitters. Using a muddler, rolling pin or anything remotely similar, crush the sugar cube and grind it into the orange zest. The aim is to dissolve the sugar and get some of the orange oil into the glass. It's worth spending a minute dissolving the sugar, because if you don't the drink won't be sweet enough.

•

Add the whiskey and some cubed ice to the glass. Stir all the ingredients together for 2 whole minutes (it's only after that time that the drink will have sufficiently diluted and be chilled enough), then serve.

Case closed then. Well, no. For the drink to be called 'Old Fashioned', it must be, well, old – right? Correct. Before being known as an Old Fashioned, the drink was simply known as a 'Whiskey Cocktail' (which is exactly what it is) – here it is featured in Jerry Thomas's original *How to Mix Drinks or the Bon Vivant's Companion* (1862):

Take 3 or 4 dashes of gum syrup.
2 dashes of bitters (Boker's)
1 wine glass of whiskey
Fill one-third full of fine ice; shake and strain in a fancy red wine glass. Put a piece of twisted lemon peel in the glass and serve.

ISOAMYL ACETATE OLD FASHIONED

This variation on an Old Fashioned is based on the Jack Daniel's drink that I entered CLASS Bartender of the Year with (and subsequently won)

in 2011. The drink is romantically named after an ester (powerful flavour molecule) called isoamyl acetate that I find to be particularly pronounced on the aroma of Jack Daniel's Old No. 7. The smell of this particular ester is best described as banana. If ever you have had a banana-flavoured sweet, you probably declared it to taste of nail varnish (if you're a girl) or model aircraft glue (if you're a boy). That's because synthetic isoamyl acetate is used to flavour banana candy and milkshakes as well as being a solvent for glues and varnishes.

Interestingly, isoamyl acetate also serves as a pheromone for honey bees, released into the air as they sting you to attract more bees to the party.

In alcohol, isoamyl acetate is formed when amyl alcohols, which make up part of the wonderfully dirty flavour-giving alcohols we call fusel oils, react with acid in a process called esterification. Fermentation, distillation and ageing of bourbon

ISOAMYL ACETATE OLD FASHIONED

For the Banana Syrup
200 G/7 OZ. (CASTER) SUGAR • 200 G/7 OZ. DRIED BANANA • 400 ML/14 OZ. WATER

50 G/2 OZ. CLEAR RUNNY HONEY (NOT WANTING TO LEAVE THE BEES OUT)

Blitz the sugar and banana together in a food processor until it forms a fine powder. Immediately transfer to an airtight container and store in the fridge for at least 2 days.

Put the banana powder and water in a saucepan and gently heat until it forms a gloopy syrup and all the sugar is dissolved. Pass the hot mixture through a MUSLIN CHEESECLOTH to filter the banana out, then stir in the honey while it's still warm. Bottle and store in the fridge for up to 4 weeks.

For the Walnut Bitters
40 G/1½ OZ. TOASTED WALNUT HALVES • 15 G/½ OZ. BURDOCK ROOT • 10 G/⅓ OZ. GRAPEFRUIT ZEST

10 G/⅓ OZ. ORANGE ZEST • 5 G GRATED NUTMEG • 5 G VANILLA SEEDS • 5 G GENTIAN FLOWERS

5 G GROUND CINNAMON • 3 G STAR ANISE • 3 G CLOVES • 2 G CARDAMON SEEDS • 2 G SALT

400 ML/14 OZ. OVERPROOF ALCOHOL (WHITE RUM SUCH AS WRAY & NEPHEW DOES THE TRICK)

Add all of the ingredients except the alcohol to a food processor or SPICE BLENDER and grind to a coarse powder. Add the the overproof alcohol, transfer to a bottle or storage jar and leave to infuse for at least 2 weeks. (To speed things up, you can use a CREAM WHIPPER to pressurize the contents – see page 32). Once infused, pass through a COFFEE FILTER and store in a DROPPER BOTTLE for as many years as you like.

For the Isomyl Acetate Old Fashioned
50 ML/2 OZ. JACK DANIEL'S OLD NO. 7 WHISKEY • 12 ML/½ OZ. 'BANANA SYRUP' • 2 DASHES OF 'WALNUT BITTERS'

Stir all the ingredients together in a chilled old fashioned glass for 9 seconds with a single piece of hand-cracked ice.

whiskey triggers thousands of reactions that develop complex flavour compounds.

With this drink I wanted to play off the banana thing and throw a Tennessee-style (home of Jack Daniel's) twist in there. Since an Old Fashioned typically only has three ingredients, there isn't a lot of room for manoeuvre, so it's a case of tweaking the sugar and the bitters to best suit my needs.

First, I set about making a banana sugar. Now, there's a few options here... One way would be to use a centrifuge. Centrifuges work by exerting huge gravitational forces onto a liquid by spinning it, causing it to separate into components of different densities – an awesomely extreme way of making a banana-flavoured sugar. I could mash up a couple of bananas in warm water, then put it through a centrifuge to separate the water from the mush. I would then have a nice banana-flavoured water, which I could sweeten into a sugar syrup.

A much cheaper and maybe even more effective way would be to use dried banana. Storing the dried banana with sugar for a length of time would impart a significant flavour to the sugar and the process is a lot simpler than using a centrifuge.

I tried blending banana chips with sugar, then storing them together in an airtight container for a week. Upon opening the container I got a waft of banana-scented air, so I had to work quickly to avoid any more aromatics escaping. I added some water to kick-start the extraction of flavour and to contain all those lovely volatiles. I then heated the solution gently so that the sugar dissolved, but the banana just went a little mushy. After filtering out the banana through a muslin cheesecloth, I was left with an intense banana-flavoured syrup. Perfect.

As previously mentioned, I wanted to impart a touch of the famed Tennessee hospitality to the drink, and after searching for ideas for only a few minutes, I came across Tennsessee walnut and banana bread. This seemed like the perfect route: combine my banana sugar with the ripe nuttiness of walnut bitters, which, in turn, should complement the corn characteristics of the whiskey perfectly.

Manufacturing your own bitters requires only some careful measurement, a few choice ingredients and a bit of patience – it's really very easy. First, select a nice strong spirit, as they extract the most flavour – an overproof rum, or some of that rocket fuel your brother-in-law brought back from Poland will do nicely. (Taste is not important, believe me, since it'll all be covered up ten times over by the powerful roots, barks and spices used to make the bitters.) Add your aromatics and seal for a period of weeks. You can choose to infuse each ingredient separately and then blend together afterwards to form a desirable taste profile.

ROB ROY

50 ML/2 OZ. SCOTCH WHISKY

25 ML/1 OZ. MARTINI ROSSO VERMOUTH

2 DASHES (2 ML) OF ORANGE BITTERS

A TWIST OF ORANGE ZEST, TO GARNISH

Stir all the ingredients together with cubed ice for around
90 seconds. Strain into a chilled coupe glass and garnish with
a small twist of orange zest.

NB: You might like to add a touch of sugar syrup if you have
a sweet tooth, or depending on what Scotch you use.

Rob Roy Macgregor (*Raibeart Ruadh* in Gaelic, meaning 'Red Robert') was an early 18th-century outlaw and, by all accounts, the Scottish version of Robin Hood (i.e. he was handy with a sword and a bow and prone to starting fights with people who had more money than he did – which was more or less everyone.) Try as I might, I could not find any connection between this ginger-haired man (hence the 'Red' in his name) and perfectly refined mixed drinks... Until 1894 that is.

Around 150 years after Red Robert died, the story of his life was made into an operetta by the American composer Reginald De Koven. During the late 19th century, it was common for drinks to be created in honour of new musicals or plays (the trend continued into the early years of cinema, with drinks like Blood & Sand, Greta Garbo and Mae West). This cocktail is thought to have been created at the Waldorf Hotel in New York, just around the corner from Herald Square, where the *Rob Roy* show first opened.

One notable difference between the Rob Roy and the Manhattan is that the former historically calls for orange bitters instead of the Angostura or Boker's bitters used in a Manhattan. This adds a slightly fresher note to the drink that, depending on what Scotch you use, can do a fantastic job of brightening the drink and avoiding the sticky-sweet spice bog that Manhattans are sometimes guilty of verging on.

'INSTA-AGE' ROB ROY

I got the idea for this drink from chatting to some friends about the idea of extracting the 'age essence' from whisky. Looking back, I think the conversation itself had spawned from something that Nathan Myhrvold (author of *Modernist Cuisine*, 2010) had come up with a few years back. Ideally, the process requires a rotary evaporator, so is limited only to those folks who have access to one, but I wanted to talk about this recipe, since it really is a fantastic concept.

The premise is that you redistil the whisky, which separates the light, alcoholic part of the product from the heavy, sweet oaky stuff that won't evaporate. In the collecting vessel you are left with something not dissimilar to vodka, and in the evaporation flask you'll find a concentrated whisky essence! This age essence can then be used to flavour anything from ice cream to haggis, or it can be used to instantly add an aged effect to a cocktail or spirit.

I absolutely loved the idea of creating a cocktail that could be served with the 'age' on the side, perhaps in a pipette or a separate vessel. But then it occurred to me, why not freeze the age essence into a kind of age pastille? I could make the drink as normal, but using the Scotch distillate in place of regular Scotch. The cube could then be added to the finished drink and allowed to melt, simultaneously both chilling and ageing the drink, like a journey through the life of the product.

To make the 'age cube', I distil a bottle of Highland Park 15-year-old whisky though my rotary evaporator (see page 52), which leaves me with my light vodka-like distillate and the gooey 'age concentrate'. The distilate from 1 bottle (700 ml) of Scotch has a volume of 600 ml/20 oz. – enough to make 12 drinks. My age cubes need to be able to make a similar quantity of cocktails so that once the age cube melts entirely, the whisky has returned to its original state. So, to 100 g/3½ oz. age essence I add 100 ml/3⅓ oz. water and 20 g/⅔ oz. sugar, then portion the mixture into 12 separate ice cubes, each of around 15 g/½ oz. and freeze.

If you do want to try it at home, you can create a similar whisky 'age essence' by simply reducing the product down in a pan. But this is not ideal, as the flavour is altered a bit and it would need to be reduced on a low heat over the course of around 10 hours (so that it doesn't burn).

For the cocktail, I use 50 ml/2 oz. of my Scotch distilate, 25 ml/1 oz. Vermouth Gancia Bianco and 4 drops of Bob's Abbotts Bitters. I use Gancia Bianco vermouth, since it's nice and sweet, yet almost completely clear. This further highlights the colour change (and corresponding age change) of the drink as the age cube melts. I stir these ingredients with cubed ice for about 90 seconds, then strain into a chilled coupe. Pop an age pastille into the glass and enjoy over the course of ten minutes as the whisky magically ages in front of your eyes!

For an extra twist on this drink, you can skip diluting the age essence prior to freezing. The result is a turbo-aged cocktail older than its years!

RUM

There is no other spirit, nay – drink, that can claim to have shaped modern civilization to such an extent as rum. This is the liquid responsible for fuelling a navy that ruled the high seas for 300 years, it contributed to the sale and enslavement of an entire race of people and even affected government policy and taxation, ultimately leading to the independence of the most powerful nation on earth today.

Rum's story begins with the colonization of the New World. In 1501, a mere nine years after Columbus's first voyage, sugar cane was successfully planted on the island of Hispaniola (now Haiti and the Dominican Republic). The cane grew furiously and started a domino effect: within 100 years, most of the eastern coast of the Americas and almost every Caribbean island had a sugar cane plantation.

This sugar revolution needed a workforce, and the 'infernal triangle' obliged. Sugar and its products were among the most valuable and hotly traded commodities on the new global trading platform. In many instances, slave-made rum was traded directly with Ivory Coast chiefs for human cargo, further strengthening rum's grip on slave trading.

At some point in the mid-16th century, Brazil, colonized by the Portuguese, began distilling cachaça – a crude style of rum made from fermented sugar cane juice. Later, the French took a similar approach on the Caribbean island of Martinique; they named it '*rhum agricole*'. British and Spanish colonies saved their precious cane juice for the valuable raw sugar that it contained. But the by-product of the refinery process, molasses – a thick, treacle-like substance – had no further uses and could also be fermented and distilled into rum.

The word rum itself dates back to the mid-17th century, and is likely to have spawned from the Devonish word *rumbullion* (a great tumult or uproar). Other etymological possibilities are that the name of the drink was derived from the Latin word for sugar, *saccharum*, or perhaps even named after a Dutch drinking vessel called a *rommer*.

In 1655, Vice-Admiral William Penn, who later became the founder of the US state of Pennsylvania, issued a ration of rum to the sailors in his British Naval fleet. Their long voyage across the Atlantic had exhausted rations of beer and wine, and after taking the island of Jamaica, rum was a cheap and plentiful option. By the end of the 17th century, rum rations (or tots) were a staple that continued up until 1970. The ration was reduced and diluted over time, with the most significant of these changes brought about by Admiral Edward Vernon in 1740. Aware of the heightened state of inebriation onboard British ships, Vernon halved the daily 1-pint ration of rum and diluted it with water and citrus juice (arguably the first Daiquiri – see pages 160– 161). The mariners weren't impressed; they named the new drink 'grog' after Vernon's thick grogham coat. But the introduction of lime or lemon juice (and thus vitamin C) into their diets significantly reduced instances of scurvy, saving countless lives.

Meanwhile, there were upsets in the colonies. Strict laws and heavy taxes on molasses and sugar (needed to produce rum) in North America spurred a revolutionary spirit. America's war for independence had begun.

During the 1800s, rum became a dirty word. Used as a scapegoat by the temperance movement, the spirit was nicknamed 'demon rum.' By 1900 it it lost favour to gin, whiskey and brandy – but rum was biding its time, and once Prohibition struck the US in 1920, the Caribbean became a tempting retreat. The hot climate, latino flair and flowing rum cocktails made islands like Cuba the party goer's first-choice destination. Rum's association with tropical lifestyle and laid-back attitude continued into the 1940s and 50s with the rise of Tiki culture, inspired by the Polynesian way of life and liberally garnished with gallons of rum punch.

MOJITO

The Mojito has the ability to ruin an evening shift behind the stick with incredible ease – 'Five Mojitos please, mate' – and there goes ten minutes of your life (if you're as slow as me), wasted in the familiar tedium of muddling mint, squeezing limes and building a crushed ice tower. Try to sell them a different drink and they will almost always drag their heels, but it's not surprising really. This drink is very tasty when made correctly and evokes all those lovely memories of endless summers, good company and undercooked barbecue sausage.

So why the love affair with the Mojito? What makes it so popular? The fact that it is incredibly refreshing is a good place to start. Lime, soda, light rum and mint make for a crisp drink with the added benefit of menthol's cooling effect. The mint also suggests super freshness and, dare I say it, the illusion of healthiness and nutrition. Then there is the element of ritual; the gentle muddling of the

mint, the squeezing of the lime and the building and churning of the ice. This is a drink that is purpose made for each and every guest. It isn't dispensed from a machine (well, there are exceptions) and it doesn't come in a carton. No, not the Mojito; each one of these beauties is hand-crafted with love, care and affection... ahem.

The Mojito works on the same principles as the Collins and Fizz families of cocktail – four parts of something strong, two of something sour, one of something sweet, top it up with soda. But the affinity between rum, lime and sugar seems to be a special one. Those three ingredients were meant to abide with each other.

The Mojito can trace its roots back to the 16th century and its great-great-great-grandfather, El Draque ('The Dragon') – a drink named after Sir Francis Drake and purportedly created by the British privateer Richard Drake. Records show that El

10 FRESH MINT LEAVES, PLUS A LARGE MINT SPRIG TO GARNISH

50 ML/2 OZ. BACARDI SUPERIOR RUM

25 ML/1 OZ. FRESH LIME JUICE

12.5 ML/½ OZ. SUGAR SYRUP (SEE PAGE 204)

SODA WATER, TO TOP UP

Gently muddle the mint in the base of a chilled highball glass. (Crushing the mint too much releases chlorophyll, which makes the drink taste bitter and covers up the subtle menthol aromatics of the herb. We are looking at doing no more than softening the hairs on the outside of the leaves.)

Add the rum, lime juice and sugar syrup. Stir gently and add a little crushed ice. Stir some more and continue adding ice until the glass is full. Give everything a good churn and add a splash of soda. Cap off with more crushed ice and add a sprig of mint on top. (Give the mint sprig a slap on a firm surface just before serving to release some of the aroma into the air.)

Draque was, in principle, a Mojito – Lime? Check. Mint? Check. Sugar? Check. Aguardiente? Ch… Whoah, what's that? History tells us that rum, as we know it, didn't surface until the beginning of the 17th century. Before rum there existed aguardiente, a cruder, harsher elder sibling, the troublemaker of the family who has since been told to stay in his room, shut the door and be quiet.

It's not surprising that lime and mint have been bedfellows on many occasions since El Draque – in all likelihood, the Mojito was probably conceived simply because it seemed more natural to do it than not to. The etymology of the name itself is still in question: it could come from the Spanish word *mojadito* (meaning 'a little wet'), or it might have evolved from a recipe for 'Mojo', a lime and mint-based salsa. Blanche Zacharie de Baralt published *Cuban Cookery: Gastronomic Secrets of the Tropics* with an Appendix on Cuban drinks in 1931,

which included a recipe for 'Rum Cocktail (Cuban Mojo)' and directions to make what is quite clearly a Mojito. The famous Havana bar Sloppy Joe's, aka 'The Crossroad of the World', can lay claim to the first published use of the word 'Mojito' to describe the same drink in their 1934 Sloppy Joe's bar menu.

These days, it is La Bodeguita del Medio that lays claim to being the spiritual home of the Mojito in Havana. Steeped in history and covered head to toe in the rum-fuelled pen strokes of its former patrons, La Bodeguita del Medio is as atmospheric as its Mojito is bad (sadly). If you happen to visit the bar, expect to see bludgeoned mint stalks, bottled lime juice-or-something, and lashings of rum. Having said that, La Bodeguita del Medio cannot be beaten for whiling away an afternoon in a haze of cigar smoke and rum fog. Just make sure you're sober enough to sign the wall before leaving.

CLARO MOJITO

◆

It always seemed such a shame that the mint in a Mojito doesn't fit up the straw. Not because I want it stuck in my teeth, but because those little pockets of fresh menthol goodness would sing on the palate and make each sip a potential flavour explosion. With that in mind, I created a version of the ultimate Mojito, using a great number of different techniques. This recipe is inspired by previous Mojito creations from Eben Freeman (New York), Bramble Bar (Edinburgh) and my own findings – it makes 4 Claro Mojitos.

I use the rotary evaporator for the rum, and distil 500 ml/17 oz. Bacardi Superior, along with a handful of fresh mint leaves, through the rotary evaporator at 30°C/85°F (around 30mbar pressure) collecting 90% of the liquid. I cut this distillation with regular rum until the desired mintiness is achieved. This gives a subtle mint backbone to the drink.

For those extra bursts of menthol I use an edible spherification of mint. These little green balls stand out visually, and provide flavour when sucked up the straw. The good thing about spherification is that the centre of the pearls remains liquid, so when they hit the palate they explode with flavour!

To make the mint balls, I mix 50 ml/2 oz. of the Mint Bacardi Superior with 1 ml peppermint flavouring, 1 ml green food colouring, and 100 ml/3½ oz. water. (Food colouring is not essential, but I can assure you that green things do taste more minty.) Using a stick blender or aerolatte, I blend the solution while slowly dispersing 1 g sodium alginate powder over the surface. Once all lumps are gone, I put the solution in the fridge overnight to complete hydration.

When it comes to preparing the cocktail, I mix 1 g calcium chloride with 200 ml/7 oz. water in a short glass. Using a syringe, I slowly dispense droplets of the mint alginate solution into a calcium chloride bath, one at a time (making 50 balls for the 4 drinks), then strain the balls out of the bath and rinse them briefly in cold water.

So that the balls of mint are as visually prominent as possible, I clarify the lime juice to remove the 'dishwater' opacity that citrus juice adds to a cocktail. To achieve this, I use an agar clarification process. (For more on see clarification, see pages 41–43)

To create the Mojito formula, I combine 100 ml/ 3½ oz. of the lime water with 200 ml/7 oz. of mint rum and 50 ml/2 oz. sugar syrup, and put it in the fridge to chill until needed.

I want the clarity and contrast of this drink to define it. For this to happen I wave goodbye to the ice. Yes, I use clear ice, but the ocular spectacle of a totally clear drink with green balls hanging in stasis is a greater goal. The main challenge is to get the mint balls to suspend throughout the length of the glass. Particles in a liquid tend to either float or sink; this means that they'll fill your mouth on either the first sip or the last sip. Not good. To get this to work, I change the viscosity of the cocktail. There are a few hydrocolloids that would do the trick here. I use xanthan gum, a thickening agent that in small quantities provides no distinguishable change in texture, but alters viscosity sufficiently to suspend the mint balls. One of the main advantages of xanthan is that it doesn't need to be heated to hydrate, so there is no danger of spoiling my liquids through heat damage. 1 g xanthan gum per 1 litre/34 oz. of Mojito is enough to suspend the spherification. I've found that tiny air bubbles get easily trapped in the liquid once the xanthan gum has been blended in; the best way to get rid of them is to put the liquid in a vacuum chamber, which lowers the pressure and boils all the bubbles out very effectively.

To build the cocktail, I add 80 ml/2⅔ oz. of the chilled Mojito formula to a small highball glass and top up with 40 ml/1⅓ oz. soda water. I deposit about 12 mint balls into each glass and stir gently. The balls neither sink nor float, but remain in stasis throughout the length of the drink.

DAIQUIRI

Anyone fortunate enough to have spent an evening in the Cabinet Rooms, the home of *Diffordsguide to Cocktails* creator Simon Difford, will at some point, have witnessed a 'Daiquiri-off'. It simply involves mixing a perfect straight-up Daiquiri by eye, then tasting and comparing the results. Since this is a drink that contains only three ingredients, it might seem like a pointless exercise, but slight shifts in the proportions of this cocktail result in huge differences in the final flavour. It's revelling in the unique profile of every variation that has made us return to the exercise time and time again.

Most people will tell you that the Daiquiri was invented around the beginning of the 20th century by an American engineer in Cuba called Jennings Cox. This is more than likely to be true, since there exists a written recipe by him from around that time. But it doesn't take a mining engineer to work out that a drink as simple as this probably pre-

dates Jennings Cox, albeit under different titles. Surely many a rum punch has existed containing only rum, lime, sugar and water? And you only need to look at the Brazilian Caipirinha to see a cousin of the Daiquiri, comprising many of the same ingredients, all served over ice.

Of course, the fact that Hemingway was a serious advocate of the Daiquiri has firmly placed it in the cocktail hall of fame. He once famously wrote: 'My Mojito in La Bodeguita, My Daiquiri in El Floridita', his favourite Havana hang out (which even today has a full-size statue of the man propping up the bar). Indeed, despite the Daiquiri being invented around 500 miles away, near the town of Santiago on the south-east coast, El Floridita lays claim to being *La Cuna del Daiquiri* or 'The cradle of the Daiquiri'. Order a Daiquiri at El Floridita today and you're likely to be served a blended abomination presented in an over-sized

50 ML/2 OZ. BACARDI SUPERIOR RUM

12.5 ML/½ OZ. FRESH LIME JUICE

7.5 ML SUGAR SYRUP (SEE PAGE 204)

5 ML WATER

A LIME WEDGE, TO GARNISH

•

Shake all the ingredients together with cubed ice and fine
strain into a chilled coupe glass. Garnish with a lime wedge
on the rim (so that the acidity can be adjusted if necessary).

---

coupe glass. But if you get a bit more specific and tell them that you want a natural, or *papa doble*, they will make you (often begrudgingly) a nice (expensive) drink. But it's worth it.

The best Daiquiri that I've had in Cuba was actually served to me in a wine glass from the rooftop bar at the Hotel Ambos Mundos, which is at the other end of Calle Obispo to El Floridita. Most cocktails in Cuba are overly sweetened, but I recall it being well balanced, cold, without being overly diluted, and the perfect aperitif to fit the soft sounds of jazz and the setting Cuban sun.

SPARKLING DAIQUIRI SORBET

There's only one thing that can spoil an afternoon sat at a rooftop bar in Havana: warm Daiquiris. Here is a drink that benefits from being as cold as is feasibly possible. At around 30% ABV, it slips down a hell of a lot easier when cold enough to make an Eskimo weep an icy tear. This twist on a Daiquiri, I believe, is quite simply one of the most refreshing things you will ever try.

While ice is usually sufficient for good chilling, dry ice takes things to the next level (see pages 44–45 for more information and safety tips). By harnessing the incredible chilling power of dry ice, I can make a Daiquiri that is so cold it'll freeze solid (impossible to achieve in a household freezer). And by combining the cocktail in a stand mixer, I'll be able to control the formation of ice crystals and chill the cocktail to a fizzy sorbet.

I'm adding in a couple of extra ingredients to the sorbet, paying homage to Hemingway's *papa doble* Daiquiri, which normally includes grapefruit juice and a dash of maraschino liqueur.

This is a brilliant drink to make en masse for a party, since it can be batched up in a stand mixer and refrozen if necessary.

SPARKLING DAIQUIRI SORBET

◆

For the Ultra-thick Maraschino Liqueur

100 G/3½ OZ. WHOLE (UNPITTED) MARASCA CHERRIES • 500 ML/17 OZ. LIGHT RUM

200 ML/6¾ OZ. WATER • 500 G/1 LB. 2 OZ. SUGAR

ZEST OF 1 LEMON • ZEST OF 1 SMALL ORANGE

•

Add the cherries, rum and water to a **HEAVY-DUTY BLENDER*** and mix on a pulse grinding setting until puréed. Allow to settle for a day, then strain through a **MUSLIN CHEESECLOTH**, ensuring that you get as much of the flavoursome juices out as possible. If small particles or cherry pulp are still present in the liquid, try passing it through a **PAPER COFFEE FILTER**.

•

Add the citrus zests and sugar to the liquid and heat or **SOUS VIDE** (see pages 31–32) at 65°C/150°F for 1 hour. Allow to cool, **FILTER**, then bottle and refrigerate for up to 1 month.

•

*NB: If you don't have a heavy-duty blender, such as a Blendtec (lesser blenders may struggle, or even break grinding cherry stones/pits), you can infuse the mixture for 2 weeks instead (see pages 30–32).

For the Sparkling Daiquiri Sorbet

500 ML/17 OZ. BACARDI SUPERIOR RUM • 100 G/3½ OZ. CRUSHED ICE

100 ML/3⅓ OZ. FRESH LIME JUICE • 50 ML/2 OZ. SUGAR SYRUP (SEE PAGE 204)

5 G THIN-CUT GRAPEFRUIT ZEST SQUARES • 2 G SALT • ROUGHLY 200 G/7 OZ. DRY ICE PELLETS

'ULTRA-THICK MARASCHINO LIQUEUR', TO SERVE

•

Makes 10 servings

•

Mix the rum, ice, lime juice, sugar syrup, grapefruit zest and salt in a jug/pitcher and chill for 1 hour.

•

Put the chilled liquid in a stand mixer along with the dry ice and set to a low/medium speed. As the liquid begins to freeze, increase the speed slightly and continue to mix until all dry ice has evaporated away.

•

Scoop into frozen coupe glasses and drizzle the Ultra-thick Maraschino Liqueur over the top.

◆

MAI TAI

◆

25 ML/1 OZ. TROIS RIVIERES BLANCO RUM • 25 ML/1 OZ. MYERS'S JAMAICAN RUM

12.5 ML/½ OZ. ORANGE CURAÇAO • 25 ML/1 OZ. FRESH LIME JUICE

8 ML ORGEAT SYRUP • 8 ML SUGAR SYRUP (SEE PAGE 204)

A PINEAPPLE WEDGE AND CHERRY, TO GARNISH

A SPLASH OF OVERPROOF RUM, TO FINISH

•

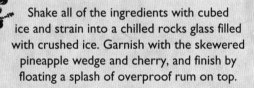

Shake all of the ingredients with cubed
ice and strain into a chilled rocks glass filled
with crushed ice. Garnish with the skewered
pineapple wedge and cherry, and finish by
floating a splash of overproof rum on top.

◆

The Mai Tai is often mistaken for being a long, fruity punch-style drink. It is not. It is actually a very strong drink, based loosely around a Daiquiri on the rocks, but with a few added extras.

The origin of the drink is contested between two men, Victor 'Trader Vic' Jules Bergeron and Ernest 'Don Beachcomber' Raymond Beaumont Gantt. The evidence points towards Vic being the true creator in 1944, but Don Beachcomber argues that he invented it ten years before that. The story goes that Vic was entertaining Tahitian guests one evening, when he served the yet-to-be-named Mai Tai, and one of the guests exclaimed '*Mai Tai-Roa Aê*', which in Taihitian means, 'Out of this world – the best!' So Vic named the drink Mai Tai.

Don Beachcomber's recipe is unrecognizable from Vic's, though not a bad drink. It includes most of Vic's ingredients, plus grapefruit, bitters, pastis, Falernum (a spiced low-alcohol cordial) and a healthy dash of water. Search long enough and you'll see variations of the Mai Tai with everything from pineapple juice and bitters, to Malibu and lemonade. In fact, the Mai Tai has a strong claim to being the most messed-around-with cocktail out there. This is hardly surprising, given the influence that it had on the rise of Tiki culture in the US.

As air travel and air conditioning became a reality for the common American, so, too, did experiences of exotic locations with wholly unusual cultural traits. The likes of Don and Vic made these experiences available in towns and cities throughout North America. Bars were constructed from driftwood and palm leaves, walls were draped with fishing nets and the whole thing was lit from a blowfish lampshade. Tiki was undeniably one of the first and best multi-sensory drinking experiences to exist.

The two rums I've listed here go some way towards emulating Wray & Nephew 17, the rum that Vic originally used to make the drink. Wray & Nephew 17 has been out of production for quite some time now, and even Vic himself was forced to use a combination of Martinique and Jamaican rums to emulate its style.

MAILLARD TAI

If you're planning on making a good Mai Tai at home, it shouldn't be too much trouble to get hold of some nice bottles of rum, curaçao and limes. Acquiring a decent bottle of orgeat, however, can prove to be a little more tricky.

Orgeat is a milky-coloured, almond-flavoured syrup. It's different from other flavoured syrup as it is made from almond milk and usually contains rose water or orange flower water. The name 'orgeat' is derived from the French word for barley (*orge*), which is traditionally used in the production of the syrup. The problem is that most commercially available orgeats are sweet, insipid and generally quite uninspiring. So I set about making my own...

The name of this drink comes from the 'Maillard reaction', a complex set of chemical changes that take place every time you toast bread, fry steak or roast potatoes. Maillard reactions are also known as 'browning reactions' and are named after French chemist Louis-Camille Maillard. The Maillard flavour is thought to derive from complex reactions between sugar and amino acids when food is cooked. With this drink, I set about trying to add some extra juicy brown flavours to the classic Mai Tai.

MAILLARD TAI

◆

For the Brown Orgeat

20 G/³/₄ OZ. WHOLE MALTED BARLEY • 20 G/³/₄ OZ. BUTTER • 800 G/1 LB. 12 OZ. (CASTER) SUGAR

1 LITRE/1 QUART UNSWEETENED ALMOND MILK • 2 G SALT • 5 ML ORANGE FLOWER WATER • 20 ML/²/₃ OZ. VODKA

•

Gently brown the barley, butter and 20 g/²/₃ oz. of the sugar in a frying pan for 5 minutes. Transfer the toasted barley to a KILNER JAR SUITABLE FOR PRESSURE CANNING and add the almond milk. Seal, then put the jar on a canning rack in a PRESSURE COOKER with 300 ml/10 oz. water. Bring up to pressure and cook for 30 minutes. Depressurize and filter the infusion through MUSLIN CHEESECLOTH while still warm. Finally, add the rest of the sugar, salt, orange flower water and vodka. Store in a glass bottle in the fridge for up to 1 month.

For the Maillard Tai

1 LIME • A GENEROUS TEASPOON OF BROWN SUGAR • 25 ML/1 OZ. EL DORADO 10-YEAR-OLD RUM

25 ML/1 OZ. TROIS RIVIERES BLANCO RUM • 12.5 ML/½ OZ. GRAND MARNIER • 12 ML/½ OZ. 'BROWN ORGEAT'

A SLICE OF DEHYDRATED PINEAPPLE (SEE PAGE 40)
AND A SLICE OF TOASTED PINEAPPLE (USE A CHEF'S BLOWTORCH), TO GARNISH

•

Dice the lime, then dust it with the brown sugar and toast using a CHEF'S BLOWTORCH.
Add the lime to a shaker and crush the juices out using a muddler.

•

Add the remaining ingredients to the shaker and shake with cubed ice. Strain into a rocks glass filled with crushed ice. Garnish with a slice of toasted pineapple and a slice of dehydrated pineapple.

◆

FISH HOUSE PUNCH

The success and longevity of a cocktail is sometimes down to the name its given. If that's true Fish House Punch must be a tasty drink, since it certainly hasn't relied on its name to attract drinkers over the years.

Punches pre-date 'Cock-Tails' by a good 200 years. The name probably comes from the Hindi word *panche*, which means 'five', and references the number of ingredients in a standard punch recipe. Counting on your fingers, you would normally have: a strong ingredient (spirit), a long ingredient (tea, water, juice), a sweet ingredient (sugar, liqueur), a sour ingredient (citrus) and a spiced ingredient (bitters, herbs, spices). There are a lot of historical punch recipes, some of which are attached to specific societies, cultures and [ahem] fishing clubs.

Back in 1732, a group of high-society types from Philadelphia got together and formed a club called the 'State in Schuylkill Fishing Corporation'. The clubhouse was on the bank of the Schuykill (pronounced 'Skookul) River and they celebrated their self-proclaimed mastery of aquatic beasts by mixing up a punch. The Fish House Punch was born.

Traditionally, Fish House Punch should be served in a large punch bowl with a single, huge chunk of ice. The recipe however, is at odds with the punch bowl size, since this is quite a strong drink.

A quick note on peach brandy: this is very different from peach liqueur. Peach brandy is much drier and has actually seen a peach in its lifetime (unlike many of the liqueurs).

GOLDFISH HOUSE PUNCH

It doesn't take a marine biologist to work out that serving the Fish House Punch directly out of a fish bowl instead of a punch bowl is a cool idea. But replacing the individual glasses with a clear plastic bag and putting fish-shaped pieces of ice

120 G/4 OZ. SUGAR

400 ML/13½ OZ. WATER

200 ML/6¾ OZ. FRESH LEMON JUICE

400 ML/13½ OZ. APPLETON ESTATE V/X RUM

200 ML/6¾ OZ. HENNESSY FINE DE COGNAC

35 ML/1¼ OZ. PEACH BRANDY

•

Makes 10 servings

•

The day before you wish to serve the cocktail, prepare a large lump of ice by freezing water in a plastic container.

•

To construct the cocktail, add the sugar, water and lemon juice to a **PUNCH BOWL** and whisk until all the sugar is dissolved (sugar doesn't dissolve as easily in alcohol or in cold liquids). Add your prepared lump of ice, followed by the rum, Cognac and peach brandy. Give everything a really good stir and serve in **PUNCH CUPS**.

(complete with 'fish food') in there takes a little more imagination.

Rather annoyingly, Fish House Punch is a muddy brown (thanks to the citrus, aged rum and Cognac), so we'll need to work out a way of making a clarified version to emulate the water in a fish bowl. Back in 2010, I was lucky enough to try a new Cognac product on the market called Godet Antarctica Folle Blanche. Cognac has to be aged for a minimum of two years and this one is aged for seven, but then filtered prior to bottling to take the colour out (while still retaining character). There is a whole range of rums on the market that undergo a similar process to Godet Antarctica; I'm choosing to use Pampero Añejo Blanco, which is a Venezuelan rum that's aged for two years before being filtered and bottled.

For the straw-coloured peach brandy, I'll DIY it and follow the lead of Godet and Pampero by

passing it through a home water filter to remove the colour. Most filters use activated charcoal to remove colour and impurities. Activated carbon (charcoal) is incredibly porous; if you could unfold 1 g activated carbon to reveal all of its surfaces, it would cover in excess of 500 m². This makes it great for adsorption, whereby the tiny particles that give a liquid its colour adhere to the creases and folds of the charcoal. This type of filtering inevitably removes flavour-giving molecules. The trick is to filter enough to remove the colour and not so much that the taste is too compromised.

The imitation fish food is crushed dried tarragon, which resembles the real thing and tastes great with the lemon and peach in the punch, giving a subtle grassy aniseed/anise quality that's not a million miles from the absinthe I like to add to the classic. Finally, the lemon juice is clarified using agar-agar (see page 35) so it looks like water.

GOLDFISH HOUSE PUNCH

❖

For the Fish Food

10 G/⅓ OZ. FRESH TARRAGON LEAVES

•

Dry the tarragon leaves in an oven set to 40°C/105°F, or on your oven's lowest setting, for 6 hours. (You could also use a **DEHYDRATOR**.)

•

Once dried, grind the leaves briefly with a mortar and pestle. Aim for 3-mm/⅛-inch-sized pieces.

For the Fish House Punch

400 ML/13½ OZ. PAMPERO ANEJO BLANCO RUM • 400 ML/13½ OZ. WATER

200 ML/6¾ OZ. GODET ANTARCTICA FOLLE BLANCHE COGNAC

100 ML/3⅓ OZ. FILTERED LEMON JUICE (SEE PAGE 41)

40 ML/1⅓ OZ. FILTERED PEACH BRANDY • 100 ML/3⅓ OZ. SUGAR SYRUP (SEE PAGE 204)

'FISH FOOD', TO SERVE

•

Makes 10 servings

•

The day before you wish to serve the cocktail, prepare a large lump of ice by freezing water in a plastic container. Prepare gold fish ice cubes by freezing water in a suitable novelty **FISH ICE CUBE MOULD**.

•

Mix all of the punch ingredients together in a **SMALL FISH BOWL** and add the block of ice and the fish ice cubes.

•

When you're ready to serve, ladle 150-ml/5-oz. servings of the punch into **SMALL PLASTIC BAGS**, along with a couple of ice goldfish. Add a pinch of the Fish Food (you wouldn't want them to die of starvation) and pop a straw in each bag, then tie the bag up around the straw to seal it. When you finish the drink, you can pop the bag straight in the bin.

❖

CUBA LIBRE

I can hear the shouts from the back row already, 'It's just a rum and coke!' – but no, it's not just a rum and coke, it's a rum and coke with lime.

Despite our over-familiarity with the product, Coca-Cola is an undeniably brilliant and, dare I say it, complex product. The fact that I'm drawn to drink it on both a hot summer's day and a cold winter's evening is an achievement that cannot be ignored.

A quick scan over the key flavours of Coca-Cola – lemon, orange, lime, cinnamon, lavender, coriander, nutmeg and neroli – shows a set of ingredients that matches nicely with rum as stand-alone modifiers. Indeed, most of them have coupled historically with rum in punches. All this means that the affinity between rum and coke is no accident – it's a genetic predisposition, quite possibly hardwired into the fabric of the world.

The drink is thought to have first come to light during the Spanish-American War that granted Cuba its libre – free[dom] – from Spanish rule. However, the dates don't entirely match, since the war ended on 12th August 1898 and Coca-Cola's first bottling plant didn't open until the following year. But still, what better way to celebrate a successful coalition with the *yanquis* than to mix some of their coca leaf and cola nut-inspired soft drink with a healthy glug of Cuban rum?

The Cuban civil war broke the spell and the Cuban-American embargo kicked into effect in the 1960s, which technically made it very difficult to make a true Cuba Libre (Cuban rum with real Coca-Cola) for the remainder of the century. Of course, a true Cuba Libre in its original form wouldn't have lasted long into the 1900s at all, as Coca-Cola started getting anxious about the more 'active' ingredients in their drink and their brand's ability to 'keep people up all night'. The coca leaf was subsequently, and quietly, all but phased out.

15 ML/½ OZ. FRESH LIME JUICE, PLUS THE LIME SHELL TO GARNISH

50 ML/2 OZ. BACARDI SUPERIOR RUM

150 ML/5 OZ. COCA-COLA

•

Take a highball and fill it with ice. Squeeze the juice the lime half in there (which should be about 15 ml/½ oz.), then drop the spent lime shell in the glass. Add the rum and coke, stir well and serve. Cuba Libre!

—◆—

C L   1 9 0 0

For this drink, I intend to perfect a Cuba Libre by combining white rum with a made-from-scratch cola that is as close to the cola of the era in which the drink was invented as possible. The formula for Coca-Cola has changed over the years, and I'm going to recreate one of John Pemberton's original cola formulas from the late 19th century. Once mixed with rum, I'll have a replica of a 1900 Cuba Libre.

The Coca-Cola Company are legendary for guarding their recipes with Fort Knox-level security. But search long and hard enough and you'll find that on a number of occasions the cat has been let out of the bag. One such occassion was in 1979, when a picture of an old notebook was published in the *Atlanta Journal-Constitution*. Strangely, no-one recognized that the grainy photo listed the recipe for 'Coco-Cola Improved' at the time, but three decades later it was discovered that the image of the notebook actually held the secret to one of the early Coca-Cola formulas.

The recipe contains one ingredient that I won't be able to use: coca leaves. Coca-Cola once contained a natural extract of coca leaves (the natural source of the coca alkaloid used to make cocaine), but it was changed to a 'decocanized' version in1903. Given that, it is likely that the first Cuba Libres, which appeared a few years earlier, would have had traces of coca leaves in them.

Since I can't include coca leaves in my formula, I'm going to replace them with an extract of basil and bay leaf. Both of these leaves contain eugenol, a naturally occurring molecule that has a distinctive spicy, clove-like aroma, and is also responsible for the mild-anasthetic properties of cloves. An extract of these leaves should give the slight numbing sensation that the coca leaves might have provided over 100 years ago.

CL 1900

For the 7X Flavour

0.2 ML (4 DROPS) ORANGE OIL • 0.1 ML (2 DROPS) CINNAMON OIL • 0.3 ML (6 DROPS) LEMON OIL

0.05 ML (1 DROP) CORIANDER OIL • 0.1 ML (2 DROPS) NUTMEG OIL • 0.1 ML (2 DROPS) NEROLI OIL

50 ML/2 OZ. VODKA • 2 G GUM ARABIC

•

Mix all of the oils together with the vodka and gum arabic using a stick blender or AEROLATTE. Ensure that the mixture is completely emulsified (it should be a cloudy yellow colour) and not split if left to rest.

For the Cola Formula

5 G FINELY GROUND DRIED BAY LEAVES • 7.5 G FINELY GROUND DRIED BASIL LEAVES • 25 ML/1 OZ. VODKA

8.5 G VANILLA SEEDS • 1.35 KG/2 LB. 15½ OZ. SUGAR • 950 ML/32 OZ. WATER

95 ML/3¼ OZ. FILTERED FRESH LIME JUICE (SEE PAGE 41) • 5 G CARAMEL COLOURING • 6 ML '7X FLAVOUR'

8.5 G CITRIC ACID POWDER • 2.75 G POWDERED CAFFEINE

•

Infuse the ground bay leaf and basil in the vodka for 48 hours (you can speed this up with a CREAM WHIPPER (see page 48), then filter through a MUSLIN CHEESECLOTH and reserve the liquid.

•

Gently heat the vanilla seeds, sugar and water in a pan for 30 minutes, then strain to remove the seeds.

•

Put 100 ml/3⅓ oz. of the strained vanilla syrup in a blender and add the lime juice, colouring, 7X Flavour, citric acid and caffeine powders and 2.5 ml of the bay and basil infusion. Blend together, then stir this back into the remaining vanilla syrup. Pour into a glass bottle and store in the fridge for up to a month. This recipe makes roughly 2 litres/2 quarts – enough for about 12 litres/3 gallons CL 1900.

For the CL 1900

50 ML/2 OZ. BACARDI 1909 RUM • 25 ML/1 OZ. 'COLA FORMULA' • 125 ML/4 OZ. SODA WATER

•

Build the cocktail ingredients together in a highball glass with cubed ice, and garnish with a lime wedge.

•

NB: You could also add the syrup to a SODA SIPHON with water in a ratio of 1:5, then carbonate it ready for use.

FLIP

◆

50 ML/2 OZ. BACARDI 8 RUM

200 ML/6¾ OZ. DARK ALE

10 G/⅓ OZ. SUGAR

10 G/⅓ OZ. MOLASSES

A GRATING OF NUTMEG

•

Add all the ingredients to a large, HEATPROOF TANKARD. Be sure to leave at least 2.5 cm/1 inch of head space in the cup to accommodate the expansion of the liquid. Heat a POKER on an open fire, barbecue or gas hob/stove until glowing red hot. Wear GOGGLES for protection and handle the poker with HEAT-RESISTANT GLOVES. Plunge the poker into the centre of the liquid, then slowly stir as the liquid froths and bubbles. The smell itself is incredible. Drink as soon as it is cool enough to do so.

◆

The Flip is possibly the earliest significant use of rum in a mixed drink. Flips date back to the colonial taverns of mid-17th century America (as it would later be known) and formed a staple part of colonial drinking culture in the New World.

These days, the Flip is commonly made with a whole egg, but this is a later evolution of a drink that was served warm and without egg in it. So where did the egg come from? Well, the original Flip consisted of a large bowl to which rum, sugar (or molasses), ale and spices were added. The mixture would be stirred and then heated using a hot poker. The poker affects the drink in a number of ways (see right), one of which was to add a foamy, creamy texture. Later, when hot pokers seemed a little impractical, an egg was added in its place in order to achieve the same creamy consistency.

But there's no substitution for a hot poker in life, and it affects more than just the texture and temperature of the drink.

The Flip was popular in a time where adding hops to beer was not a common practice. Many beers were bland concoctions, occasionally flavoured with bitter ingredients, including roots, barks and wormwood. In a Flip this was not so essential, because aggressively heating a Flip mixture with a hot element has the effect of caramelizing and then burning the sugar present within the mixture, which in turn adds balance and structure to the drink. Heating it on a hob/stove would not achieve the same effect as a red-hot poker. This angry heating of the liquid also went some way towards sterilizing the drink (beer was generally more sterile than water anyway) – meaning a lesser chance of issues further down the line. Couple that with some aromatic spices, the rich fortification of rum and a warm, silky texture that slides a healthy dose of alcohol swiftly into the bloodstream, and you have a formidable winter mixture fit for any table, old or new.

FLIPPING WONDERFUL

I must confess that I am a huge fan of the original Flip. For such an old libation, it still has great relevance for today's palate (especially given the popularity of bitters in recent years). However, I am also a fan of the humble egg, and it would be foolish to ignore the rise of the egg-based Flip and some of its more delicious variants. My Flip will build off the backbone of beer and rum used in the traditional Flip, but will include some choice magical ingredients, resulting in a vibrant, velvet concoction that could just as easily double up as a dessert.

The rum I'm using is Ron Zacapa 23, a unique Guatemalan rum aged in a variety of sherry barrels. This gives it a nutty and dried fruit quality that will couple nicely with a dark porter or stout. Sweetness is provided by muscovado sugar, which has some of the rich molasses character, and a touch of Pedro Ximenex sherry, a sweet Spanish sherry with tons of dried fruit characteristics. For colour, I'm going to add some fresh beetroot/beet juice, this will not only tint the drink nice shade of purple, but also add a dry earthiness that will cut through some of the richer ingredients.

Finally, I'm going to serve the drink with some edible meringue toadstools that will set the mood for the cocktail. Rather ironically, however, these meringues don't contain any egg!

FLIPPING WONDERFUL

◆

For the Meringue Toadstools

150 ML/5 OZ. WATER • 2 G METHYLCELLULOSE • 200 ML/6¾ OZ. BEETROOT/BEET JUICE
1 G XANTHAN GUM • 1 G SALT • 60 G/2 OZ. ICING/CONFECTIONERS' SUGAR • CREAM, TO SERVE

•

Boil the water and blend the methyl-cellulose into it. Once cooled, add the beetroot/beet juice, xanthan gum and salt and whisk in a stand mixer. Slowly add the sugar and whisk until the mixture forms stiff peaks. Spoon tall cone-shaped dollops onto non-stick baking parchment and bake in the oven (or use a DEHYDRATOR) at 60°C/140°F for 10 hours.

•

To serve, stack the meringue cones in pairs and use a little cream, dispensed from a SYRINGE, to blob little dots of cream onto the top of each toadstool.

For the Flipping Wonderful

50 ML/2 OZ. RON ZACAPA 23 RUM • 1 EGG • 50 ML/2 OZ. BEETROOT/BEET JUICE • 75 ML/2½ OZ.
PORTER OR STOUT (GUINNESS) • 15 ML/½ OZ. PEDRO XIMENEZ SHERRY • 10 ML/⅓ OZ.
MUSCOVADO SUGAR SYRUP (SEE PAGE 204) • COCOA POWDER, TO DUST • 'MERINGUE', TO SERVE

•

Shake all the ingredients together for 10 seconds. Strain into a separate shaker and whisk with an AEROLATTE for 10 seconds to aerate. Pour into a stemmed glass and dust with cocoa powder. Serve with the Meringue Toadstools.

◆

ZOMBIE

—◆—

35 ML/1¼ OZ. JAMAICAN DARK RUM • 35 ML/1¼ OZ. BACARDI GOLD RUM • 25 ML/1 OZ. DEMERARA 151 RUM

20 ML/⅔ OZ. FRESH LIME JUICE • 15 ML/½ OZ. FALERNUM • 10 ML/⅓ OZ. GRAPEFRUIT JUICE

5 ML CINNAMON GOMME • 2 DASHES OF ANGOSTURA BITTERS • A SPLASH OF ABSINTHE • A SPLASH OF GRENADINE

HALF A PASSIONFRUIT, A PINEAPPLE LEAF AND A TWIST OF ORANGE ZEST, TO GARNISH

•

You can either blend or build this drink. The blended version is much lighter on the alcohol kick and requires only a quick blitz of all the ingredients in a blender with a scoop of ice and for the mixture to be poured into a **TIKI MUG** or long glass.

•

To make the built version, add all the ingredients, except the Demerara rum, to a **TIKI MUG** or highball glass filled with cubed ice, stir, and finish by floating the Demerara rum on top.

•

For both methods, garnish with the passionfruit, pineapple leaf and twist of orange zest.

—◆—

Almost as much mystery and as many horror stories surround this drink as its undead, rag-clad namesake. The Zombie has developed quite a reputation over the years due to its titanic alcohol content, mysterious origins and the spectacular nose dive effect it can inflict on anyone crazy/ heroic enough to drink one.

A true Zombie should contain around 75 ml/3 oz. rum as well as a further 15 ml/½ oz. overproof rum. Most bars charge a decent wedge for one of these, but many will reduce the rum to a more sensible quantity and lengthen the drink with extra fruit juice. If you're served one in a highball, don't mistake this drink for a long, diluted cocktail – it's mostly rum in that glass! And it's for this reason that Zombies are almost universally listed with a 'maximum of one per person' warning.

The Zombie is normally accredited to Ernest Raymond Beaumont Gantt aka Don Beachcomber,

who purportedly invented the drink in 1934. There is no evidence to actually back this up other than the fact that Don states in his book, 'I originated and have served this "thing" since 1934... Anyone that says otherwise is a liar!'.

A notebook dated 1937 goes some way towards qualifying the tale: it was owned by one of Beachcomber's waiters and does list a recipe for a Zombie. But as a footnote to that, a recipe for a Zombie was published in Patrick Gavin Duffy's 1934 book, *The Official Mixer's Manual*. Even though Duffy's recipe is not exactly the same, there are clear similarities.

Regardless of who the true inventor of the drink was, the Zombie undoubtedly played a leading role in the rise of the Tiki boom throughout the 1940s and 50s (it was famously served at the 1939 World's Fair in New York), and that was largely down to the success of Don Beachcomber's restaurant empire.

UNDEAD DRUNK

◆─────◆

I want my Undead Drunk cocktail to live up to the 'shock and awe' of Tiki style, so I will serve it in a crystal carafe, sat on a bed of edible charcoal. I'll also include a plume of dry ice 'smoke' and I'm going to use a bit of science to facilitate a spooky colour-changing effect. This is going to be awesome!

I start by making the edible charcoal, which is made by colouring a brioche dough with squid ink, breaking it into lumps and baking until dry and crispy.

I mix 7 g dried baker's yeast and 50 g/2 oz. sugar into 130 ml/4⅓ oz. warm milk and set aside for 5 minutes.

Next I put 500 g/1 lb. 2 oz. bread flour, 6 g salt and 60 g/2 oz. softened butter into the bowl of a stand mixer, and mix, then add the yeast mixture and 2 beaten eggs. I mix again until everything comes together, then add 15 g/½ oz. squid ink and set it to knead for 10 minutes. The mixture is left to prove for 1 hour, before I knock it back and divide it into 6 individual portions. These are set on a greased baking sheet, covered with greased clingfilm/plastic wrap and allowed to sit in a warm place for a further hour. I then preheat the oven to 180°C/350°F and bake the brioche for 16 minutes, then turn it out onto a cooling rack. Once cool, the brioche is broken into charcoal-shaped pieces, sprayed with vegetable oil, and returned to the oven for 10 minutes more to crisp up, then left to cool completely.

To create the colour-changing effect in the drink, I'm going to go back to high-school chemistry and the bizarre property of anthocyanin. As mentioned in Seasoning Cocktails (see pages 27–29), anthocyanin is a naturally occurring pigment that changes colour based on acidity and alkalinity (or how sour the drink is): when in an acidic solution, it's red, and when in an alkaline, it's blue. If I add concentrated anthocyanin to a drink along with an alkaline (bicarbonate of soda/baking soda in this instance), the drink will be blue, but if I then neutralize the drink with acid, it will

turn purple. Add even more acid and it will eventually turn red. This fantastic theatrical effect is both safe and incredibly easy to do since many common ingredients contain anthocyanin, including red cabbage, blood orange and purple corn. The most dramatic colour changing I have witnessed has come from dried berries such as blackcurrant, maqui berry, açaí, wild blueberry and chokeberry. Simply hydrate the dried berry and add some acids and alkalines to watch the colour-changing show!

To make the indicator solution, I combine 4 g freeze-dried maqui berry with 25 ml/1 oz. water and 3 g bicarbonate of soda/baking soda in a small bowl.

For the colour-changing solution, I combine 35 ml/1¼ oz. filtered fresh grapefruit juice (see page 41) with 2 g citric acid and 1 g malic acid in a separate small bowl.

In a carafe, I combine 150 ml/5 oz. Pampero Blanco rum, 50 ml/2 oz. El Dorado 3-year-old rum, 50 ml/2 oz. Trois Rivières Rhum Agricole, 75 ml/2½ oz. Falernum, 5 ml La Clandestine absinthe, 100 ml/3½ oz. clear lemonade, 50 ml/2 oz. gomme and 100 ml/3½ oz. water, then refrigerate until ready to serve.

I arrange my 'charcoal bricks' and dust with icing/confectioners' sugar, a touch of ground cinnamon and some dehydrated blood orange powder (see page 40 for more on dehydrating). The carafe is placed on top of the charcoal, then I pour in the indicator solution and the drink turns from clear to blue. When I add 10 g/⅓ oz. dry ice (see pages 44–45) the drink will begin to change to purple, because the dry ice releases carbonic acid, neutralizing the liquid. Finally, when the colour-changing (acid) solution is added, the drink will turn bright red.

Once the dry ice has finished bubbling, the drink is safe to consume. I pour through a tea strainer (to ensure that no dry ice finds it's way into the glass) into a suitable drinking vessel and enjoy.

HOT BUTTERED RUM

One of my favourite things about mixed drinks from days gone by is their use of dairy products. Milk, cream and butter form the basis of many drinks from the early modern period and colonial times, but why is this?

Well, it's certainly in part due to availability of ingredients. We take it for granted these days that yuzu juice can be delivered to your door and that the fruit market stocks eight varieties of cherries. Back in the day, however, transport and shipping networks were sketchy to say the least, plus essentials like tobacco, cotton, weapons and booze were prioritized. Moving fresh, perishable products around the world was all but impossible before the invention of fridges or freezers, so the mixologists of the day relied on what they could get hold of locally.

So let's take a look at a typical winter back bar in colonial America... Ok, we've got some rum distilled by the guy two doors down – [sniff] nasty, it'll need cutting back with some water (hot, because it's cold outside now). [Slurp] hmm, tastes a bit bland, let's add some of those dried spices that came in six months ago... [sip] better, needs some sugar to take the edge off though... [gulp] now we're making progress... Just needs a finishing touch... something to soften it... make it slip down nicely... butter! [glug].

The truth is that as a creative type with a limited larder, you're likely to experiment with any and every combination of everything you've got. Hell, if I only had five ingredients to play with and one of them was rat saliva, I'd probably give it a try! Couple that with the fact that humans are a highly adaptable species, quick to jump on the next trend and to overlook imperfections, especially when alcohol is involved, and you have a good argument for a Hot Buttered Rum.

50 ML/2 OZ. BACARDI 8 RUM

15 G/½ OZ. SOFT BROWN SUGAR

150 ML/5 OZ. HOT WATER

15 G/½ OZ. BUTTER

A GRATING OF NUTMEG

•

In a tall, handled glass, mix the rum, sugar and hot water until the sugar is dissolved. Add the butter on top, then grate over a little nutmeg. Commence drinking once the butter has melted – you might like to give it a stir if you don't want a mouthful of butter fat...

When we think of rum, we generally think of countries like Jamaica, Barbados and Puerto Rico, but the American colonies also distilled, traded and drank a huge amount of rum. Places like New England played a large hand in perpetuating the triangular trading of human workers for rum and molasses. Indeed, many of the colonial rum brands were prized more highly than that of the inferior gut rot that the Caribbean islands churned out. Fact. By the time America had won its independence and gone through a civil war, production of rum had all but ceased. Bourbon was the US poster boy – after all, it had none of that 'Britishness' attached to it and could be made from the tons of corn grown in the South.

So it's kind of cool that there's a few distillers in the US who have started making rum recently, including Prichard's in Tennessee, Railean in Texas and Montanya in Colorado.

HOT BATTERED RUM

Charles Browne, the author of the 1939's *Gun Club Cook Book*, remarked that the main purpose of the butter in a Hot Buttered Rum was to lubricate one's moustache. As desirable as a well-lubricated moustache (or indeed a greased upper lip) is, it does turn the drink into a somewhat fatty affair. The truth is that the exact purpose of the butter is not wholly known, but in my mind it is to aid with texture, so that the drink slips down the gullet nice and easily. In this respect, a Hot Buttered Rum fails, and here's why...

Fat and water do not mix. The oxygen in a water molecule is charged positively and the hydrogen is charged negatively – this essentially turns a water molecule into a small magnet that attracts other water molecules. Fats and oils are generally neutral, with no electromagnetic charge. As such, the water in a Hot Buttered Rum sticks

HOT BATTERED RUM

— ◆ —

For the Strawberry Jelly

500 G/1 LB. 2 OZ. FRESH STRAWBERRIES • 300 ML/10 OZ. APPLE JUICE • 2 G AGAR-AGAR POWDER

5 G GELATINE LEAF • 30 G/1 OZ. (CASTER) SUGAR

•

Purée the strawberries with the apple juice in a blender and pass through a coarse sieve/strainer.

•

Put one-quarter of the strained liquid in a saucepan and heat to boiling point, then add the agar-agar powder. Remove from the heat and add the rest of the liquid, then allow to cool in an **ICE BATH** until set.

•

Once set, gently break up the jelly with a whisk. Pass the jelly through a **MUSLIN CHEESECLOTH** to collect the juice, which should be a pale pink colour and devoid of any particles or lumps. Agitate the jelly to release as much liquid as possible whilst avoiding lumps.

•

Heat one-quarter of the filtered liquid to 70°C/160°F and add the gelatine and sugar. Once dissolved, remove from the heat and add the rest of the liquid. Transfer to a **SHALLOW BUTTER PORTION MOULD** and refrigerate until completely set.

For the Hot Battered Rum

150 ML/5 OZ. HOT BLACK TEA • 45 ML/1½ OZ. BACARDI 8 RUM • 10 G/⅓ OZ. SUGAR

2 G LECITHIN • 20 G/¾ OZ. BUTTER • 1 G SALT • 'STRAWBERRY JELLY', TO SERVE

•

Add the hot black tea, rum and sugar to a blender along with the lecithin and blitz for 30 seconds, or until the lecithin is fully dissolved.

•

Gently melt the butter in a saucepan, then slowly pour the melted butter into the blender whilst continuing to mix. Blend for a further 20 seconds and the liquid should be fully emulsified.

•

To serve, transfer the mixture back to the pan and heat to around 70°C/160°F, or just below a simmer. Pour into a heatproof mug, and garnish with a piece of the Strawberry Jelly.

•

NB: If you have access to a **THERMOMIX** (see page 48), the heating and blending can take place at the same time.

— ◆ —

together and the fat is shunned, left to reside on the surface of the drink. From both a tactile and flavour standpoint, this is not a good thing. Texturally, the drink has a greasy surface and the bulk of the drink is watery. In sipping the drink, the drinker is likely to taste either the watery (rum, sugar, water) components OR the fatty. In the event that a single sip does contain both elements, the brain is able to separate the two components effectively and register a sensation of fatty and aqueous solutions in a crude mixture. This effect is similar to that of eating a split hollandaise sauce. When a hollandaise is well made, it tastes rich without feeling fatty or greasy despite it containing a lot of fat. When a hollandaise fails (splits) and the fat leaches out of the emulsion, it immediately tastes greasy and unpleasant. By creating an emulsion (a fine mixture of oil and water molecules), both the texture and the flavour of the ingredients will be noticeably better.

So how do you create an emulsion of butter and water? In a hollandaise (or a mayonnaise), this is achieved with egg yolks, which contain a compound called lecithin. Lecithin is a surfactant (see pages 48–51), a long molecule with hydrophilic (water-loving) and lipophilic (fat-loving) ends. As such, it allows water and fat to live in harmony when mixed together. This type of oil-in-water emulsion involves mixing the two liquids together in the presence of a surfactant until the molecules of oil become incredibly fine, resulting in an opacity and thick, creamy texture.

Using egg yolks to achieve this in a Hot Buttered Rum would undoubtedly result in a kind of rum/water omelette! But lecithin and other similar surfactants can be used in their raw powdered form. In cookery, this opens up hundreds of emulsion recipe opportunities. For bartenders, it means we can make a fully emulsified Hot Buttered Rum!

For my recipe, I'm going to add a few extra ingredients into the fold that will complement the rum and the butter nicely.

Both black tea and strawberry couple beautifully with the rum and the butter. This recipe certainly puts a slightly breakfast slant on the classic Hot Buttered Rum, but the combination works at any time of the day and pretty much all the time when it's cold outside! You'll notice a decent richness in the taste of this drink, but with none of the oily residue found in the original. Both butter and sugar levels can be adjusted according to taste. The jelly will slowly melt, emulating the butter in the original drink and providing an increasing level of fruitiness as you sip.

TEQUILA

No other spirit can claim to be as so completely intertwined with its country of origin as tequila.

It all starts with the humble agave, or maguey. Ancient civilizations have risen to power and toppled into obscurity off the back of this plant. Aztec, Toltec and Olmec societies all had a strong reliance on the agave, attributing its creation to the gods and holding the plant in the highest-possible esteem. The agave is a large fibrous plant with thick barbed leaves. It's often mistakingly described as a cactus, but actually belongs to the monocot family of flowering plants, being closely related to the yucca (Joshua tree), and a cousin of asparagus.

The Spanish conquistadors arrived in 1521 and brought to Mexico the technology of distillation. Shipping brandy across the Atlantic to the colonies would be an expensive business, so much better for the New-Worlders to make their own with whatever fermentable materials existed locally. In Mexico it was the agave, and mescal was born: the fermented and distilled juices of the roasted agave heart.

Jump forward a couple of hundred years and the small town of Tequila in Jalisco has become famous for the quality of its mescal, made from the cooked juices of the blue agave. The first licence to produce tequila was granted by King Carlos IV in 1795.

There are many varieties of agave grown in Mexico, but only the blue agave can be used to make tequila. Besides the state of Jalisco, which is responsible for over 90% of all tequila, there are four other Mexican states that can legally produce tequila: Guanajuato, Michoacán, Nayarit and Tamaulipas.

Blue agave take 7–10 years to reach maturation, at which time they are harvested by a *jimador* (plantation worker). The jimador uses a *coa* (disc-shaped blade on a long pole) to swiftly cut away the thick *penca* (leaves) from the heart of the plant. The pencas can be recycled into all manner of things including fuel, twine, weapons or even moisturizer, which was once proudly offered to me by Jose Cuervo's most famous jimador, Ishmael. Indeed, in 1615 the Spanish priest Francisco Ximénez wrote of the agave: 'The plant alone would be sufficient to provide all things necessary for human life'.

The trimmed-down heart of the plant, or piña, which can weigh up to 115 kg/250 lb., is then taken for processing. First, they are cooked, which converts the starch into fermentable sugar. The cooked piña are chopped, squashed or shredded, then water is used to flush out the fermentable *aguamiel* (honey water). Fermentation then takes place, resulting in a pungent agave wine. This wine is then distilled at least twice. Some tequilas are distilled three times, further purifying the liquid.

There are two main categories of tequila: mixto (mixed) and 100% agave. Mixto accounts for the vast majority of tequila sold around the world. By law, it must be made from a minimum of 51% sugars derived from the blue agave – the rest of the sugar can come from any other source except other varieties of agave (typically, it's derived from cane or corn). As the name suggests, 100% agave tequila is made from only sugars of the blue agave. Mixto tequilas tend to be a little softer due to the use of non-agave products, while 100% agave tequilas are often more characterful. If the bottle doesn't state 100% agave, the tequila is a mixto.

Tequila production is strictly controlled by the CRT (Consejo Regulador del Tequila). I know of no domain-classified product, spirit or otherwise that is so closely governed as tequila. Unbelievably, all 75(ish) of the operating tequila distilleries in Mexico must be visited daily by a CRT representative.

Tequila has three main classifications of age: Blanco – usually unaged, but can be aged for up to 60 days; Reposado – meaning 'rested', for between two months and one year in oak casks up to 20,000 litres/5,000 gallons in size; and Añejo – meaning 'aged', for between one and three years in barrels up to 600 litres/160 gallons in size.

MARGARITA

The Margarita hails from the curaçao/Sour family of drinks, and can name such cocktails as the Sidecar (see pages 117–118) and Cosmopolitan (see page 102) as siblings. The Margarita is undoubtedly the youngest member of this socially diverse family, with virtually no mention of the drink prior to the 1970s. Having said that, Charles H. Baker refers to a tequila drink with lime as far back as 1939. The truth is that if you pick up a cocktail book published before the 1970s, it's unlikely to mention tequila at all – not surprising given that good-quality 100% agave tequila had been all but unavailable in North America and Europe until modern times.

Now, even though the Margarita is the grimy, salt-caked young tearaway of the family, she also happens to be universally better loved and an altogether more rounded, well-balanced individual. Lime and tequila have a powerful affinity and the

dry orange note from the triple sec/curaçao does a great job of lifting the vegetal, earthy characteristics of a good tequila. The (optional) salt buffers the acidity of the lime, actually lessening its tongue-shrivelling effect. For this reason alone, I am of the opinion that a Margarita with sugar added requires no salt rim. That's not to say that a Margarita without sugar must have a salt rim; it's really a preference thing. If you do opt for a salt rim, use flakes and not table salt, which is far too fine and will make the drink taste like a fisherman's sock.

Margaritas can be blended, but shaking is where it's really at. The good news is that a classic 2:1:1 ratio is a fairly reliable one-size-fits-all that can be applied to virtually any tequila/curaçao/lime combination, regardless of brand. Ultimately, what you end up with is a cocktail that charms the pants off you while you steadily slip into an inebriated state of being.

20 ML/²/₃ OZ. FRESH LIME JUICE, PLUS A WEDGE OF LIME

SEA SALT FLAKES

40 ML/1¼ OZ. CALLE 23 REPOSADO TEQUILA

20 ML/²/₃ OZ. DRY ORANGE CURAÇAO

•

Using the lime wedge, wet the edge of a coupe glass and then dip the rim (exterior only) into flakes of sea salt.

•

Shake all the liquid ingredients together with cubed ice. Strain into the prepared glass and serve immediately.

•

NB: For a rather excellent variation, substitute the curaçao for 10 ml/⅓ oz. agave nectar and serve on the rocks. This is known as a Tommy's Margarita and is widely accepted by the bartending fraternity to be, well, better than the original.

◆

CURED MARGARITA

This twist on a classic Margarita was born out of a sensory analysis of a range of tequilas that got me thinking about interesting flavours that work well with tequila. Tequila has a very unique flavour profile, a hand-me-down from the agave plant itself, and the steaming or cooking process that turns the starch in the plants piña into fermentable sugar. The distillate can reveal funky vegetal notes, often accompanied by floral sweetness, bright citrus, spice, black pepper, dry earth, brine, tropical fruit, baked fruit, fermented fruit, freshly cut fruit or over-ripe fruit. During one tasting session, I noticed a very interesting briny characteristic in the glass that was reminiscent of a dry Manzanilla sherry, or even of fresh fish arriving at a harbour. This twist on a Margarita plays off that characteristic, which crops up occasionally in some Blanco tequilas.

I first looked at sherry, which seemed like an obvious partner to the tequila, given the dry and sometimes salty flavours that some sherry has. This got me thinking about the connection between Spain and Mexico, and the conquistadors of the 16th century. During this time, distillation was encouraged in Spanish colonies, but many products were shipped across the Atlantic ocean, too. In 1587, Sir Francis Drake's looting awarded him 2,900 sherry butts from Spanish fleets bound for Central American colonies. Trade ships also carried preserved fruits for sale in Europe, sometimes dried, sometimes steeped in alcohol or vinegar. This practice of pickling fruit for preservation and transportation was not a new one, but was certainly a useful one in an era when an Atlantic voyage could take over six weeks. At some time or other, these pickled-fruit cordials became known as shrubs, and while their main purpose was to preserve fruits and vegetables prone to spoilage, the fortunate by-product was the flavouring of the vinegar itself. These days, some bartenders actually set out with the aim of flavouring a vinegar for use in cocktails.

Vinegar in a cocktail may sound bizarre, but it makes more sense than you might think. For a start, vinegar is made from alcohol, whether it be wine, beer (malt) or sherry, and some of the distinguishing components of the product carry through to the vinegar. Also, vinegar is sour, just like lemons or limes. Sure, it's a different kind of sourness, acetic acid instead of citric, but when balanced correctly, vinegar can add a very interesting twist to a cocktail. For this drink, I made a lime shrub using sherry vinegar. I wanted to keep the lime dominant in the cocktail, but for the oils in the zest to contribute just as much as the juice.

For the drink in the picture here, I chose a glass that seems to be etched with leaves like that of the agave plant. The soil in and around the Tequila valley has a strange quality to it that I only noticed upon my first visit to Mexico. The ground kind of sparkles with a deep red, almost burnt, effect. I wanted the service ware for this drink to somehow bring a piece of that unique terroir to the table too so on the side of the drink I'm serving some fish escabeche in a small terracotta dish. Escabeche is basically fish preserved with citrus juice, vinegar and seasoning and the flavours should complement the drink nicely.

CURED MARGARITA

◆

For the Lime Shrub

150 G/5 OZ. LIME ZEST • 5 G SALT • 400 ML/14 OZ. SHERRY VINEGAR

•

Combine the lime zest, salt and sherry vinegar. SOUS VIDE (see pages 31–32) at 60°C/140°F for 3 hours, then strain. Bottle and store the Lime Shrub in the fridge and it should keep for years.

For the Cured Margarita

40 ML/1¼ OZ. OCHO ANEJO TEQUILA • 20 ML/⅔ OZ. PIERRE FERRAND DRY CURAÇAO

10 ML/⅓ OZ. FRESH LIME JUICE • 5 ML GOMME • 10 ML/⅓ OZ. 'LIME SHRUB'

•

Shake all the ingredients together with cubed ice and strain into a chilled glass.

◆

TEQUILA AND SANGRITA

◆

440 ML/15 OZ. TANGERINE OR CLEMENTINE JUICE

200 ML/6¾ OZ. TOMATO JUICE • 150 ML/5 OZ. POMEGRANATE JUICE

100 ML/3⅓ OZ. FRESH LIME JUICE

70 ML/2⅓ OZ. SUGAR SYRUP
(SEE PAGE 204)

4 G SEA SALT • 2 G GROUND BLACK PEPPER

5 ML TABASCO (OR ALTERNATIVE SPICE)

50 ML/2 OZ. OCHO BLANCO TEQUILA
(EL PUERTOCITO), TO SERVE

•

For the Sangrita, put all the ingredients (except the tequila) into
a suitable clean bottle. Shake well and refrigerate for 12 hours.

•

Serve 50 ml/2 oz. of the Sangrita with 50 ml/2 oz. tequila
in seperate chilled shot glasses.

◆

In my humble opinion, there is no better way to enjoy tequila than with a side shot of Sangrita: earthy peppery Blanco tequila matched with intense, sweet and sour spiced fruit. It baffles me that there aren't more bars that encourage this style of drinking, since it is very easy to prepare and the result is one of those perfect harmony moments when you realize that two contrasting liquids were simply made to be together.

The word *sangrita* translates to 'little blood' (not to be confused with *sangria*, which means 'bleeding').

Historically, the Sangrita was a well-guarded secret – few people other than the Jaliciense (people who originate from the Mexican state of Jalisco) knew of Sangrita's existence, and even

fewer were privy to the recipe. However, as tequila's popularity grew, so too did the efforts of the larger brands to promote Mexican culture, and that included the ritual of the Sangrita. Traditionally, it's thought that a Sangrita would be a 'leftovers' drink, comprising of the leftover juices from a spiced Mexican salsa called *pico de gallo* ('cockerel's beak' – curiously similar to 'cocktail'). Sangritas developed and commonly used fruits such as mango, papaya, pomegranate, tangerine and cucumber. These days, tomato juice is often used to provide the deep red hue, but in the past this was achieved using only chilli and pomegranate. Some might say that many of the Sangritas served across Europe and the US are not a true representation of the classic Mexican

Sangrita. I would argue that the tequila and Sangrita ritual has got off lightly in comparison to other traditional drinking customs from around the world (Mojito and Daiquiri spring to mind).

The truth is that there is still a level of secrecy, a tap on the nose, a wink and a nudge when it comes to the Sangrita. Many bars do not serve them or have never heard of them. I put this down to the need for preparation. Ideally, it is not a drink that is prepared from scratch, on the spot. It requires the perfect balance of sweetness, acidity, fruit, and most important of all, spice. Many of the bars who do serve Sangritas will guard the recipe with their lives. It's a cocktail bar faux pas to ask a bartender for their Sangrita recipe, like asking a magician how he did his last trick – they won't tell you.

LIGHTNING SANGRITA

The aim of this drink was to create an accompaniment to tequila that targeted all the major taste senses – sweet, sour, salt, umami, bitter, astringent, metallic, fatty, cooling and spicy. The idea is for the tequila to excite the palate, whilst the Sangrita effectively resets it by overstimulating the palate – kind of like a full body massage for the tongue. The name of the drink reflects the intense flavour of the liquid, but also pays homage to a [probably] mythical story that tells of the first-ever pulque (agave-based) wines being produced by lightning striking the agave plant.

The human affinity with smoky flavours is a strange one. Whether it be a rich peated Scotch, sticky barbecue ribs or creamy smoked cheese, there is something about the carbonyls and phenols produced by burning wood that relaxes and comforts. Perhaps a few thousand years' worth of campfires and wood-fired stoves have ingrained the smell and taste of smoke firmly into the 'this is a good thing' area of our brains.

For my Lightning Sangrita, I intend to serve the drink under a glass cloche filled with smoke. The idea here is that the surface of the drink is slightly affected by the ambient clouds of smoke, but the remainder of the liquid is not forced to succumb to the overpowering wafts of wood flavour.

Next, I wanted to bring an earthy, mineral-like flavour to my drink. The flavour of stone is a difficult one to contain, but flint has become a popular ingredient in recent times due to its clean, mineral taste. For this drink I made a simple flint sugar syrup that adds sweetness, dryness and a crisp, almost metallic finish to the drink.

Last but not least, I'm using a tiny pinch of aluminium salt, an ingredient often used to preserve crispiness in pickling and brining, to add a drying astringency to the Sangrita.

LIGHTNING SANGRITA

◆

For the Flint Syrup

200 G/6 OZ. POWDERED FLINT • 500 ML/17 OZ. WATER • 700 G/1 LB. 8¾ OZ. SUGAR

•

Soak the powdered flint in the water for 24 hours.

•

Add the flint to a saucepan along with the soaking water and heat to a boil. Strain through a **PAPER COFFEE FILTER**, then immediately stir in the sugar until dissolved. Refrigerate for up to 1 month.

For the Lightning Sangrita

150 ML/5 OZ. FRESH BLOOD ORANGE JUICE

100 ML/3⅓ OZ. PRESSED CUCUMBER JUICE (SEE PAGE 38)

100 ML/3⅓ OZ. PRESSED POMEGRANATE JUICE • 100 ML/3⅓ OZ. 'SPICED

TOMATO WATER' (SEE PAGE 108) • 50 ML/2 OZ. FRESH LIME JUICE • 50 ML/2 OZ. 'FLINT SYRUP'

25 ML/1 OZ. OLIVE OIL • 3 ML TABASCO • 3 G FRESH MINT LEAVES

3 G GROUND BLACK PEPPER • 2 G SEA SALT • 0.2 G ALUMINIUM SALT

50 ML/2 OZ. OCHO BLANCO TEQUILA (EL PUERTOCITO), TO SERVE

•

For the Sangrita, blend all the ingredients (except the tequila) together and refrigerate for up to 5 days.

•

To serve, pour 50 ml/2 oz. of the Sangrita mix and 50 ml/2 oz. of tequila into seperate chilled shot glasses. Place both glasses under a **GLASS CLOCHE** and use a **SMOKE GUN** to smoke with a good helping of mesquite wood (see page 47).

◆

LA PALOMA

Paloma is Spanish for 'dove' – a lovely name for a drink – but try as I might, for a long time I struggled to find a connection between the bird and the drink. After some extensive research, I managed to track down a link between the agave plant and certain species of pigeon, including a bunch of 'paloma' varieties, whose highly corrosive droppings can wreak havoc on agave plantations. So if you've got corroded penca on your agave plantation (it happens), the problem is quite possibly paloma. The connection is, however, a little tenuous, and when I questioned my friend and tequila expert Tomas Estes on the subject, he told me that the word 'paloma' is sometimes crudely used to refer to the female nether-region, in Mexico. Case closed.

In most of the Western world, we drink tequila in Margaritas or as some kind of ritualistic shot (salt and lemon, or slammer). In Mexico, however, by far the most popular way to drink tequila –

other than swigging it straight out of the bottle – is in this fine drink. Sweetness, acidity, bitterness and salt come together in a chorus of refreshing goodness, which in the heat and humidity of a Mexican rainy season is very much called for.

Typically, the drink is made with tequila, fresh lime, effervescent grapefruit soda and salt (optional). In Mexico, the most popular brand of soda used is Squirt. There are other brands too, Jarritos and Ting being two popular ones. If you can't get hold of any of them, equal parts fresh grapefruit juice and soda, with a touch of sugar, also works well too.

Sadly, the inventor of this drink remains a mystery. Some accredit it to Don Javier, proprietor of the famous La Capilla (The Chapel) in the town of Tequila. But this seems unlikely, since The Don is famed for the invention of a less popular (but just as good) drink called Batanga, which is made using tequila, lime, cola and salt.

50 ML/2 OZ. OCHO REPOSADO TEQUILA

10 ML/¹⁄₃ OZ. FRESH LIME JUICE, PLUS A LIME WEDGE TO GARNISH

EFFERVESCENT GRAPEFRUIT SODA, TO TOP UP

•

Build the ingredients over cubed ice in a chilled highball glass.
Garnish with the lime wedge.

•

NB: You can substitute the grapefruit soda with 75 ml/2½ oz. fresh
grapefruit juice, 75 ml/2½ oz. soda and 10 ml/¹⁄₃ oz. sugar syrup.

AVANT-GARDE PALOMA

Props for this drink must go to Thomas Aske, as this is a variation on a cocktail that he came up with in 2009. The original drink was a sharing cocktail that featured on the first-ever cocktail list at Purl.

The original drink was served from a soda siphon, but with fresh grapefruit juice in place of grapefruit soda – since the siphon would provide the fizziness. It worked well, since the cocktail could be prepared and balanced prior to evening service, then, when ordered, it could be quickly served with assurance of quality.

I'm bottling the cocktail in the hope that it will give the drink a feel that it's a commercially sold, quality-assured product. It's a shame that many of the old glass bottle sodas have now moved over to plastic bottles. The aim of this drink is to evoke that sense of nostalgia, when you crack the lid off the bottle and hear the ttssssss sound of gas escaping!

Carbonation is the process of dissolving carbon dioxide molecules (CO_2) into a liquid. Most of us have owned or used a household carbonator, SodaStream™ being the most famous brand. CO_2 weakly dissolves into water, but when pressurized – as is the case with commercially sold sodas, Champagne and beer – it dissolves much more readily. When you crack open the bottle of soda, the pressure is released and the CO_2 immediately begins to precipitate out of the solution. The more you open a bottle, the flatter it gets because every time it's sealed the headspace (space not filled with liquid) fills with CO_2, which escapes as soon as you open the bottle. Soda siphons are much better at keeping liquids fizzy, since they don't allow air to enter the system once it's sealed, meaning that the system remains pressurized with CO_2 (and uses the pressure to eject the liquid through the nozzle) for a long time.

AVANTE GARDE PALOMA

---◆---

For the Grapefruit Infusion

2 LITRES/2 QUARTS FRESH PINK GRAPEFRUIT JUICE

3 G GROUND PINK PEPPERCORNS • 2 G GROUND CORIANDER SEEDS

5 G SALT • 25 G/1 OZ. AGAVE NECTAR • 2 G CITRIC ACID • 1 G ASCORBIC ACID

•

Heat the grapefruit juice, peppercorns, coriander seeds and salt up to 62°C/145°F and hold the temperature for 30 minutes to pasteurize the juice. (Try not to overheat the juice, as it can impair the flavour.)

•

Filter the pasteurized juice through a **MUSLIN CHEESECLOTH**, followed by a **PAPER COFFEE FILTER**. While the liquid is still warm, stir in the agave nectar and acids, then allow to cool.

For the Avant Garde Paloma

1.5 LITRES/1.5 QUARTS 'GRAPEFRUIT INFUSION'

500 ML/17 OZ. CALLE 23 REPOSADO TEQUILA

•

Makes enough for 10 bottles*

•

Mix the Grapefruit Infusion with the tequila and leave in the fridge to chill.

•

Pour the drink into a **SODA SIPHON** and shake. Funnel the drink into **200 ML/7 OZ. BOTTLES**, following the guidelines on pressure – do not over pressurize! – and seal. Serve in chilled highball glasses with cubed ice.

•

*NB: Always use strong bottles, with no cracks or scratches. Check with the manufacturer that the glass or plastic is suitable for the task. If you are serving the drink within 24 hours, there is no need to sterilize the bottles.

---◆---

GLOSSARY

Acetone Flavourful ketone produced during the fermentation process.

Acid phosphate Traditional mixture of phosphoric acid and mineral salts of magnesium, potassium and calcium. Commonly used as a soda souring agent in early 20th-century America.

Absorbtion Process of a solid, liquid or gas being 'taken in' by another solid, liquid or gas.

Adsorption Adhesion of particles to a surface. Principle mechanism of charcoal filtration.

Agar Gelling agent (hydrocolloid) derived from red seaweed. Used for creating heat-stable gels and for clarification. Typical usage 0.5–2%.

Agave Thick fibrous plant, the heart (or piña) of which is cooked and used to make tequila.

Albumin Egg white protein, used for stabilizing foams, airs and in place of egg white in cocktails that call for it. Mix with water before using.

Atomize To spritz or spray aroma, usually directed at glassware or the surface of a drink.

Bar Measurement of air pressure equal to 14.5 psi (pounds per square inch); 1,000 bars = 1 mbar.

Botanical Fruit, herb, flower or spice used to flavour gin during distillation process.

Brix Measurement of sugar present within a solution, syrup, product or infusion. 50 brix is equivalent to 50% of the total weight of the product being made up of sugar.

Calcium chloride Mineral salt often used for firming cooked vegetables. Commonly used as a catalyst for sodium alginate in spherification (see page 36). Also used as a mineral salt in acid phosphates (see page 27).

Case-hardening The phenomenon of a product's exterior surface drying during dehydration, slowing migration of moisture from the interior of the product (see page 40).

Chemesthesis The irritation or burn of a chemical (including alcohol) on the palate or skin.

Citric acid Acid found in lemons and other citrus fruit (see pages 27–29).

Column still Large distillation apparatus that rectifies a wash into more than 96% spirit. Uses steam and bubble plates in a continuous process.

Distillation Process of separating alcohol and/or other volatile compounds from a mixture, based on their boiling points. Controlled through heat and air pressure. Most commonly used to extract ethanol from an ethanol–water mixture.

Fusel oils Generic term describing heavy (high boiling-point) alcohols produced during fermentation that add characterful, heavy flavours to distillations.

Gelatine Collagen-based gelling agent, usually derived from fish or pig skins. Check bloom strength and adjust according to the texture you want to achieve.

Gellan Carbohydrate-based gelling agent. Great for making fluid gels and brittle jellies. Comes in two varieties: low-acyl and high acyl (see page 36).

Gum arabic Derived from the sap of the acacia tree. Useful for oil in water emulsions such as those in soft drinks. Also decreases surface tension and improves fizz in soft drinks.

Dry ice CO_2 (carbon dioxide) in solid state. At approximately -79°C/-110°F, it sublimates into gas and can be used for a variety of applications (see pages 44–45).

Ethanol (ethyl alcohol) Flavourless and colourless alcohol found in all spirits and liqueurs. Boiling point of 78.3°C/173)°F and freezing point of -114°C/-173°F.

Emulsion Mixture of water and oil, or water and gas in a suspended state (see page 48).

Fermentation Conversion of carbohydrates to alcohol (ethanol)/organic acids, heat and CO_2 through microbiologial organism (yeast).

Foam Air in water emulsion, where air is the suspended phase and water is the continuous (see pages 48–49).

Fructose Fruit-derived sugar, almost twice as sweet as sucrose.

Glucose Very simple sugar, 75% the sweetness of sucrose.

Gomme Sugar syrup used to sweeten drinks containing an emulsifier such as gum arabic.

Heat of fusion Energy (joules) required to convert 1 g ice to 1 g water; also applicable to other elements and compounds (see pages 22–23).

Hydrocolloid Any type of gelling agent that slows down or 'sets' an aqueous solution, eg. gelatine, agar-agar (see pages 34–37).

Ketone Organic, often flavour-providing compound.

Lecithin Phospholipid-based emulsifier found in egg yolks. Used for creating airs and foams and for stabilizing fat in water solutions. Typically used in levels of 0.1–1%. Commonly available unbranded, or as Lecite from Texturas range.

Lemon powder Dried ground lemon peel used as a flavouring.

Lignin Compound present in plants and wood that makes up part of secondary plant cell structure. Responsible for much of the aromatic compounds produced when wood is charred or burned (see page 47) and also a big player in the realms of barrel ageing (see pages 53–55).

Liquid nitrogen (LN_2) Nitrogen in liquid form at approximately -196°C/-320°F. Used for a variety of chilling applications (see page 44).

Maillard reaction Complex reaction between sugars and amino acids. Responsible for the 'brown' or toasted flavour of cooked meats, vegetables etc.

Malic acid Acid particularly prevalent in green apples. More tart than citric and longer flavour.

Maltodextrin Starch derivative (commonly from corn), used to thicken mouthfeel. Behaves in much the same way as sugar, but not as sweet.

Meat Glue see Transglutaminase

Methanol Volatile light alcohol produced in small quantities during fermentation. Toxic when consumed in large quantities.

Methyl cellulose Derived from cellulose (plant cell walls), it sets when hot and melts when cool. Useful for heat-stable ice creams and hot jellies (see page 36).

Nitrous oxide (N_2O) Gas used for pressurizing a cream whipper.

Nitrogen cavitation Sudden and violent effervescence of nitrogen bubbles in a liquid. Used to speed up infusion times (see page 32).

Nucleation site Localized formation of bubbles dissolved in a gaseous liquid, eg. bubbles appearing on the inside of a champagne flute.

Olefactory epithelium Smell pad located between the eyes and the first stage of the brain, for detecting aroma.

Orthonasal (smell) Aroma carried through the front of the nose up to the olefactory epithelium.

Osmotic pressure Force required for a liquid to break through a semipermeable membrane. In the case of fruit, it is the force required for a liquid to leach out through the skin or membrane of the fruit (see page 38).

Papillae Visible collection of taste buds on the tongue.

Pot still Traditional kettle-style still.

Retronasal (smell) Aroma carried through the back of the mouth and into the nasal passage.

Rotary evaporator (rotovap) Low-pressure distillation apparatus. Facilitates distillation of liquids at low temperatures ($<40°C/104°F$). Allows concentration and preservation of temperature-sensitive ingredients (see page 52).

Salinity Proportion of salt present within a liquid, solution or product.

Shrub Preservation of fruit in either vinegar or alcohol. A method of infusing flavour into vinegars for use in cocktails.

Sodium alginate Carbohydrate-based gelling agent extracted from certain types of brown seaweed. Requires presence of calcium to set, and is therefore useful for spherification of liquids that do not contain calcium (see pages 36–37).

Sous vide ('under vacuum') Practice describing both the sealing of ingredients in a vacuum pouch and the heating/cooking of ingredients in a water bath. Very useful for controlled concentration of aromatics in alcoholic and non-alcoholic infusions (see pages 31–32).

Specific heat Energy (joules) required to heat 1 g of a material by 1°C.

Spherification Process of forming liquid-filled spheres (or other shapes) through bonding of calcium and alginate (see page 36).

Sublimation Transition of a substance directly from a solid to a gas (skipping liquid phase), most notably in dry ice (see page 44).

Sucrose Simple sugar

Sugar syrup A simple syrup used to sweeten drinks with a 2:1 ratio of sugar to water. To make about 1 litre/1 quart sugar syrup, gently heat 660 g/23¼ oz. caster/granulated sugar (you can also use soft brown/muscovado sugar) with 300 ml/10 oz. water and 30 g/1 oz. vodka in a saucepan. Once all the sugar has dissolved, bottle it and pop it in the fridge for up to 6 months.

Sialagogue Food or drink that promotes the production of saliva in the mouth.

Synesthesia Concept of the brain combining sensory input to create a 'flavour image' (see page 14).

Tartaric acid Grape acid – tart and short-lived.

Triangular taste tests Three samples are presented to the subject: two are the same and one is different. The subject is required to pick the odd one out, indicating that there is a tangible difference.

Transglutaminase (or 'meat glue') Protein-bonding enzyme used for sticking meat together and for bonding gelatin-infused fruit and vegetables. Available under the Activa brand.

Xanthan gum Polysaccharide of bacterial origin. Useful for gelling and thickening liquids without the need for heat.

Wormwood (artemesia absinthium) Shrub used in the production of absinthe and vermouth and famed for its powerful herbal bitterness. It was historically used to bitter ale, before the practice of using hops became common in the 19th century. It's important to use only the specified quantity of wormwood as large doses can be dangerous.

EQUIPMENT & SUPPLIERS

General Equipment & Glassware

Cocktail Kingdom Supplier of quality bar equipment – Yarai mixing beakers, Gallone mixing glasses, all manner of cobbler and Parisienne shakers, jiggers, strainers and kit bags. Also reproduction vintage cocktail books. www.cocktailkingdom.com

Drinkshop General glassware and cocktail equipment – absinthe fountains, large selection of glassware and basic equipment. www.drinkshop.com

Chef Steps (US) Sous vide, handheld smokers, scales and thermometers. www.store.chefsteps.com

WMF Reliable German kitchen equipment – pressure cookers, pans, utensils. www.wmf.com

Fisher Scientific (UK) One-stop shop for lab-grade equipment and sundries. www.fisher.co.uk

Specialist Ingredients

MSK Ingredients Large range of own-brand powdered flavours, gelling agents and emulsifiers. www.msk-ingredients.com

Infusions 4 Chefs Specialist ingredients, equipment and serviceware. Stockist of Texturas, Mugaritz, Lyo and Sosa ranges of products. Also stocks 'meat glue'. www.infusions4chefs.com

Modernist Pantry (US) Full range of modernist ingredients for all manner of applications. www.modernistpantry.com

Cream Supplies (UK) Molecular gastronomy ingredients and lots of gadgets. Cuisine Innovation and Kalys branded products. www.creamsupplies.co.uk

Brew UK (UK) Home-brew suppliers – sterilization, containers, filters, yeast, ingredients, bottles. www.brewuk.com

Witchcraft Shop (UK) Unexpected supplier of a vast range of quality dried herbs, spices, flowers, roots and barks (including cinchona bark). www.witchcraftshop.co.uk

Baldwins (UK) Long-time purveyors of ingredients, tinctures and infusions. www.baldwins.co.uk

Specialist Equipment

Kitchen Aid The classic food mixer. Useful for ice creams, sorbets and emulsions. www.kitchenaid.com

Buchi The original rotary evaporator manufacturer – rotary evaporators, chillers, vacuum pumps. Lots of other specialist lab equipment. www.buchi.com

Thermomix Jack-of-all-trades food mixer, used for blending, emulsifying, infusing and heating and much more besides. www.thermomix.com

Sous Vide Supreme Manufacturer and supplier of affordable sous vide equipment – non-circulating water baths and vacuum packers. www.sousvidesupreme.com

Polyscience High-end professional kitchen technology – sous vide, food smokers, rotary evaporators. www.polyscience.com

Cream Supplies (UK) Molecular gastronomy ingredients and lots of gadgets – cream whippers, soda siphons, lab beakers, scales, smoking gun, magnetic stirrers, sous vide, sundries. www.creamsupplies.co.uk

Polybags (UK) Good value supplier of many types of bag, including all kinds of sous vide applications. www.polybags.co.uk

Cheftools (UK) Supplier of Pacojet (ice cream and sorbet mixer), sous vide, smokers and Superbags (for filtering). www.cheftools.co.uk

ACKNOWLEDGMENTS

This book would not have been possible without the encouragement and support of my wife, Laura.

Thank you to my mum, for all the sacrifices made and the introduction to flavour!

Thanks must also go to all the people in this amazing industry who have inspired and helped me along the way. Most notably: Addie Chinn, Agostino Perrone, Alex Kratena, Angus Winchester, Barrie Wilson, Claire Smith, Craig Harper, Daryl Haldane, Dave Broom, Erik Lorincz, Ian Burrell, James Hoffmann, James Petrie, Jeff Masson, Justin Smyth, Max Helm, Polly Dent, Ryan Chetiyawardana, Simon Difford, Simone Caporale, Spike Marchant, Thomas Aske, Tom Nichol, Tomas Estes, Tony Blake, Tristan Welch and Wayne Curtis.

Finally, a big thank you must go to the team at RPS, especially Julia Charles and Rebecca Woods, for allowing me to write the book I dreamed of writing!

ABOUT THE AUTHOR

Tristan Stephenson has been involved in the hospitality industry for over 10 years and is renowned as one of the leading experts in the bar community on cocktail science and molecular mixology. In 2005, he set up the bar at Jamie Oliver's Fifteen Cornwall, before taking on a role as a Brand Ambassador for the Reserve Brands Group in 2007, training bartenders at some of the highest regarded bars and restaurants in the UK, including The Ritz. In 2009, Tristan co-founded Fluid Movement, a breakthrough events and consultancy company for the drinks industry. This lead to the opening of his first bar Purl in 2010, the Worship Street Whistling Shop in 2011, and in 2012, Dach & Sons (a New York inspired hot dog, beer and bourbon bar), all of which have been greeted with critical acclaim. Tristan has travelled to distilleries and breweries all over the world in his research, worked closely with critically acclaimed writers and flavour perception expert Tony Blake, and was a speaker at Tales of the Cocktail in New Orleans in 2012. Tristan was also awarded UK Bartender of the Year in 2012 by Class Magazine (having been a runner up in 2011) and was also included in *Evening Standard*'s 2012 top 1000 most influential people in London. Tristan appears regularly on TV and is a regular contributor to various print and online drinks publications. Tristan spends most of his time involved with bar consultancy, writing and training, and travelling. This is his first book.